Eindhoven, 16 June 1999

Dear David,

Thanks for everything and up to the future!

Harrie & Rob

Nederland

land in beweging

The Netherlands, *country on the move*

Die Niederlande, *Land in Bewegung*

Les Pays-Bas, *pays en mouvement*

Los Países Bajos, *país en movimiento*

Países-Baixos, *país em andamento*

Nederland
land in beweging

The Netherlands, *country on the move*

Die Niederlande, *Land in Bewegung*

Les Pays-Bas, *pays en mouvement*

Los Países Bajos, *país en movimiento*

Países-Baixos, *país em andamento*

TIRION

Planned and produced by Canal House Publishers
Concept and text by Joop van der Liet
Cover design by Rob Buschman
Pagemaking by Electronic Publishing Services BV

ISBN 90.51.21.74 6.3
Nugi 672
SBO 35

Inhoud

Inhaltsverzeichnis

Sumario

Contents

Table des matières

Índice

Voorwoord

Nederland kan niet bogen op een lange geschiedenis. De mens achtte het niet als zijn hoogste prioriteit om zich permanent te vestigen op de drassige delta van de Rijn en de Maas. Eerst toen de eerste stammen kunstmatige heuvels en dijken konden bouwen, was er sprake van bewoning.
Door stormvloeden kwam de zee weliswaar telkens weer terug, maar toch raakten de bewoners gewend aan de gedachte dat het water op de lange duur niet onoverwinnelijk behoeft te zijn.
Het is een de mengeling van initiatief en doorzettingsvermogen dat door de eeuwen heen kenmerkend voor de Nederlanders is gebleken. De gemeenschappelijke vijand, het water, was niet individueel te bestrijden. Onderlinge menings-verschillen moesten wijken voor de gezamenlijke aanpak. Het schiep een vorm van saamhorigheid waarbij altijd het eigen belang bleef meetellen: het behoud van eigen erf..
Nederland werd zo bij uitstek een land waar sprake was van consensus.
Het fenomeen doet zich reeds gelden in de benadering van de Romeinen, later bij de vrijmaking van Spanje en het uitroepen van de Republiek, maar vooral ook in de handel. De Nederlandse Gouden Eeuw was nooit zo profijtelijk geweest als de kooplieden èn de politici zich geen gezamenlijke doelen hadden gesteld.
De laatste jaren wordt deze consensus wel het 'poldermodel' genoemd. Niet alleen waar het de economie betreft, maar ook in de dagelijkse politiek. Zijn het in economisch opzicht de werkgevers en de werknemers die samen afspraken maken over de inkomens, in de gemeenteraden en in het parlement zijn het afgevaardigden van maar liefst een tiental partijen die uiteindelijk de politieke koers moeten bepalen.

Foreword

The Netherlands does not have a very long history. People were not that interested in settling permanently on the boggy delta of the Rhine and the Maas. The area was not really inhabited until the first tribes were able to build artificial mounds and dykes. While the sea sometimes broke through with the spring tides, people became used to the idea that, given time, it would not be impossible to conquer the water. Over the centuries the Dutch have been characterized by a mixture of initiative and perseverance. Their common enemy, the water, could not be tackled by an individual. Differences of opinion had to be put aside in the interests of the common approach. It created a form of solidarity where one's own interests always continued to count: preservation of one's own property.
And so the Netherlands became a country that excelled in consensus. The phenomenon can be found as far back as the approach to the Romans, later on when liberated from Spain and the declaration of the Republic, but above all in trade. The Dutch Golden Age would never have been so profitable if the merchants and politicians had not set themselves joint objectives. In recent years this consensus has been called the 'polder model'. And not just in economic matters, but in day-to-day politics as well. When it comes to economics, the consensus relates to agreements between employers and employees about wage restraint. In local councils and the parliament there are representatives of no fewer than ten political parties who between them have to set the political course.

Vorwort

Die Niederlande können sich nicht mit einer langen Geschichte brüsten. Der Mensch hielt es nicht für besonders erstrebenswert, im Mündungsdreieck von Rhein und Maas dauerhafte Niederlassungen zu gründen. Erst als die ersten Stämme künstliche Hügel und Deiche aufschütten konnten, war eine Besiedlung möglich. Bei Sturmfluten kam das Meer zwar immer wieder zurück, aber die Bewohner gewöhnten sich mit der Zeit an den Gedanken, daß das Wasser langfristig nicht unüberwindbar sein mußte. Diese Mischung aus Tatkraft und Durchsetzungsvermögen erwies sich im Laufe der Jahrhunderte als kennzeichnend für die Niederländer. Der gemeinsame Feind, das Wasser, ließ sich nicht vom Einzelnen bezwingen. Meinungsverschiedenheiten mußten dem gemeinsamen Ziel weichen. So entstand eine Form der Zusammengehörigkeit, bei der stets auch das eigene Interesse gewahrt wurde: der Erhalt des eigenen Besitzes.
Auf diese Weise wurden die Niederlande zu einem Land, das wie kein anderes nach Konsens strebte.
Das Phänomen zeigte sich bereits beim Umgang mit den Römern, später bei der Befreiung von Spanien und dem Ausrufen der Republik, aber vor allem auch im Handel. Das niederländische Goldene Zeitalter wäre niemals so glorreich verlaufen, wenn nicht Kaufleute und Politiker dieselben Ziele verfolgt hätten.
In letzter Zeit wird dieser Konsens oft "Poldermodell" genannt. Nicht nur in der Wirtschaft, sondern auch in der Tagespolitik. Sind es im wirtschaftlichen Bereich Arbeitgeber und Arbeitnehmer, die gemeinsame Absprachen in Tarifverhandlungen treffen, so sind es in den Gemeinderäten und im Parlament die Abgeordneten von gut und gerne zehn verschiedenen Parteien, die sich letztendlich auf einen politischen Kurs einigen müssen.

Préface

Les Pays-Bas ne peuvent se prévaloir d'une longue histoire. Les premiers hommes n'avaient pas choisi en priorité de venir s'installer durablement dans le delta marécageux du Rhin et de la Meuse. Ce n'est que lorsque les tribus maîtrisèrent la construction de digues et de collines artificielles, qu'il fut question d'une occupation permanente. Certes, la mer revenait sans cesse avec les marées de tempête, mais peu à peu les habitants se familiarisèrent avec l'idée que les eaux n'étaient pas forcément invincibles.

C'est un mélange d'esprit d'initiative et de ténacité qui, au cours des siècles, a caractérisé les Néerlandais. L'ennemi commun à tous, l'eau, ne pouvait être combattue individuellement. Les divergences d'opinion devaient s'effacer devant une approche collective, ce qui engendra une forme de solidarité, qui tenait toujours compte de l'intérêt individuel : la conservation de sa propre terre. Les Pays-Bas devinrent ainsi le pays du consensus par excellence.

Cet état d'esprit se fait déjà sentir dans la façon d'aborder les Romains, il s'affirme plus tard, lorsque le pays se libère des Espagnols et se proclame République, mais surtout à travers le commerce. L'Age d'Or aux Pays-Bas n'aurait jamais été si profitable, si marchands et hommes politiques n'avaient pas poursuivi des objectifs communs. Dernièrement, ce consensus a été baptisé le 'modèle du polder', et il s'applique non seulement dans l'économie, mais aussi dans la politique de tous les jours. De la même manière que le patronat et les salariés, menant ensemble les négociations sur les revenus, ainsi les orientations politiques sont-elles définies, dans les assemblées locales et au parlement, par les représentants d'une dizaine de partis politiques.

Prólogo

Holanda no puede vanagloriarse de tener una historia muy antigua. Los antiguos pueblos no tuvieron intención de establecerse en el pantanoso delta del Rín y el Mosa. Hasta que las primeras tribus no construyeron cerros artificiales para la asentamiento de sus cabañas, no se puede hablar de que este pais fuera habitado. Debido a las tempestades, el mar inundaba cada vez una parte de la tierra, pero sus habitantes se fueron convenciendo de la idea de que el mar no era invencible. Se trata de la mezcla de iniciativa y perseverancia la que ha quedado como característica propia de los holandeses a través de los siglos. El enemigo común, el agua, no se podía combatir de forma individual. Las diferencias de criterio se tuvieron que adaptar para poder desarrollar una estrategia común. Se creó una especie de solidaridad en donde siguió contando la conveniencia propia: la conservación de su propio terreno. Holanda se convirtió en el pais en donde por excelencia prevalecía el consenso.

Este fenómeno se vió ya en la relación de sus primeros pueblos con los romanos y mas tarde en su liberación de España y proclamación de la República; pero donde mas se aprecia es en el comercio. El Siglo de Oro holandés no hubiera sido nunca tan provechoso si los políticos y comerciantes no hubieran establecido un objetivo común. Este tipo de consenso se ha dado por llama en los últimos años el modelo 'poldermodel'. Su uso no se limita al comercio sino que los políticos lo usan a diario tambien. Si en sentido económico son empresarios y asalariados los que deben llegar a un acuerdo sobre sus ingresos, en los ayuntamientos y en el parlamento son una decena de partidos los que finalmente deben ponerse de acuerdo para establecer el curso político a seguir.

Prefácio

A Holanda não se pode regozijar de uma história muito longa. As gentes antigas não tinham como mais alta prioridade fixarem-se permanentemente no delta pantanoso dos rios Reno e Mosa. Só depois das primeiras tribos terem construído elevações e diques, é que se começou a pensar em morar lá. Por causa das inundações com tempestades o mar voltava muitas vezes, mas no entanto os moradores habituaram-se à ideia de que a água no decorrer de muito tempo não poderia ser invencível.

É uma mistura de iniciativa e de perseverança, o que pelos séculos fora se demonstrou ser uma característica dos holandeses. O inimigo comum, a água, não se podia combater individualmente. Diferenças de opinião tiveram que ceder a um empreendimento colectivo. Criou-se uma forma de homogeneidade, na qual o interesse próprio sempre prevalecia: a conservação da sua propriedade.

A Holanda tornou-se assim um país onde há, pode-se dizer, um consenso.

O fenómeno sentiu-se já na maneira de abordar os romanos, mais tarde na libertação do domínio dos espanhóis e na proclamação da República, mas muito em especial também no comércio. A Época Áurea Holandesa nunca teria sido tão vantajosa se os comerciantes e os políticos não tivessem determinado uma finalidade comum.

Ultimamente chamam a este consenso o 'modelo do pólder'. Não só no que diz respeito à economia, mas também na política do dia a dia. No ponto de vista económico são os patrões e os empregados que em conjunto fazem contratos para os salários; nos concelhos municipais e no parlamento são os deputados de, pelo menos, dez partidos, que finalmente determinam o curso político a seguir.

Leven met het water

Co-existing with water

Leben mit dem Wasser

Vivre avec l'eau

La convivencia con el agua

Viver com a água

Nederland ligt op de plek waar de Rijn en de Maas in de Noordzee uitmonden. In het verleden had de zee hier vrij spel. De oerbewoners konden weinig anders uitrichten dan hun nederzettingen bouwen op hoger gelegen gronden of zich vestigen op kunstmatig opgeworpen heuvels, terpen.
Zo troffen de Romeinen deze delta aan toen zij hun rijksgrens tot ver in noordelijke richting uitbreidden. Als commandant van een ruitereenheid verbaasde Plinius de Oudere zich in 47 v Chr over het feit dat 'op deze troosteloze vlakten mensen konden wonen'.

Vrijwel gelijk met de kerstening in de achtste eeuw kwam ook de gerichte strijd tegen het water op gang. Om meer land in gebruik te kunnen nemen werden kleine gebieden bedijkt en in de waterlopen werden primitieve sluisdeuren aangebracht om het water bij eb te kunnen spuien. Langzamerhand koloniseerden de bewoners van het hoger gelegen oostelijk deel van het land het westen.
Het was een strijd met wisselend succes. Toen rond het jaar 1200 de temperatuur iets opliep, rees de zeespiegel. Als gevolg hiervan werden grote gebieden weer prijsgegeven aan het water. De oorspronkelijke Middelzee, nu het IJsselmeer, werd bijna driemaal zo groot. In het zuidwesten woedde in de nacht van 18 op 19 november 1421 de St.-Elizabethsvloed. Dorpen en landerijen werden verzwolgen.
De Biesbosch, een natuurgebied met kreken en moerasbossen bij Dordrecht, is ontstaan na deze ramp.

The Netherlands is located on the delta of the Rhine and Maas rivers. In the past, the sea held reign over the land. The first inhabitants could do little else than build their houses on higher ground or construct artificial mounds, known as terpen. This is what the Romans found on this delta when they expanded the boundaries of their empire far to the north.As commander of a calvary unit, Plinus the Older was surprised to find in 47 BC that 'people could live on these desolate spots.'

At about the same time as they converted to Christianity in the 8th century, the inhabitants began their battle with the water. In order to make more land usable, small parts were enclosed by dykes and primitive sluis doors were built to drain the water. Very slowly, the inhabitants colonised the higher land in the west.
It was a battle with varying degrees of success. When temperatures rose around 1200, sea levels rose. As a result, large tracts of land were again lost to the sea. The original Middle Zee, now the IJsselmeer, was nearly three times as large. The St Elisabeth flood covered the land in the southwest on the night of November 18, 1421. Villages and land were drowned. The Biesbosch, an area of marshes and creeks near Dordrecht is still a reminder of this disaster.

Die Niederlande liegen an der Stelle, an der Rhein und Maas in die Nordsee münden. In der Vergangenheit war das Meer hier wild und ungebändigt. Den Ureinwohnern blieb nichts anderes übrig, als ihre Häuser an höhergelegenen Orten zu errichten oder sich auf künstlich aufgeschütteten Hügeln - sogenannten Wurten - niederzulassen.
So fanden die Römer dieses Flußdelta vor, als sie die Grenze ihres Reiches nach Norden hin ausbreiteten. Als Befehlshaber einer Reitereinheit war Plinius der Ältere im Jahre 47 v. Chr. erstaunt darüber, daß 'in dieser trostlosen Gegend Menschen wohnen können'.

In etwa zur Zeit der Christianisierung begann im 8. Jahrhundert auch der gezielte Kampf gegen das Wasser. Um mehr Land nutzen zu können, wurden kleine Flächen mit Deichen geschützt, und in die Wasserläufe wurden primitive Schleusentore eingebaut, damit das Wasser bei Ebbe abfließen konnte. Langsam besiedelten die Bewohner des höher gelegenen östlichen Landesteils den Westen.
Dieser Kampf war von wechselndem Erfolg gekrönt. Als um das Jahr 1200 die Temperatur etwas anstieg, stieg auch der Meeresspiegel an. In der Folge wurden große Gebiete wieder vom Meer verschluckt. Die ursprüngliche Middelzee, das heutige IJsselmeer, vergrößerte sich auf fast das Dreifache. Im Südwesten wütete in der Nacht vom 18. auf den 19. November 1421 die St. Elisabeths-Flut. Dörfer und Ländereien wurden von den Fluten verschlungen.
Das Biesbosch, eine Naturlandschaft mit Prielen und Sumpfwäldern bei Dordrecht, entstand nach dieser Katastrophe.

Les Pays-Bas se situent à l'endroit où le Rhin et la Meuse se jettent dans la mer du Nord. Dans les temps anciens, la mer avait ici champ libre et les premiers occupants durent construire leurs habitations sur des terres élevées, ou s'installer sur des collines artificielles, les tertres.
C'est ainsi que les Romains ont découvert ce delta lors de l'élargissement des frontières de l'empire vers ces lointaines contrées nordiques. Commandant de cavalerie, Pline le Vieux s'étonnait en 47 avant J.C. du fait que 'des hommes pouvaient vivre sur cette plaine désolante'.

Pratiquement en même temps que la christianisation au 8e s., la lutte intentionnelle contre l'eau commença. Pour gagner de nouvelles terres, des petits bassins furent endigués, et on installa dans les cours d'eau des vannes primitives afin de pouvoir évacuer les eaux à marée basse. Petit à petit les habitants des hautes terres situées dans l'Est du pays colonisèrent l'Ouest.
La lutte eut un succès inégal. Vers l'an 1200 la température augmenta légèrement et le niveau de la mer s'éleva. En conséquence, de grandes parties de terres durent être restituées aux eaux. L'ancien 'Middelzee' (mer du milieu), devenu aujourd'hui lac d'IJssel, tripla de surface. Le 19 novembre 1421, jour de la Sainte Elisabeth, une terrible marée se déchaîna, engloutissant des villages entiers. Un des résultats de cette catastrophe est le Biesbosch, un parc naturel composé d'étangs et de marécages.

Holanda se encuentra situada en la desembocadura al Mar del Norte de los rios Rin y Mosa. En el pasado este lugar era juguete de las olas del mar. Sus antiguos moradores no podían hacer otra cosa que construir sus moradas o bien en sitios naturales elevados o construyendo ellos mismos estas elevaciones que llamamos cerros.
De esta forma, al extender sus fronteras hacia el norte, encontraron los romanos este delta.
Plinio el Viejo, comandante de una unidad de caballeria en el año 47 a.C., se sorprendía por el hecho de que "pudieran vivir gentes en esta planicie tan desolada".

Conjuntamente con la cristianización en el siglo octavo se empezó también la lucha expresamente dirigida contra la subida del agua. Para poder apropiarse de tierra, se construyeron diques protegiendo territorios asi como unas primitivas esclusas en los cauces fluviales para poder desaguar durante el reflujo.
Gradualmente los pobladores de la parte alta oriental, fueron colonizando la tierra que se iba secando en la parte occidental.
Esta lucha contra el agua no fue fácil y de resultados diversos. Cuando alrededor del año1.200 subió algo la temperatura, ascendió el nivel del mar. Por ello volvieron a inundarse de nuevo grandes extensiones de tierra ya secada. El mar Middenzee original, el actual IJsselmeer, se triplicó en extensión. En el sudoeste se desencadenó durante la noche del 18 de noviembre de 1.421 la marea alta llamada de Sta. Isabel que se tragó pueblos y fincas rurales.
La región del Biesbosch con sus arroyos y lugares pantanosos, en los alrededores de Dordrecht, es aún un remanente de dicho desastre.

A Holanda encontra-se no sítio onde o Reno e o Mosa desaguam no Mar do Norte. No passado o mar reinava aqui completamente. Os habitantes primitivos pouco mais podiam fazer do que construir os seus povoados em terrenos altos ou fixar-se em pequenos montes de terra artificiais, outeiros. Assim encontraram os romanos este delta, quando eles alargaram as fronteiras do seu estado em direcção ao norte longínquo. Como comandante de uma unidade de cavalaria, Plinius Senior admirou-se, no ano 47 a.C., sobre a facto de como é que "as pessoas podiam viver nesta planície desolada".

Practicamente ao mesmo tempo que a cristianização, no século oito, começou o combate orientado contra a água. Para poder usar mais terrenos, foram feitos diques à volta de uma pequena região e nas correntes dos rios foram construídas comportas, para poder manter a água durante as marés baixas. A pouco e pouco os habitantes das regiões mais altas na parte leste do país, foram colonizando o ocidente. Foi uma luta de êxitos variáveis. Quando por volta do ano 1200 a temperatura aumentou um pouco, o nível do mar subiu. Por esta causa, foram perdidas ao mar grandes superfícies de terreno. O Lago Central, de então, e agora chamado o Lago Eissel, tornou-se quase três vezes maior. No sudoeste deu-se, na noite de 18 para 19 de Novembro de 1421, a Inundação de Santa Isabel. Aldeiamentos e campos foram cobertos pela águas. O "Biesbosch", uma região natural com enseadas e pantanais, nas proximidades de Dordrecht, apareceu depois dessa catástrofe.

De Nederlandse kust wordt bijna over de hele lengte beschermd door duinen met zandstranden. Waar dit, zoals bij Petten, niet het geval is werd een hoge zeedijk aangelegd. Ook langs de voormalige Zuiderzee hebben de dijken een indrukwekkende hoogte. De vuurtoren van het vroegere eiland Urk waakt nu over de scheepvaart op het IJsselmeer.

Nederland heeft met het water een soort haat/liefde verhouding. Beelden van historische scheepswerven, drogende netten van palingvissers, schaatsers en die enkele boer die zijn koeien nog per boot vervoert zijn net zo realistisch als de merktekens op een boerderij, die de hoogten markeren van het water bij de diverse overstromingen. (volgende bladzijden)

The Dutch coast is protected by dunes and beaches over nearly its entire length. In other places, such as Petten, a high sea dyke has been built. Along the former Zuider Zee the dykes also are impressively high. The lighthouse on the former island of Urk now overlooks shipping in the IJsselmeer.

The Netherlands has a sort of love/hate relationship with water. Prints of historical shipyards, drying nets of eel fishermen, skaters and the few farmers who continued to move their cattle by boat are as realistic as the signs on a farm house which mark the water levels in times of flood.

Die niederländische Küste wird fast auf ihrer gesamten Länge von Dünen und Sandstränden geschützt. Wo dies nicht so ist, wie beispielsweise bei Petten, wurde ein hoher Seedeich angelegt. Auch entlang der ehemaligen Zuiderzee erreichen die Deiche eine beeindruckende Höhe. Der Leuchtturm der früheren Insel Urk wacht nun über die Schiffahrt auf dem IJsselmeer.

Mit dem Wasser verbindet die Niederlande seit jeher eine Art Haßliebe. Bilder, die historische Schiffswerften, trocknende Aalfischernetze, Schlittschuhläufer oder den einzelnen Bauern zeigen, der seine Kühe noch mit dem Boot transportiert, sind ebenso realistisch wie die Markierungen auf einem Bauernhof, die den Wasserstand bei Überschwemmungen angeben. (Folgende Seiten)

Un cordon de dunes protège la côte néerlandaise sur presque toute sa longueur. Aux endroits où ce cordon est interrompu, comme à Petten, une haute digue de mer fut érigée. Les digues autour de l'ancien Zuiderzee impressionnent également par leur hauteur. Le phare d'Urk, autre fois une île, veille aujourd'hui sur la navigation du lac d'IJssel.

Les Pays-Bas ont un rapport 'haine-amour' avec les eaux. Un chantier naval historique, le sêchage des filets des pêcheurs d'anguilles, ces patineurs et ce paysan qui transporte ses vaches par bateau, toutes ces images sont aussi réelles que la borne-repère à côté d'une ferme indiquant le niveau des eaux lors d'inondations successives. (Pages suivantes)

Practicamente la totalidad de la costa holandesa está protegida por dunas y playas arenosas.
A falta de ello, como por ejemplo en Petten, se ha construido un alto dique marítimo. Tambien se han construido estos diques preventivamente alrededor del antiguo Zuiderzee. El faro de la vieja isla de Urk guía ahora la navegación en el IJsselmeer.

Desde siempre Holanda ha mantenido una relación de amor y odio con el agua. Las imágenes de históricos astilleros, redes de pescadores de anguilas secando al sol, patinadores sobre hielo y al mismo tiempo señales en las paredes de las granjas marcando el nivel al que había llegado el agua en cada inundación dan clara muestra de dicha relación. (Páginas siguientes)

A costa holandesa é protegida quase na sua totalidade por dunas com praias de areia. Onde estas não existem, como em Petten, foi construído um dique marinho. Também ao longo do ex- Mar do Sul foram construídos diques de uma altura impressionante. O farol da ex-ilha Urk, vela agora pela frota do Lago Eissel.

A Holanda tem com a água uma espécie de relacionamento de amor/ódio. Imagens dos estaleiros históricos, das redes dos pescadores de enguias, a secar, de patinadores e de um camponês transportando as suas vacas de barco, são tão realistas como as marcas nas casas das quintas, mostrando as alturas a que a água subiu nas diversas inundações. (Páginas seguintes)

1740 EN EEN
STOND HET WATER
AAN DESEN STEEN.
1819 EN EEN
STOND HET WATER
AAN DESEN STEEN
1809 IS HET WATER
AAN DESEN STEEN
GESTEGEN

De waterzijde van een stad was vroeger vaak belangrijker dan de landzijde. Over het water kwam de handelswaar per schip zoals het geval was bij de Koppelpoort te Amersfoort over het riviertje de Eem en de Koornmarktpoort te Kampen die de stad opende voor het graan dat de Hanzekoggen in de Middeleeuwen over de IJssel aanvoerden uit de Oostzeelanden. (beide links) Harderwijk en Elburg waren van oudsher vissersplaatsen. De rechts afgebeelde poorten worden dan ook in beide stadjes Vispoort genoemd.

Les villes d'antan accordaient plus d'importance à leur côté tourné vers l'eau, qu'à celui vers les terres, car c'est en bateau qu'arrivaient les marchandises. C'était le cas à Amersfoort avec sa Koppelpoort, porte située sur l'Eem, et à Kampen où la Koornmarktpoort (porte du marché au blé), au moyen âge, ouvrait la ville aux navires de la Hanse, qui apportaient par l'IJssel le blé des pays baltiques. Harderwijk et Elburg (g.) étaient depuis toujours des ports de pêche. Ainsi, dans ces deux villes, les portes représentées à droite, ont été nommées 'Vispoort' (porte aux poissons).

The water side of a city was often more important than the land side. Merchandise was landed by ship as in the case of the Koppelpoort at Amersfoort where the ships moved through th small Eem river, and the Koornmarktpoort in Kampen whch opened the city to grain shipments from the Baltic states via the IJssel river in the Middle Ages. (both left) Harderwijk and Elburg were originally fishing villages. The gates seen at the right were called Vispoorts where fish were landed in both cities.

Antiguamente la parte que daba al agua de una ciudad era más importante que su parte de tierra. Navegando por el agua llegaban los barcos y el comercio y asi por ejemplo navegando por el riachuelo Eem entraban por la puerta Koppelpoort de Amersfoort; en la Edad Media en Kampen la puerta Koornmarktpoort abría la ciudad al transporte de grano que las naves hanseáticas navegando por el Ijssel traían de los países Bálticos. (Ambos izquierda) Tradicionalmente fueron siempre Harderwijk y Elburg pueblos pesqueros. Ambas puertas representadas a la derecha son llamadas por ello Vispoort (puerta del pescado).

Die dem Wasser zugewandte Seite einer Stadt war früher häufig wichtiger als die Seite zum Landesinneren hin. Über Wasser kam die Handelsware mit dem Schiff, wie zum Beispiel durch das Koppelport in Amersfoort über das Flüßchen Eem und das Kornmarkttor in Kampen, durch das das Getreide der Hansekoggen im Mittelalter über die IJssel aus den Ostseeländern in die Stadt kam. (Beide links)
Harderwijk und Elburg sind alte Fischerorte. Die rechts abgebildeten Tore wurden deshalb auch in beiden Städten Fischtor genannt.

A parte da cidade que mostra para a água era antigamente mais importante do que o lado interior. Pela água vinham os produtos comerciais de barco, como se dava no Portal Koppel, em Amersfoord, através da ribeira Eem e o Portal do Koornmarkt, em Kampen que dava entrada à cidade para os cereais que os Hanzekoggen transportavam,
na Idade Média, através do rio Eissel, vindos dos Países do Mar Báltico. (Ambos à esquerda) Hardewijk e Elburg eram antigamente aldeias de pescadores. Os portais que figuram no lado direito receberam por isso o nome de "Vispoort" (Portais dos Pescadores).

COVA

Oude kaarten van Nederland uit de 16de eeuw tonen een land met grote inhammen en binnenmeren in open verbinding met de zee. Waterbouwkundige en molenbouwer Jan Adriaansz. Leeghwater ontwikkelde plannen met een groep Amsterdamse financiers om de binnenmeren ten noorden van de stad droog te leggen. Voor de toenmalige stand der techniek een geweldig project Met behulp van honderden molens werden in een periode van 20 jaar duizenden hectaren land op het water gewonnen.
Een bedreiging vormde de Haarlemmermeer tussen de plaatsen Haarlem, Leiden en Amsterdam. De westenwind zweepte de golven op en van de oostelijke oever ging steeds meer land verloren. Er was berekend dat drooglegging met windmolens hier geen haalbare kaart was. Het duurde tot 1852 eer met behulp van stoomgemalen ook deze waterwolf was getemd. Slechts weinigen zullen dit beseffen als zij landen op de luchthaven Schiphol.
Door al dit menselijk ingrijpen kreeg Nederland zijn huidige vorm. Twee projecten bleven een doorn in het oog van de ondernemende waterbouwers: de Zuiderzee en de Zeeuwse Stromen.
Na de Eerste Wereldoorlog ontwikkelde ir. Lely plannen voor het inpolderen van deze binnenzee. De aanleiding vormde de voedselschaarste tijdens de oorlogsperiode. Het project werd in fasen uitgevoerd. In 1932 werd de Afsluitdijk voltooid en de laatste polder, Zuidelijk Flevoland, viel droog in 1968. Totaal een landwinst van 1650 km^2.
Na de grote overstromingsramp in februari 1953 werden de Zeeuwse Stromen aangepakt. Om het water buiten te houden werden de eilanden met dammen verbonden en werd in 1997 als slotstuk een enorme beweegbare schuif in de Nieuwe Waterweg aangebracht.

Old maps of the Netherlands dating from the 16th century show a country with large lakes and bays in open contact with the sea. Hydraulic engineer and windmill builder Jan Adriaansz. Leeghwater developed plans with Amsterdam financiers to drain the lakes north of the city. It was a tremendous project given the then-current techniques. With the help of hundreds of windmills thousands of hectares of land were created from water over a period of 20 years. The Haarlemmermeer was a threat to the cities of Amsterdam, Haarlem and Leiden. Westerly winds pushed the waves to the eastern edge of the lake and more land was lost. It took until 1852, but this 'beast' was tamed with the help of steam-driven pumps. Only a few people know that Amsterdam's Schiphol Airport has been built on what was once the bottom of this lake, six metres below sea level.
The Netherlands got its present form from all this human activity. Two projects proved to be a thorn in the eye of the developers: the Zuider Zee and the Zeeuwse Stromen - inlets in Zeeland.
After World War I, the engineer Cornelis Lely developed plans to empolder the inland sea then known as the Zuider Zee. The food shortages during the war made this necessary. The project was carried out in stages. The enclosing dam known as the Afsluitdijk was completed in 1932 and the last polder in the sea, the southern part of Flevoland was completed in 1968. The project created 1650 hectares of land.
After the great flood of 1953, the Zeeuwse Stromen were attacked. In order to keep the water at bay, the islands were linked by dams culminating in the huge flood barrier in the Nieuwe Waterweg leading to Rotterdam which was completed in 1997.

Ältere Karten von den Niederlanden im 16. Jahrhundert zeigen ein Land mit großen Buchten und Binnenseen, die offen mit dem Meer verbunden sind. Der Wasserbautechniker und Mühlenbauer Jan Adriaansz. Leeghwater entwickelte zusammen mit einer Gruppe Amsterdamer Kaufleute einen Plan zur Trockenlegung der Binnenseen im Norden von Amsterdam. Für den damaligen Stand der Technik ein gigantisches Vorhaben. Mit Hilfe Hunderter von Mühlen wurden in einem Zeitraum von 20 Jahren tausende von Hektar Land dem Wasser entrissen. Eine Bedrohung bildete das Haarlemmermeer zwischen den Orten Haarlem, Leiden und Amsterdam. Der Westwind peitschte die Wellen auf und am östlichen Ufer ging immer mehr Land verloren. Anhand von Berechnungen erkannte man, daß eine Trockenlegung mit Windmühlen hier nicht durchführbar war. Es dauerte noch bis 1852, bis mit Hilfe dampfgetriebener Schöpfwerke auch dieser "Wasserwolf" gezähmt wurde. Nur sehr wenige Menschen sind sich dessen bewußt, wenn sie auf dem Flughafen Schiphol landen.
Durch all diese Eingriffe des Menschen erhielten die Niederlande ihre heutige Form. Zwei Projekte blieben den tatkräftigen Wasserbauingenieuren jedoch ein Dorn im Auge: die Zuiderzee und die seeländischen Meeresarme.
Nach dem 1. Weltkrieg entwickelte der Ingenieur Lely Pläne für die Einpolderung dieses Binnenmeers. Anlaß dazu war die Lebensmittelknappheit während des Krieges. Das Projekt wurde in Etappen durchgeführt. 1932 wurde der Abschlußdeich fertiggestellt, und der letzte Polder, das südliche Flevoland, wurde bis 1968 trockengelegt. Insgesamt konnten so 1650 km^2 Land gewonnen werden.
Nach der großen Flutkatastrophe im Februar 1953 wurde auch das Projekt der seeländischen Flußmündungen in Angriff genommen. Um das Wasser abzuwehren, wurden die Inseln mit Dämmen verbunden, und 1997 ließ man als Abschluß ein riesiges bewegliches Schütz in den Nieuwe Waterweg ein.

Les anciennes cartes des Pays-Bas du 16e s. montrent un pays de grands golfes et de lacs en communication ouverte avec la mer. Hydraulicien et constructeur de moulins, Jan Adriaansz. Leeghwater, soutenu par des financiers amstellodamiens, développa un plan d'assèchement des lacs situés au nord de la ville. Ce fut un projet gigantesque, si l'on tient compte du niveau de la technique de l'époque. A l'aide de centaines de moulins, on a gagné sur l'eau des milliers d'hectares de terres sur une période de vingt ans. Une autre menace était le lac de Haarlem, situé entre les villes de Haarlem, Leiden et Amsterdam. Le vent d'ouest soulevait les vagues et les rives orientales perdaient de plus en plus de terrain. Une étude montra que la mise à sec par moulins à vent n'était point réalisable ici. Et on dut attendre 1852 avant que ce 'waterwolf' (loup d'eau) soit apprivoisé à l'aide de pompes à vapeur. Peu de gens s'en rendront compte en atterrissant à l'aéroport de Schiphol.
Toutes ces interventions humaines donnèrent aux Pays-Bas sa forme actuelle. Cependant, il restait une épine dans le pied des ingénieurs : le 'Zuiderzee' (mer du Sud), et les bras de mer de Zélande.
Proposé par l'ingénieur Lely, un projet de poldérisation pour le golfe fut adopté après la 1ere Guerre Mondiale. Il devait également résoudre les problèmes de pénurie alimentaire. Les travaux d'aménagement furent entrepris par étapes. La 'afsluitdijk' (digue de fermeture) fut achevée en 1932, et le dernier polder, Flevoland-Sud, fut asséché en 1968. Au total, une récupération de 1650 km^2 de terres.
Suite au désastre des inondations de février 1953, on s'attaqua au problème des bras de mer de Zélande. Pour se protéger des eaux, les îles furent reliées par des barrages. L'étape finale fut la pose d'une gigantesque vanne mobile dans le Nieuwe Waterweg en 1997.

Mapas antiguos de Holanda del siglo 16 nos muestran un país con grandes ensenadas y mares interiores en conexión abierta con el mar.
El arquitecto hidráulico y constructor de molinos Jan Adriaansz. Leeghwater ideó un plan, ayudado por un grupo de financieros de Amsterdam, para desecar los mares que se encontraban al norte de la ciudad. Un proyecto grandioso si se tiene en cuenta el desenvolvimiento técnico en dicha época. Con la ayuda de cientos de molinos bombeando agua y en un periodo de tiempo de 20 años, se desaguaron miles de hectáreas de tierra. El mar Haarlemmermeer situado entre las ciudades de Haarlem, Leiden y Amsterdam formaba una gran amenaza ya que con vientos del oeste el azote de sus olas en la orilla oriental hacia perder tierra en su favor. El desecado de este mar por medio de molinos era imposible de realizar tecnicamente. Es por ello que no se logró dominar este mar hasta el 1.852 con la ayuda de la maquina hidráulica para el desagüe. Pocos viajeros se dan cuenta de ello al aterrizar en el aeropuerto de Schiphol.
A traves de todas estas intervenciones humanas, se fué dando forma a la actual Holanda.
Sin embargo quedaron dos proyectos como espinas en los ojos de los arquitectos hidráulicos, a saber, el Zuiderzee y las corrientes de Zelanda.
Acabada la Primera Guerra Mundial, el ingeniero dr. Lely concibió los planes para el desecado del mar interior Zuiderzee. La razón de este proyecto se derivó de la falta de alimento durante el periodo de la mencionada guerra debido a la falta de tierras de cultivo.
El proyecto se llevó a termino en diversas fase. En 1.932 se terminó el Afsluitdijk, dique que cerraba el Zuiderzee del mar abierto y en 1.968 se desecó el último polder, el Zuidelijk Flevoland habiendose ganado un total de 1.650 km cuadrados.
Despues de las grandes inundaciones de febrero del 1.953, se dedicó toda la atención a las corrientes de Zelanda. Para impedir el paso del agua se unieron las diversas islas por medio de diques y en 1.997 como final de proyecto se instaló en el Nieuwe Waterweg una enorme compuerta movible.

Mapas antigos da Holanda, do século 16, mostram terras com grandes baías e lagunas, com ligação ao mar. O Engenheiro de Hidráulica e Constructor de Moínhos, Jan Adriaansz Leeghwater desenvolveu uns planos, com um grupo de financeiros de Amesterdão, para secar os lagos ao norte da cidade. Considerando a situação técnica dessa altura era um projecto enorme. Com a assistência de centenas de moínhos ao vento, num período de 20 anos foi conquistada ao mar uma grande quantidade de terreno. Uma ameaça passou a ser o Lago de Haarlem, entre os lugares Haarlem, Leiden e Amesterdão. O vento de Oeste açulou as ondas e na margem ocidental perdeu-se cada vez mais terreno. Tinha-se calculado que a dessecagem com os moínhos aqui era impossível. Chegou-se a 1852 antes que, com auxílio de bombas a vapor, se dominasse este "monstro aquático". Pouca gente estará consciente deste facto, quando aterrem no Aeroporto de Schiphol.
Devido a todas estas intromissões humanas, a Holanda foi recebendo a sua forma actual. Dois projectos tornaram-se "uma espinha na garganta" dos constructores activos: O Mar do Sul e as Correntes da Zelândia.
Depois da Primeira Guerra Mundial, o Eng. Lely desenvolveu planos para a polderização deste mar interno. O motivo foi a grande falta de alimentos durante o período da guerra. O projecto foi realizado em fases. Em 1932 foi terminado o "Afsluitdijk" (Dique de Encerramento), e o último pólder, o Flevoland do Sul, foi ressecado em 1968. Um ganho de terreno de 1650 km2. Depois da grande inundação catastrofal de Fevereiro de 1953, iniciaram-se os trabalhos nas Correntes da Zelândia. Para se manterem as águas no exterior, as ilhas foram ligadas entre si com diques e em 1997 foi montada, como apoteose, uma enorme comporta movediça, no Canal Novo (Nieuwe Waterweg).

De loop van rivieren is altijd bepalend geweest voor de plaats van de nederzettingen die later uitgroeiden tot steden. De buitenbochten van de rivieren creëerden goede aanlegplaatsen voor schepen. Nederland heeft talrijke steden met een prachtig waterfront. Goede voorbeelden zijn de historische steden Deventer (l.) en Nijmegen (r.)

The courses of the rivers determined the location of the settlements which later became cities. The outer curves of the streams created good landing stages for ships. The Netherlands has many cities with splendid waterfronts. Good examples are the historic cities of Deventer (left) and Nijmegen (right).

Der Lauf der Flüsse war schon immer entscheidend für die Wahl der Niederlassungen, die später zu Städten heranwuchsen. Ausbuchtungen von Flüssen waren stets gute Anlegeplätze für Schiffe. In den Niederlanden gibt es zahlreiche Flüsse mit wunderschönen Uferfronten. Hervorragende Beispiele dafür sind die historischen Städte Deventer (l.) und Nimwegen (r.).

Les cours d'eau ont toujours défini les lieux d'implantation, qui se développèrent plus tard en villes. Sur les rives extérieures des boucles des fleuves furent créés des appontements. Les Pays-Bas possèdent de nombreuses cités dotées de quais remarquables, comme les villes historiques de Deventer (g.) et Nimègue (dr.).

El cauce de los rios ha marcado siempre el lugar donde se establecían primero colonias que mas tarde por su crecimiento se convertían en ciudades. El recodo que formaban los meandros de los rios era lugar ideal para establecer amarraderos para los barcos y por consiguiente colonias y ciudades. En Holanda se encuentran numerosas ciudades con hermosas fachadas en su parte ribereña. Buenas muestras de ello las encontramos en las ciudades de Deventer (izq.) y Nimega (d.)

O curso dos rios foi sempre determinante para a posição das povoações, que mais tarde chegavam a cidades. As curvas exteriores dos rios criavam boas oportunidades para amarragem dos barcos. A Holanda tem imensas cidades com magníficas condições fluviais. Bons exemplos disso são as cidades históricas Deventer (esq.) e Nimega (dir.).

Het water fungeerde tijdens een groot aantal eeuwen als de natuurlijke infrastructuur. De Waal, de Rijn en de Lek zijn de hoofdverbinding tussen de havens van Rotterdam en Amsterdam en het Duitse Ruhrgebiet. Bij de sluizen van Wijk bij Duurstede passeert dagelijks een groot aantal tank- en containerschepen.
De waterstand in de grote rivieren moet in droge tijden worden gereguleerd. Grote stuwen zoals deze in de Lek bij Hagestein dragen bij tot een goed waterniveau op de zeer drukbevaren Waal. Waar de rivier een belemmering vormt voor het verkeer en er geen noodzaak bestaat om een brug te bouwen, wordt de oeververbinding onderhouden door een ouderwetse veerpont.

L'eau a fait fonction d'infrastructure naturelle pendant de longs siècles. Le Waal, le Rhin et le Lek sont les liens principaux entre les ports de Rotterdam et Amsterdam et ceux du bassin de la Ruhr en Allemagne. Les écluses de Wijk bij Duurstede voient passer quotidiennement un grand nombre de porte-conteneurs et de tankers.
Le niveau de l'eau doit être régulé pendant les périodes de sécheresse. A cet effet, de grands barrages comme celui de Hagestein dans le Lek, montrent leur efficacité sur les fleuves au trafic intense. Là, où le fleuve fait obstacle à la circulation routière, et s'il n'y a pas nécessité de construire un pont, la liaison entre les rives est confiée à un bac à l'ancienne.

Water functioned as the natural infrastructure for a good many centuries. The Waal, Rijn, Lek and IJssel rivers are the main links between the ports of Rotterdam and Amsterdam and Germany's Ruhr industrial area. A large number of tankers and container vessels pass by the locks at Wijk bij Duurstede every day.
Water levels in the big rivers have to be regulated in dry periods of weather. Large dams such as this near Hagestein on the Lek river help maintain a good water level on the very heavily trafficked Waal river. Where the river becomes an obstacle for traffic and there is no need to build a bridge, crossings are maintained by old-fashioned ferries.

En el transcurso de muchos siglos, el agua formó la infraestructura natural del pais. Los rios Waal, Rin y Lek son las rutas principales entre los puertos de Rotterdam y Amsterdam y la zona industrial del Ruhr. Muchos barcos contenedores y cisternas pasan diariamente por las esclusas de Wijk bij Duurstede.
En tiempos de sequía es necesario regular el nivel del agua de los grandes rios. Grandes presas como ésta en el Lek a la altura de la ciudad de Hagestein contribuyen a mantener el nivel de agua adecuado para facilitar la navegacion tan activa que se da en el Waal. Cuando un rio forma un obstáculo para el tráfico terrestre y no hay necesidad de construir un puente, se opta entonces por facilitar el tráfico entre las dos márgenes del rio por medio de un clásico pontón

Wasser bildete viele Jahrhunderte lang eine natürliche Infrastruktur. Waal, Rhein und Lek sind die Hauptverbindung zwischen den Häfen von Rotterdam und Amsterdam und dem Ruhrgebiet. Zahlreiche Tank- und Containerschiffe passieren Tag für Tag die Schleusen von Wijk bei Duurstede.
Der Wasserstand der großen Flüsse muß in trockenen Zeiten reguliert werden. Große Stauwerke wie das in der Lek bei Hagestein tragen zu einem brauchbaren Wasserstand auf der äußerst vielbefahrenen Waal bei. Wo der Fluß ein Hindernis für den Verkehr darstellt und die Errichtung einer Brücke nicht notwendig ist, werden die Ufer mit einer altmodischen Fähre miteinander verbunden.

A água teve, durante muitos séculos, a função de infraestrutura natural. Os rios Waal, Reno e Lek formam as ligações principais entre os portos de Roterdão e Amesterdão e a Região alemã do Ruhr. Nas comportas de Wijk bij Duurstede passa todos os dias uma grande quantidade de navios de contentores e de tanques. O nível da água nos rios grandes tem que ser regulado, nos períodos de secura. Enormes comportas, como esta no rio Lek, próximo de Hagestein, contribuem para a manutenção de um nível adequado, no rio Waal de muito movimento. Onde o rio forma um impedimento para o trânsito e não existe a necessidade de se construir uma ponte, regula-se o transporte entre as margens por meio de embarcações especiais

Dommelsch Bier

Tot in de 14de eeuw was de Middelzee een groot binnenmeer dat werd gevoed door het water van de IJssel, de Eem, de Vecht en de Overijsselse Vecht. Ook de landengte tussen Westfriesland en Friesland was niet zo breed als nu. Door zware noordwesterstormen werden grote stukken land verzwolgen en vormde zich de Zuiderzee. Slechts twee hoger gelegen plekken bleven gespaard: de eilanden Schokland en Urk. In de jaren twintig, toen de behoefte aan een groter landbouwareaal zich aandiende, werd de beslissing genomen grote delen van de Zuiderzee in te polderen. Het plan omvatte in eerste instantie 5 polders, maar van inpoldering van de laatste, de Markerwaard werd vanwege landschap en milieu na 1968 afgezien.
De twee eilanden zijn nu volledig opgenomen in het polderlandschap. Het kanon van Schokland waarschuwt niet langer tegen het water en op de zeebodem ploegt nu een tractor. De Unesco gaf Schokland de status van internationaal erfgoed. Urk, vanouds reeds een kleine vissershaven, heeft zich ontwikkeld tot een belangrijk centrum voor de visserij en de visverwerking.

Until the 14th century, the Middel Zee was a vast inland sea fed by the IJssel, Eem, Vecht and Overijsselse Vecht rivers. The isthmus between Westfriesland and Friesland was not always as broad as it is now. Heavy northwest storms swallowed up large tracts of land and formed the Zuider Zee. Only two higher spots remain, the former islands of Schokland and Urk. It was decided to empolder large parts of the Zuider Zee in the 1920s when there was need for more agricultural land. The plan called for five large polders in the first stage, but the empoldering of the last, the Markerwaard was called off in 1968 because of the need for recreational water and the environment. The two islands are now included in the polder landscape. Schokland's cannon no longer warns its inhabitants against high waters and tractors now plow the former sea bed. Unesco has named Schokland an international heritage site. Urk, formerly a fishing port, has developed into a major centre for the fishing and fish processing industry.

Bis in das 14. Jahrhundert war die Middelzee ein großer Binnensee, in den das Wasser von IJssel, Eem, Vecht und Overijsselse Vecht strömte. Auch die Landenge zwischen Westfriesland und der niederländischen Provinz Friesland war nicht so breit wie heute. Durch schwere Nordwest-Stürme wurden große Landstriche verschlungen, und es entstand die Zuiderzee. Nur zwei höhergelegene Flecken blieben verschont: die Inseln Schokland und Urk. Als in den zwanziger Jahren mehr landwirtschaftliche Flächen benötigt wurden, beschloß man, große Teile der Zuiderzee einzupoldern. Der Plan sah ursprünglich 5 Polder vor, doch der letzte, der Markerwaard-Polder, wurde schließlich aus landschafts- und umweltschützerischen Gründen nach 1968 nicht mehr eingepoldert. Die beiden Inseln sind heute vollständig in die Polderlandschaft integriert. Die Kanone von Schokland warnt nicht mehr vor den Fluten, und den Meeresboden pflügt der Bauer nun mit seinem Traktor. Die Unesco erklärte Schokland zum Weltkulturerbe. Urk, das von alters her ein kleiner Fischerhafen war, entwickelte sich zu einem wichtigen Zentrum der Fischerei und der Fischverarbeitung.

Jusqu'au 14e s., le Middelzee était une sorte de grand golfe, alimenté par les eaux de l'IJssel, l'Eem, le Vecht et le Vecht d'Overijssel. L'isthme entre la Frise et la Frise occidentale n'était pas si large qu'aujourd'hui. De grands morceaux de terre furent engloutis à cause des tempêtes de nord-ouest, et le Zuiderzee se forma. Seules les îles de Schokland et d'Urk furent épargnées . Dans les années vingt fut entrepris l'assèchement d'une grande partie de cette mer, suite à un besoin grandissant de superficie agricole. Cinq polders étaient prévus dans les plans initiaux, mais pour des raisons de protection de paysage et de l'environnement, on renonça à assécher le dernier, le Markerwaard, en 1968. Les deux îles sont aujourd'hui complètement intégrées dans le paysage des polders. Le canon de Schokland ne donne plus l'alerte contre les assauts de la mer, et un tracteur laboure les anciens fonds marins. L'Unesco a attribué le statut de patrimoine mondial à Schokland. Urk, jadis petit port de pêche, s'est développé en un centre important de pêche et de transformation du poisson.

Hasta el siglo 14, el Middenzee fué un gran mar interior que se veía alimentado por las aguas de los rios IIssel, Eem, Vecht y Overijsselse Vecht. Tampoco el istmo entre la Frisia Occidental y Frisia era tan ancho como en la actualidad. Las fuertes tormentas procedentes del noroeste que inundaron grandes extensiones de terrenos llevaron consigo la formación del Zuiderzee. Solamente sobresalían dos elevaciones de terreno: las islas de Schokland y Urk. Cuando en los años 20 se acentuó la necesidad existente de terreno agrícola, se tomó la decisión de convertir grandes trozos del Zuiderzee en pólderes. En principio el plan constaba de 5 pólderes pero finalmente en 1.968 se renunció al último poder, el de Markerwaard, por razones paisajistas y de medio ambiente. Las dos islas mencionadas están ahora completamente incorporadas al paisaje del pólder en donde se encuentran. El cañon de Schokland no avisa ya del peligro del agua y el fondo marino de antaño es labrado ahora por un tractor. La Unesco concedió a Schokland el título de patrimonio internacional. Urk, desde antiguo una poblacion pesquera, ha sabido desarrollarse hasta convertirse en un importante centro de pesca y elaboración de productos derivados de la misma.

Até ao século 14, o Mar Central foi um lago, que era alimentado pelas águas dos rios Eissel, Eem, Vecht e o Vecht de Overeissel. Também o istmo entre a Frísia Oriental e a Frísia não era tão largo como agora. Devido a tempestades do noroeste foram arrancados grandes pedaços de terra e assim se formou o Mar do Sul. Apenas dois sítios mais altos foram poupados: as ilhas Schokland e Urk. Na década dos vinte, quando havia uma grande necessidade de terrenos para a agricultura, foi tomada a decisão de polderizar grandes partes do Mar do Sul. O plano continha em primeira instância 5 pólderes, mas a polderização do último, o Markerwaard, foi anulada em 1968 por motivo da paisagem e do ambiente. As duas ilhas estão presentemente incluídas na paisagem rural do pólder. O canhão de Schokland já não precisa de avisar pelo risco de uma inundação e no fundo do mar lavra agora um tractor. A UNESCO deu a Schokland a qualidade de património internacional. Urk, já em tempos passados um pequeno porto piscatório, desenvolveu-se a um centro importante de pesca e de elaboração de peixe.

De voltooiing van de Afsluitdijk op 28 mei 1932 maakte een eind aan de vaak onstuimige Zuiderzee. In 5 jaar tijd werd 42 miljoen kubieke meters grond aangevoerd ten behoeve van deze 32 kilometer lange dijk. Voor die tijd was het project dermate kolossaal dat vrijwel alle Nederlandse baggeraars moesten toetreden tot het consortium dat door de regering met de uitvoering werd belast.
De dijk vergrootte niet alleen de veiligheid van het achterliggende gebied, maar verkortte tevens de afstand tussen de provincies Noord-Holland en Friesland.

The completion of the Afsluitdijk (the IJsselmeer Dam) on 28 May 1932 signalled the end of the often tempestuous Zuider Zee. Forty-two million cubic metres of soil were transported over a five-year period to make this 32-kilometre-long dyke. It was such a colossal project for its time that virtually every Dutch dredging company there was had to join the consortium that was commissioned by the government to build it. The construction of the dyke made it safer for the areas behind it, and it also cut the distance between the provinces of North Holland and Friesland.

Die Fertigstellung des Abschlußdeichs am 28. Mai 1932 machte der oft stürmischen Zuiderzee ein Ende. In nur 5 Jahren wurden 42 Millionen Kubikmeter Erde für diesen 32 Kilometer langen Deich herangeschafft. Für die damalige Zeit war dieses Projekt so gigantisch, daß nahezu alle niederländischen Baggerführer einem Konsortium beitreten mußten, das von der Regierung mit der Durchführung dieser Arbeiten beauftragt worden war.
Der Deich vergrößerte nicht nur die Sicherheit des dahinterliegenden Gebiets, er verkürzte auch die Entfernung zwischen den Provinzen Nord-Holland und Friesland.

L'achèvement de la Digue de Fermeture le 28 mai 1932 a sonné l'heure de la fin du Zuiderzee, si souvent impétueux. En cinq ans, 42 millions m3 de terre furent transportés pour la construction de cette digue longue de 32 km. Les travaux ont été d'une ampleur extrême pour l'époque, et presque toutes les entreprises néerlandaises de dragage durent entrer dans le consortium chargé des travaux par le gouvernement. Non seulement la digue augmentait la sécurité du territoire situé en arrière, mais elle raccourcissait également la distance entre la Hollande-Septentrionale et la Frise.

La terminación del dique Afsluitdijk el 28 de mayo de 1932 puso fin al frecuentemente tempestuoso mar Zuiderzee. En 5 años se transportaron 42 millones metros cúbicos de tierra para la realización de este dique de 32 km. de longitud. Para el tiempo en que se ralizó este proyecto, era de tal magnitud que casi todas las empresas de dragados del pais formaron parte del consorcio al que el gobierno encargo el trabajo. Este dique no solo aumentó la seguridad de las tierras colindantes sino que tambien acortó la distancia que separa las provincias de Holanda Septentrional y Frisia.

O acabamento do "Afsluitdijk", em 28 de maio de 1932, pôs em termo ao, muitas vezes, impetuoso Mar do Sul. Em 5 anos foram transportados 42 milhões de metros cúbicos de terra, para formar o dique com os seus 32 quilómetro de comprimento. Antes disso, este projecto era de tal maneira monstruoso que quase todos os empresários de trabalhos de dragagem na Holanda, tiveram que participar num consórcio, que foi encarregado pelo governo holandês pela realização desses trabalhos. O dique aumenta não só a segurança das terras interiores, mas diminui também a distância entre as províncias Holanda Nórdica e a Frísia.

De Haarlemmermeerpolder is de grootste droogmaking in westelijk Nederland. Als meer strekte het zich uit tussen Leiden, Haarlem en Amsterdam. Het meer werd vaak waterwolf genoemd omdat het vanaf de 16de eeuw maar liefst 5 dorpen heeft verzwolgen. Al in 1641 werden de eerste plannen voor de drooglegging ontwikkeld, maar het duurde tot 1852 eer het gebied droog was. Drie grote stoomgemalen moesten vier jaar pompen. De polder ligt gemiddeld 4 meter onder de zeespiegel. Op de luchthaven Schiphol, in de noordwesthoek van de polder, is een merkteken aangebracht dat de diepte tegenover de zeespiegel aangeeft.

The Haarlemmermeerpolder is the largest reclaimed area in the west of the Netherlands. When it was still a lake it covered the area between Leiden, Haarlem and Amsterdam. The lake was more often than not referred to as a `water wolf' because since the sixteenth century it had swallowed up no fewer than five villages. The first reclamation plans were drawn up in 1641, but it was not until 1852 that the area was finally dry. Three huge steam-driven pumping units worked flat out for four years to remove the water. The polder is an average of four metres below sea level. At Schiphol Airport in the north-west corner of the polder there is a sign showing where sea level is.

Der Haarlemmermeer-Polder stellt die größte Trockenlegung im Westen der Niederlande dar. Der See erstreckte sich zwischen Leiden, Haarlem und Amsterdam. Er wurde häufig "Wasserwolf" genannt, da er seit dem 16. Jahrhundert sage und schreibe 5 Dörfer verschlungen hatte. Bereits im Jahre 1641 wurden die ersten Pläne für eine Trockenlegung entwickelt, doch dauerte es noch bis 1852, bevor das Land dem Wasser abgerungen werden konnte. Drei große Dampfschöpfwerke mußten vier Jahre lang pumpen. Der Polder liegt durchschnittlich 4 Meter unter dem Meeresspiegel. Am Flughafen Schiphol, in der nordwestlichen Ecke des Polders, befindet sich eine Markierung, die die Tiefe im Vergleich zum Meeresspiegel angibt.

L'assèchement le plus important dans le Ouest du pays est celui du polder du lac de Haarlem. Jadis, le lac se situait entre Leiden, Haarlem et Amsterdam. On l'appela 'loup d'eau', car il engloutit cinq villages depuis le 16e s. Dès 1641, on projeta son assèchement, mais les travaux ne furent achevés qu'en 1852. Trois grandes stations de pompage travaillèrent pendant quatre ans. Le polder se situe à 4 mètres en moyenne au-dessous du niveau de la mer. A l'aéroport de Schiphol, aménagé dans le Nord-ouest du polder, une borne-repère marque ce niveau.

El polder Haarlemmermeer es el proyecto de desecado mayor del la parte occidental de Holanda. Este mar se extendía entre las ciudades de Leiden, Haarlem y Amsterdam. Se le llamaba tambien lobo de mar porque en el siglo XVI hizo desaparecer 5 pueblos. Ya en el año 1641 se hicieron planes para el desecado de este mar pero hasta el 1852 no se llevó a término. Tres enormes máquinas hidráulicas de vapor necesitaron 4 años de trabajo continuo para llevar a término el trabajo. Este polder está a 4 metros de promedio por debajo del nivel del mar. En el aeropuerto de Schiphol, en el ángulo noroeste, se ha puesto una señal marcando la diferencia con el nivel del mar.

O pólder do "Haarlemmermeer" é a maior dessecação no ocidente da Holanda. Como lago estende-se ele entre Leiden, Haarlem e Amesterdão. O lago foi chamado muitas vezes "o lobo aquático", porque desde o século 16 já 'engoliu' 5 aldeias. Já em 1641 foram feitos planos para a sua secagem, mas teve-se que esperar até 1852 antes que a região estivesse livre da água. As bombas enormes a vapor trabalharam durante 4 anos.
O pólder encontra-se a 4 metros debaixo do nível do mar. No aeroporto de Schiphol, no ângulo a nordeste do pólder, foi colocada uma marca que indica o ponto mais baixo em relação ao nível do mar.

Zeeland is veruit de waterrijkste provincie. Het wapen van Zeeland draagt niet voor niets de spreuk: Luctor et emergo (ik worstel en kom boven). Sinds mensenheugenis is het gebied door overstromingen en door landaanwinningen van vorm veranderd. Aan het begin van de jaartelling was Zeeland een kleine archipel. Door de verzanding van de kreken groeiden de kleinere eilanden vast aan de grotere.
Reeds in de Romeinse tijd waren de hoger gelegen gebieden bewoond. Het was een welvarend gebied. Vanwege de grote vruchtbaarheid van de bodem ontwikkelde zich een sterke landbouw. Binnen de visserij lag de nadruk op de haringvangst. In de 17de eeuw maakte Middelburg deel uit van de Oostindische en van de Westindische Compagnie.
Een grote watersnoodramp voltrok zich op 1 februari 1953. Een noordwesterstorm deed op talrijke plaatsen de dijken breken en vrijwel geheel Zeeland viel ten prooi aan het water. 900 inwoners verloren het leven. Het herstel van de dijken werd energiek ter hand genomen. Op 6 november van hetzelfde jaar werd het laatste gat gedicht. Deze ramp was de aanleiding tot een groots plan om het water definitief buiten te sluiten: het Deltaplan.

Zeeland is the province with by far the most water. The Zeeland coat of arms bears the telling motto Luctor et emergo (I wrestle and I emerge). The area has been changing shape as a result of flooding and land reclamation for as far back as people can remember. In prehistoric times Zeeland was a small archipelago. The smaller islands slowly grew to meet the larger ones as a result of the silting up of streams.
The higher areas were inhabited as early as Roman times. It was a prosperous area. Agriculture was very successful thanks to the high fertility of the soil. Herring was the main fishing catch. In the seventeenth century Middelburg was part of the Dutch East Indies Company and West Indies Company.
Disastrous floods occurred on 1 February 1953. A northwesterly storm breached the dykes in many places and virtually the whole of Zeeland was submerged. Nine hundred people lost their lives. The repair of the dykes was tackled with enormous energy. The last breach was closed on 6 November that same year. This disaster was the reason behind the huge-scale plan to keep the water out for good: the Delta Plan.

Zeeland ist bei weitem die wasserreichste Provinz der Niederlande. Das Wappen von Zeeland trägt nicht umsonst den Spruch: Luctor et emergo (Ich ringe und tauche auf). Seit Menschengedenken hat dieses Gebiet immer wieder durch Überschwemmungen und Landgewinn seine Form verändert. Zu Beginn der Zeitrechnung war Zeeland ein kleiner Archipel. Durch die Versandung der Priele wuchsen die kleineren Inseln mit größeren zusammen.
Bereits zu Zeiten der Römer waren die höhergelegenen Gebiete bewohnt. Die Gegend war wohlhabend. Auf dem äußerst fruchtbaren Boden entwickelte sich eine leistungsstarke Landwirtschaft. In der Fischerei lag der Schwerpunkt auf dem Heringsfang. Im 17. Jahrhundert war Middelburg Teil der Ostindischen und der Westindischen Kompanie.
Eine große Flutkatastrophe ereignete sich am 1. Februar 1953. Ein Nordwest-Sturm brachte zahlreiche Deiche zum Brechen, und fast ganz Zeeland fiel den Fluten zum Opfer. 900 Einwohner verloren ihr Leben. Die Deichreparaturen wurden energisch vorangetrieben. Am 6. November desselben Jahres wurde das letzte Loch abgedichtet. Diese Katastrophe gab den Anstoß zu einem großen Vorhaben, mit dem das Wasser definitiv bezwungen werden sollte: dem Deltaplan.

La Zélande est la province où l'eau est la plus abondante. Aussi, ses armes portent le dicton : Luctor et emergo (je lutte et émerge). De mémoire d'homme, le territoire a constamment changé de forme par des inondations ou des conquêtes de terre. Au début de notre ère, la Zélande était un petit archipel. Par ensablement des bras de mer, les îles de petite taille se relièrent aux plus grandes. Déjà à l'époque romaine, les terres émergées furent habitées. Grâce à la fertilité de ses sols, la région prospéra et une agriculture puissante se développa. La pêche se concentra sur le hareng. Au 17e s. la ville de Middelburg faisait partie de la Compagnie Réunie des Indes orientales et occidentales. Une violente tempête de nord-ouest causa la grande catastrophe du 1er février 1953, qui fit 900 morts. Un raz de marée rompit les digues à de nombreux endroits, submergeant la presque totalité de la zone. La réparation des digues fut énergiquement menée. Ainsi, le 6 novembre de cette même année, la dernière brèche fut colmatée. Ce désastre fut à l'origine d'une entreprise ambitieuse pour exclure définitivement les eaux : le plan Delta.

Zelanda es con mucho la provincia en donde más abunda el agua. No sin razón lleva el blasón de dicha provincia la leyenda: Luctor et emergo (Lucho y salgo del agua). De tiempos inmemoriables, la fisionomía de esta región se ha visto afectada por las inundaciones y los intentos de recuperar tierra al mar. En el principio de nuestra era, Zelanda era un pequeño archipiélago. Por medio de los bancos de arena arrastrados por los numerosos rios, se unieron las islas pequeñas a las grandes.
Ya en tiempo de los romanos, las partes altas de las mismas eran habitadas. Desde siempre fué una región muy próspera. Debido a la gran riqueza de su suelo se desarrolló una gran industria agrícola. Su flota pesquera se especializó en la pesca del arenque. En el siglo XVII Middelburg formó parte de la Compañía de las Indias Orientales y Occidentales.
El 1 de febrero de 1953 tuvo lugar una desastrosa inundación. Una tempestad proveniente del noroeste rompió los diques por numerosos lugares e inundó casi la totalidad de Zelanda. Con gran energía se empezó la reconstrucción de dichos diques, trabajo que fué finalizado el 6 de noviembre del mismo año. Esta inundación fué el motivo para la creacion de un gran plan para contener el agua y evitar futuros desastre, el Deltaplan.

Zelândia é a província que tem mais água. Não é sem razão que o brasão de Zelândia tem a máxima: Luctor et emergo (eu luto e emergo). Desde tempos imemoráveis que a região foi modificada por inundações e por conquistas de terreno. No princípio da nossa era, Zelândia era um pequeno arquipélago. Devido a assoreamento das lagunas as pequenas ilhas cresceram até se ligarem às maiores. Já no tempo dos romanos as terras mais altas eram habitadas. Era uma região rica. Pela grande fertilidade do solo, desenvolveu-se uma agricultura valorosa. Na pescaria o mais importante era a pesca do arenque. No século 17 Middelburg fez parte da Companhia das Indias Oriental e Ocidental. Em 1 de fevereiro de 1953 deu-se uma grande inundação. Um vendaval do noroeste causou em vários locais roturas nos diques e quase toda a Zelândia foi submersa pelas águas. 900 habitantes perderam assim a vida. O restabelecimento dos diques foi empreendido energicamente. Em 6 de Novembro do mesmo ano foi tapado o último buraco. Esta catástrofe foi o motivo para um enorme plano que tinha como fim manter definitivamente a água fora: O Plano Delta.

W
O

PILOT 2

Het Deltaplan voorziet in het afsluiten van de zeearmen in Zuidwest-Nederland om een korte en effectieve zeewering te construeren. Het afsluiten van de Westerschelde, de vaarweg naar Antwerpen en van de Nieuwe Waterweg de vaarroute naar Rotterdam, bleef buiten beschouwing. De Zeeuwse en Zuid-Hollandse eilanden zijn verbonden met dammen. De dam in de Oosterschelde is voorzien van ingenieuze schuiven die het Noordzeewater kunnen inlaten ten behoeve van de oester- en mosselcultuur.
In de Nieuwe Waterweg zijn in 1997 beweegbare deuren aangebracht die bij hoge vloed kunnen worden gesloten. De armen van de deuren hebben de lengte van de Eiffeltoren (blz. 38).

The Delta Plan involved shutting off the sea inlets in the southwest of the Netherlands, thus producing a short and effective sea defence. Shutting off the Western Scheldt, the waterway to Antwerp, and the New Waterway, the approach route to Rotterdam, was not considered. The Zeeland and South Holland islands are joined together by dams. The dam in the Eastern Scheldt has ingenious gates that let in water from the North Sea for the oyster and mussel beds.
In 1997 movable doors were installed in the New Waterway. They can be closed if there is a flood tide. The beams of the doors are as long as the Eiffel Tower is high (page 38).

Der Deltaplan sah den Abschluß der Meeresarme in Südwesten der Niederlande vor, um eine kurze und wirksame Landbefestigung zu konstruieren. Die Westerschelde, die den Schiffahrtsweg nach Antwerpen bildete, und der Nieuwe Waterweg, der auf der Wasserstraße nach Rotterdam lag, sollten nicht abgeschlossen werden. Die seeländischen und südholländischen Inseln wurden mit Dämmen verbunden. Der Damm in der Osterschelde ist mit ausgeklügelten Schützen ausgestattet, mit denen Nordseewasser für die Austern- und Muschelzucht eingelassen werden kann. Im Nieuwe Waterweg wurden 1997 bewegliche Tore angebracht, die bei Hochwasser geschlossen werden können. Die Flügel der Tore sind so lang wie der Eiffelturm (S. 38).

Le plan Delta prévoyait la fermeture des estuaires du Sud-ouest du pays, sauf l'Escaut occidental et le Nieuwe Waterweg, voies d'accès aux ports d'Anvers et de Rotterdam. Les îles de Zélande et de Hollande-Méridionale furent reliées par des barrages. Celui de l'Escaut oriental présente d'ingénieuses vannes coulissantes, qui permettent l'entrée des eaux de la mer du Nord, afin de préserver l'ostréiculture et la mytiliculture. Depuis 1997, le Nieuwe Waterweg bénéficie d'un ouvrage, dont les portes peuvent être fermées en cas de marée de tempête. Les bras de ces portes ont la longueur de la Tour Eiffel (page 38).

El Deltaplan consistía en cerrar los brazos de mar en el suroeste de Holanda con la construccion de un corto y efectivo dique. De este plan se excluyeron el Escalda occidental (Westerschelde) y el Nieuwe Waterweg, rutas marinas a los puertos de Amberes y Rotterdam respectivamente. Las antiguas islas de Zelanda y Holanda Meridional fueron unidas por diques. El dique construido en la Escalda oriental ha sido provisto de unas compuertas movibles que permiten la entrada del agua del mar del Norte en provecho de los criaderos de ostras y mejillones. En el Nieuwe Waterweg se colocaron en el 1997 puertas movibles que pueden ser cerradas durante la marea alta. Los brazos de estas puertas tienen tanta longitad como la torre Eiffel. (pag.38).

O Plano Delta prevê o encerramento dos braços de mar, no sudoeste da Holanda, para construir uma protecção contra a água mais curta e mais efectiva. As ilhas da Zelândia e as ilhas do Sul da Holanda foram ligadas entre si, por meio de diques.
O dique no Escalda Ocidental possui umas comportas movediças engenhosas, que podem deixar entrar as águas do Mar do Norte, para favorecer a cultura das ostras e dos mexilhões.
No Canal Novo foi montada em 1997 uma comporta movediça, que pode ser encerrada em caso de águas altas. Os braços das comportas têm um comprimento igual à altura da Torre Eifel (pag. 38).

De Nederlandse geschiedenis in vogelvlucht

A birds-eye view of Dutch history

Streifzug durch die niederländische Geschichte

Esquisse de l'histoire des Pays-Bas

Panorama de la historia de Holanda

A história da Holanda em vista de pássaro

De eerste sporen van menselijke bewoning zijn in Nederland zo'n 11.000 jaar oud. Alles wat wij over onze voorouders weten hebben archeologen moeten afleiden uit vondsten: aardewerk, vuursteenbijlen en pijlpunten, later ook handgereedschappen eerst gemaakt van brons, later van ijzer.

In het neolithicum werd het noordoosten van het land bewoond door stammen van de Trechterbekercultuur. Zij begroeven hun doden in hunebedden, gestapelde zwerfstenen overdekt met aarde.

Tot de komst van de Romeinen werd het gebied bewoond door drie Germaanse stammen: de Friezen in het noorden en westen, de Saksen in het oosten en de Franken in het zuiden.

De Romeinen stichtten langs de Rijn, die toen ten westen van Leiden in zee uitmondde, een groot aantal versterkte nederzettingen, zoals Maastricht, Nijmegen, Utrecht en Leiden. In de eeuwen die volgden op de Romeinse overheersing ontwikkelden de bisschoppen van Utrecht een aanzienlijke macht. Zij werden tot het begin van de 12de eeuw gesteund door de Duitse keizers.

Op plaatselijk niveau speelden de waterschappen een belangrijke rol met hun verordeningen over dijken, waterlopen en dientengevolge landinrichting.

In de 9de eeuw verschenen de Noormannen aan de Nederlandse kusten. Zij kwamen om handel te drijven, maar als dit naar hun opvatting niet goedschiks verliep, kwam het voor dat hele nederzettingen werden gebrandschat.

In de vroege middeleeuwen trachtten de graven van Gelre, Holland en de hertogen van Brabant steeds meer macht te verwerven. Zij streden niet alleen tegen de opkomende steden, maar vooral tegen de Utrechtse bisschoppen. Rond het begin van de 15de eeuw raakten de Nederlanden onder het bewind van het Bourgondisch-Habsburgse Rijk.

De opkomende Hervorming bracht grote onrust te weeg. De afkeer van de Kerk werd versterkt door het steeds hardere optreden van de Inquisitie. Het ongenoegen over het vreemde gezag en de intolerantie van de Kerk versterkten elkaar bij de drang naar separatisme. Onder het gematigde regime van keizer Karel V was dit alles minder merkbaar dan onder zijn opvolger Philips II, die vanuit het Escorial, de Lage LaLnden rigide wilde onderwerpen. Prins Willem van Oranje, opgegroeid aan het hof van Karel V, wierp zich op als de leider van de opstandelingen en samen met zijn broer leverde hij in 1568 een eerste veldslag met de Spaanse bezetting.

The first traces of human settlement date back a maximum of 11,000 years. Everything we know about these early Dutchmen archeologically comes from discoveries: pottery, chimney pipes and arrow shafts. At a later stage there were tools first made of bronze, then of iron. In Neolithic times, the northeast part of the country was occupied by branches of the so-called 'Trechterbeker' culture. They buried their dead in megolthic tombs: connected boulders covered by earth.

Until the arrival of the Romans, the area was inhabited was three German-origin groups: the Frisians in the north and west, the Saxons in the east and the Franks in the south. The Romans settled along the Rhine when then joined the open sea to the west of Leiden. The Roman settlements were fortified and included Maastrcht, Nijmegen, Utrecht and Leiden.

In the period after the Roman dominance, authority was mostly in the hands of the bishops of Utrecht. Until the beginning of the 12th century, the bishops of Utrecht were supported by the German powers.

On a local level, the water boards played a major role with their regulations relating to the dykes and waterways and consequently last use.

In the 9th century, the Normans appeared on the Dutch coast. They came mainly for trade, but if things did not go their way, they often torched the local settlements. In the early Middle Ages, the counts of Gelre and the dukes of Brabant gained increasing strength. They fought not only against the growing cities, but also, and primarily, against the bishops of Utrecht. Around the beginning of the 15th century, the Netherlands fell under the rule of the Burgandy-Hapsburg state. Trade flourished as never before and, parallel to this, the rulers' needs for money. In exchange for money, however, they extorted increasing more privileges.

The rising reformation brought great unrest. The aversion to the church was strengthened by the increasingly harder approach of the Inquisition. The dissatisfaction over the unusual governance and the intolerance of the church strengthened each other in pressure for separatism. Under the moderate regime of King Charles V this was less notable than under that of his successor, Philip II, who from his seat in the Escorial imposed a very rigid rule over his possession in northern Europe. Prince William of Orange, who was raised by Charles V, appeared as their leader, and with his brother lead the first battle against the Spanish occupying forces in 1568.

Die ersten Spuren menschlicher Besiedlung sind in den Niederlanden etwa 11.000 Jahre alt. Alles, was wir über unsere Vorfahren wissen, mußten Archäologen aus Funden ableiten: Tonwaren, Feuersteinäxte und Pfeilspitzen, später auch Handwerkszeug, erst aus Bronze, später dann aus Eisen.

Im Neolithikum wurde der Nordosten des Landes von Stämmen der Trichterbecherkultur bevölkert. Sie begruben ihre Toten in Megalithgräbern, aufeinander gestapelten Findlingen, die mit Erde bedeckt wurden.

Bis zur Ankunft der Römer wurde das Gebiet von drei germanischen Stämmen bewohnt: den Friesen im Norden und Westen, den Sachsen im Osten und den Franken im Süden. Die Römer errichteten entlang des Rheins, der damals westlich von Leiden ins Meer mündete, eine ganze Reihe bewehrter Siedlungen, wie beispielsweise Maastricht, Nimwegen, Utrecht und Leiden. In den Jahrhunderten nach der römischen Herrschaft gelang es den Bischöfen von Utrecht, ihre Macht beträchtlich auszuweiten. Sie wurden bis Anfang des 12. Jahrhunderts durch die deutschen Kaiser unterstützt. Auf lokaler Ebene spielten die 'Waterschappen' mit ihren Verordnungen über Deiche, Wasserläufe und somit auch die Landaufteilung eine große Rolle.

Im 9. Jahrhundert tauchten die Normannen an den niederländischen Küsten auf. Sie kamen, um Handel zu treiben, aber wenn dies ihrer Auffassung nach nicht im Guten möglich war, kam es vor, daß ganze Niederlassungen gebrandschatzt wurden.

Im frühen Mittelalter versuchten die Grafen von Geldern und Holland und die Herzöge von Brabant, immer mehr Macht zu erlangen. Sie kämpften nicht nur gegen die aufstrebenden Städte, sondern vor allem gegen die Utrechter Bischöfe. Gegen Anfang des 15. Jahrhunderts gerieten die Niederlande unter den Einfluß des burgundisch-habsburgischen Reichs.

Das Aufkommen der Reformation brachte große Unruhe ins Land. Die Abkehr von der Kirche wurde durch das immer härtere Durchgreifen der Inquisition gefördert. Unzufriedenheit mit der Fremdherrschaft und Unmut über die Intoleranz der Kirche verstärkten sich beim Drang nach Separatismus gegenseitig. Unter der gemäßigten Herrschaft von Kaiser Karl V. war dies alles weniger deutlich zu spüren als unter seinem Nachfolger Philipp II., der den Niederlanden von El Escorial aus eine strenge Unterwerfung aufzwingen wollte. Prinz Wilhelm von Oranien, der am Hofe von Karl V. aufgewachsen war, machte sich zum Anführer der Aufständischen und lieferte sich 1568 gemeinsam mit seinem Bruder die erste Feldschlacht mit den spanischen Besatzern.

Les premières traces d'une occupation humaine datent de 11000 ans. Des fouilles archéologiques nous racontent l'histoire de nos ancêtres : poteries, pointes de flêche et haches en silex, outils en bronze et en fer.
Dès le néolithique, le Nord-est connaît la civilisation dite 'du gobelet en entonnoir'. Ce peuplement ensevelit ses morts dans les 'hunebedden', des salles couvertes, formées d'un alignement de dolmens et dissimulées sous un petit tumulus.
Les objets apparus au siècle dernier en déblayant les tertres en raison de leur terre fertile, donnent des informations sur la vie sur ces collines artificielles.
Jusqu'à l'arrivée des romains, le territoire fut peuplé par trois tribus germaniques : Frisons dans le Nord et l'Ouest, Saxons dans l'Est et Francs au Sud.
Le long des grands fleuves, les romains fondèrent des villes fortifiées, comme Maastricht, Nimègue, Utrecht et Leiden. Les siècles suivant l'occupation romaine furent caractérisés par un pouvoir grandissant des évêques d'Utrecht, soutenus par les empereurs germaniques jusqu'au début du 12e s. Au niveau local les 'wateringues', chargés de la réglementation et du contrôle des cours d'eau et des digues, jouèrent un rôle important dans l'aménagement du territoire.
Au 9e s., les Normands firent leur apparition sur les côtes néerlandaises. Venus en commerçants, ils se transformèrent en pilleurs de villes entières, dès que l'occasion s'en présentait.
Dans le haut moyen âge, les comtes de Gueldre et de Hollande et les ducs de Brabant tentèrent d'augmenter leur pouvoir. Non seulement ils luttèrent contre les villes en plein développement, mais surtout contre les évêques d'Utrecht. Dès le 15e s. les Pays-Bas passèrent sous la domination des Bourguignons et des Habsbourg. Le commerce prospérait, et parallèlement, les besoins d'argent des princes et des nobles s'accrurent. Cette situation permit à la population, représentée aux Etats-Généraux, d'obtenir des privilèges en échange d'argent.
La Réforme naissante occasionna une agitation croissante. L'aversion à l'égard de l'Eglise était renforcée par les actions de plus en plus dures de l'Inquisition. Le mécontentement inspiré par l'autorité étrangère et l'intolérance de l'Eglise fortifièrent le mouvement pour le séparatisme. Sous le régime modéré de l'empereur Charles Quint, cela fut moins sensible que lors du règne de son successeur Philippe II, qui, depuis l'Escurial, voulut soumettre les Pays-Bas de façon extrêmement rigide. Le prince Guillaume d'Orange, élevé à la cour de Charles Quint, s'érigea en meneur des insurgés, et, aux côtés de son frère, livra en 1568 une première bataille contre l'occupation espagnole.

Las primeras huellas de los habitantes de Holanda se fechan con un máximo de 11.000 años de antigüedad. Todos los conocimientos sobre nuestros antepasados los han sacado los arqueólogos del material encontrado en sus excavaciones: vasijas de barro, hachas de pedernal, flechas y ya de épocas posteriores, utensillos hechos primero de bronze y mas tarde ya de hierro.
Durante la época del Neolítico, la parte noreste del pais estuvo ocupada por tribus de la cultura Trechterbeker. Esta tribu enterraba sus muertos en un dolmen hecho de piedras apiladas y cubiertas de tierra.
Hasta la llegada de los romanos, esta región estuvo habitada por tres pueblos, los frisios en el norte y oeste, los sajones en el este y los francos al sur. Los romanos establecieron diversos asentamientos fortificados a lo largo del Rin, que en esa época desembocaba al mar por el oeste de la ciudad de Leiden, como son Maastricht, Nimega, Utrecht y Leiden.En los siglos siguientes a la ocupación romana los obispos de Utrecht obtuvieron un gran poder y estuvieron apoyados hasta el comienzo del siglo XII por los emperadores alemanes. A nivel local los consejos del agua tuvieron un importante papel por sus ordenanzas sobre diques, cursos de agua y por consiguiente la distribución de la tierra.
En el siglo IX aparecieron los normandos por las costas holandesas. Venían con propósitos mercantiles pero si ello no se realizaba segun su parecer de manera correcta, no dudaban en matar e incendiar a toda la colonia. Durante el principio de la edad media, los condes de Gelre y Holland y los duques de Brabant intentaron hacer acopio de poder luchando no solo contra las nuevas ciudades que iban creciendo sino tambien contra los obispos de Utrecht. Hacia el comienzo del siglo XV los holandess estaban sometidos al poder del imperio borgoñon-habsburgués.
La naciente reforma trajo consigo una gran intranquilidad social. La repulsa contra la iglesia se vió sustentada y alimentada por la cruel actuación de la Inquisición. El descontento por estar la autoridad en manos extranjeras asi como la intolerancia de la iglesia fueron las causas que reforzaron las ansias del separatismo. Este sentimiento fue menos visible durante el régimen del emperador Carlos V pero se hizo mas visible cuando su sucesor Felipe II, desde su trono del Escorial, quiso gobernar esta región con mano dura. El principe Guillermo de Orange, criado en la corte de Carlos V, se presentó como el primer lider de este sepratismo y junto con su hermano presentó en 1.568 la primera batalla contra la ocupación española.

Os primeiros vestígios de povoação na Holanda datam de à volta de 11.000 anos. Tudo o que sabemos dos nossos avós tiveram os arqueólogos que deduzir de objectos encontrados: loiça, machadas de pedra e pontas de flexas, mais tarde também ferramentas, primeiro feitas de bronze e depois de ferro.
No Neolítico, o nordeste do país foi habitado por tribos da Cultura das Copos em Funil. Eles enterravam os seus mortos em Dólmens, pedras amontoadas cobertas de terra.
Até à altura da chegada dos romanos, a região foi habitada por três tribos germânicas: os frísios ao norte e no ocidente, os saxões no oriente e os francos no sul. Os romanos fundaram ao longo do Reno, que nessa altura desaguava no mar, a sul de Leiden, uma grande quantidade de povoações reforçadas, como Maastricht, Nijmegen, Utrecht e Leiden. Nos séculos depois do domínio romano, os bispos de Utrecht criaram um poder considerável. Eles receberam, até ao princípio do século 12, apoio dos imperadores alemães. A nível local, as instâncias de protecção aos pólders, desempenharam um papel importante com os seus decretos sobre os diques, as correntes de água e, por consequência, a distribuição das terras.
No século 9 apareceram os normandos na costa holandesa. Eles vieram para fazer negócio, mas quando não negociavam à vontade deles, acontecia às vezes que eles queimavam povoações completas.
No princípio da Idade Média os condes de Gelre, Holanda, e os duques de Brabância, tentavam adquirir cada vez mais poderes. Eles lutavam não só contra as cidades em desenvolvimento, mas em especial contra os bispos de Utrecht. Por volta do princípio do século 15 os holandeses foram submetidos ao regime do Reino da Burgûndia-Habsbúrgia. O comércio cresceu e paralelamente cresceu a necessidade de dinheiro dos monarcas e fidalgos. Os vassalos, representados nos estados, foram assim colocados numa situação, na qual eles, em troca de dinheiro, exigiam cada vez mais privilégios.
As reformas que começaram a aparecer causaram grande perturbação. A aversão contra a igreja aumentou com a actuação cada vez mais rigorosa da Inquisição. O descontentamento contra a autoridade estranha e a intolerância da igreja reforçavam-se mutuamente no desejo de separação. Sob o regime moderado do imperador Carlos V, isto notava-se menos do que sob o seu sucessor Filipe II, o qual do Escorial, submetia os Países Baixos rigidamente. O Príncipe Guilherme de Orange, criado na corte de Carlos V, avançou como dirigente dos rebeldes e com o seu irmão levou a efeito, em 1568, a primeira batalha com os ocupantes espanhois.

Nederland telt 53 hunebedden. Zij dateren uit de periode 2000 -1400 v.C. en zijn gebouwd als gemeenschappelijke graven. De zwerfstenen zijn aangevoerd door het landijs in de voorlaatste ijstijd. In vroeger tijd werden de hunebedden soms door de plaatselijke bevolking gesloopt om te dienen als bouwmateriaal. In de graven zijn sieraden en aardewerk gevonden als grafgiften voor de overledenen. De meeste zijn gesitueerd in Drenthe, de provincie op de hogere zandgronden.
Op de plaatsen waar het water telkens weer een bedreiging vormde wierpen de bewoners kunstmatige heuvels op om droog te kunnen wonen.In de loop der eeuwen groeiden de terpen door het storten van mest en dagelijks afval. Vooral dit laatste stelt ons in de gelegenheid meer over de bewoners te weten te komen.

There are 53 megalithic tombs in the Netherlands. They date from the period between 2000 and 1400 B.C. and were built as communal graves. The boulders were deposited by glaciers from a previous ice age. In times past some of the megalithic tombs were demolished by the local population and used for building materials. Jewellery and pottery that had been burial gifts for the deceased were found in the graves. Most of them are to be found in Drenthe, a province with relatively high sandy ground.
In areas where water was a continuous threat, the inhabitants made artificial hillocks so they could build their homes on dry land. Over the centuries the mounds grew through the accumulation of manure and everyday waste. This waste gives us a particularly valuable opportunity to learn more about the inhabitants.

In den Niederlanden gibt es 53 Hünengräber. Sie stammen aus der Zeit von 2000 bis 1400 vor Christus und wurden als Gemeinschaftsgräber angelegt. Die Findlinge wurden durch das Inlandeis der vorletzten Eiszeit herangeschwemmt. Früher wurden die Hünengräber manchmal von der örtlichen Bevölkerung abgerissen und als Baumaterial verwendet. In den Gräbern fand man Schmuck und Tonwaren als Grabbeigaben für die Verstorbenen. Die meisten dieser Gräber liegen in Drenthe, einer Provinz auf den höhergelegenen Sandgebieten.
An Stellen, an denen das Wasser immer wieder eine Bedrohung darstellte, errichteten die Bewohner künstliche Hügel, um im Trockenen wohnen zu können. Diese sogenannten Wurten wuchsen im Lauf der Jahrhunderte durch die Ablagerung von Mist und Abfällen immer weiter an. Vor allem Letztere ermöglichen uns heute, mehr über die Bewohner zu erfahren.

On a recensé 53 'hunebedden' aux Pays-Bas. Ils datent de 2000 - 1400 avant J.C. et servaient à enterrer les morts en groupe. Les rochers utilisés sont des blocs erratiques provenant d'un glacier scandinave de l'avant-dernière glaciation. La population locale démolit les 'hunebedden' à l'époque, pour en faire usage comme matériaux de construction. Dans les tombeaux on a découvert des offrandes funéraires, poteries et bijoux, placés à côté des corps. La plupart de ces monuments sont groupés dans la Drenthe, une province aux sols sablonneux.
Là où l'eau constituait une menace régulière, les populations construisirent des collines artificielles, afin de pouvoir vivre au sec. Ces tertres s'accrurent au cours des siècles par le déversement quotidien de déchets et d'ordures ménagères, ce qui nous a permis de mieux connaître les occupants d'antan.

En Holanda encontramos 53 dólmenes. Datan del periodo 2.000 a 1.400 a. de C. y fueron construidos como tumbas colectivas. Las rocas erráticas fueron arrastradas por los hielos durante el penúltimo periodo glaciario. En tiempos pasados la población demolía los dólmenes para usarlos como material de construcción. En las tumbas se han encontrado joyas y cerámica que sirvieron como regalos mortuorios para los fallecidos. La mayoria de estos dólmenes se han encontrado en la provincia de Güeldres debido a su altas tierras.
En los lugares donde el agua formaba un constante peligro, los habitantes creaban cerros artificiales donde poder vivir. A traves de siglos, estos cerros iban creciendo debido al deposito de estiércol y residuos diarios. Sobretodo estos últimos nos ayudan a obtener información sobre la forma de vida de estos antepasados.

A holanda possui 53 dólmens. Eles datam do período entre 2000 a 1400 a.C e foram construídos como túmulos comuns. As pedras "vadias" deslocaram-se para aqui por meio dos gelos terrestes, no penúltimo período glaciário. Em tempos passados os dólmens eram, às vezes, destruídos pela população, e o material servia para a construção civil. Nos supúlcros foram encontradas joias e objectos de cerâmica, que serviram de ofertas aos falecidos. A maioria deles encontram-se em Drenthe, uma província nos terrenos arenosos mais altos. Nos lugares onde a água era constantemente uma ameaça, os moradores formavam pequenos montes, para sobre eles morarem enxutos.
Através dos séculos estes outeiros cresciam, porque os habitantes deitavam-lhes por cima estrume e o lixo diário. Em especial este último dá-nos a possibilidade de saber mais sobre os moradores.

In Noviomagum, zoals Nijmegen toen werd genoemd, hadden de Romeinen hun legerplaats. Ook in de Karolingische periode stond hier een kasteel, de Valkhof. De restanten van de kapel zijn nog aanwezig (linksboven). Waar de Rijn zich splitst in de huidige hoofdstroom de Waal en de iets minder belangrijke Beneden Rijn was een uitgezochte plaats om een kasteel te bouwen (linksonder en rechtsboven). Jacoba van Beieren was gravin van Holland, in de periode 1417- 433. Zij was een zeer strijdbare vrouw en trachtte zich te handhaven tegen de oprukkende macht van Bourgondiërs als Filips de Goede. Teylingen, bij Sassenheim, was haar laatste woonplaats (rechtsonder).

The Romans had their Noviomagum army base in Nijmegen. There was also a castle here, the Valkhof, during the Carolingian period. The ruins of the chapel can still be seen (top left). The point where the Rhine splits into the Waal and the slightly less important Lower Rhine was a perfect place to build a castle (top left and below right). Jacoba van Beieren (1417 - 1488) was Countess of Holland. She was a very warlike woman and tried to resist the aggression of the Burgundians, for example Philip the Good. She died in Teylingen, near Sassenheim (below right).

In Nimwegen hatten die Römer ihr Truppenlager Noviomagum. Auch in der karolingischen Zeit stand hier eine Burg, der Valkhof. Die Überreste der Kapelle sind noch zu sehen (links oben). Die Stelle, an der sich der Rhein in den heutigen Hauptarm Waal und den etwas kleineren Niederrhein teilt, war ein bevorzugter Ort für die Errichtung einer Burg (links unten und rechts oben). Jacobäa von Bayern war Gräfin von Holland (von 1417 bis 1433). Sie war eine sehr streitbare Frau und versuchte sich gegen die heranrückende Macht der Burgunder, wie Philipp des Guten, zu wehren. Teylingen bei Sassenheim war ihr letzter Wohnort (rechts unten).

Nimègue était un camp militaire romain du nom de Noviomagus. A la période carolingienne, un palais y fut dressé, le 'Valkhof' (Tour du faucon), dont subsistent les restes de la chapelle (g.en haut). L'endroit où le Rhin se divise en un bras principal, le Waal, et le Rhin Inférieur, s'avéra être un emplacement idéal pour la construction d'un château. (g.en bas et dr. en haut). Jacqueline de Bavière fut comtesse de Hollande de 1417 à 1433. Femme combative, elle chercha à se maintenir contre le pouvoir grandissant des Bourguignons comme Philippe le Bon. Elle mourut à Teylingen, près de Sassenheim (dr. en bas)

En Nimega establecieron los romanos su guarnición Noviomagnum. Durante el periodo carolingio hubo aquí tambien un castillo, el Valkhof. Existen aún los restos de su capilla (izquierda, arriba). En donde el Rin se divide en sus dos actuales brazos, el Waal y el menos importante Beneden Rin fue el lugar ideal para la construcción de un castillo (izquierda abajo y derecha arriba). Jacoba de Baviera fué condesa de Holanda y vivió de 1417 a 1433. Fué una aguerrida mujer que intentó mantener su condado contra el avance del poder de los borgoñones como Felipe el Bueno. Su última residencia fué Teylingen, en Sassenheim (derecha abajo).

Em Nimega os romanos tinham a sua base militar Noviomagum. No período dos Carolingos esteve aqui também um castelo, o Valkhof (Paço do Falcão). Os restos da capela ainda lá se encontram (à esquerda acima). O sítio onde o Reno bifurca na actual corrente principal o Waal e no menos importante o Reno Inferior, foi um lugar muito desejado para construir um castelo (à esquerda em baixo e à direita em cima).
A Jacoba de Bavária era a condessa da Holanda, que viveu de 1417 a 1433. Ela era uma mulher muito activa e tentou manterse contra a força crescente dos Borgonhas, como Filipe, o Bom. Teylingen, perto de Sassenheim, foi a sua última moradia. (à direita, em baixo).

De vrijmaking van Spanje

Op 1 april 1572 landde een groepje opstandelingen bij het stadje Brielle en forceerden de stadspoort. Nu sloeg de vlam in de pan. De stedelijke regeringen kwamen op 19 juli in Dordrecht bijeen en kondigden vrijheid van godsdienst af. Zij kozen Willem van Oranje als hun stadhouder. De godsdienstvrijheid was een belangrijke impuls voor de immigratie van Spaanse en Portugese joden en protestanten uit de zuidelijke Nederlanden en Frankrijk.
De oprichting van de Republiek der Zeven Vereenigde Nederlanden werd formeel in 1579 bekrachtigd door de Unie van Utrecht. De Spaanse koning Philips II stuurde meer huurlingen en gevreesd was hun legeraanvoerder, de hertog van Alva. Het land werd het toneel van hevige strijd. Onder opeenvolgende stadhouders als Maurits en Frederik Hendrik verliep de strijd steeds meer in het voordeel van de Republiek tot in 1648 de vrede van Münster een einde maakte aan deze tachtig jaar durende vrijheidsstrijd.
Tot de Franse Revolutie werd de Republiek afwisselend bestuurd door een stadhouder uit het geslacht van de Oranjes of door een raadpensionaris, een landsadvocaat. Dit hing af van de mate waarin de Staten, de vergadering van de afgevaardigden van de gewesten, al dan niet Oranjegezind waren.
In de winter van 1795 trokken Franse troepen de bevroren rivieren over en vestigden hier naar Frans voorbeeld de Bataafse Republiek. Stadhouder Willem V moest uitwijken naar Engeland.
Na de val van Napoleon werd de zoon van Willem V ingehaald op het strand bij Scheveningen en niet veel later wordt hij door een groep wijze mannen uitgeroepen tot koning Willem I.

Het begin van de parlementaire monarchie

Door de blokkade van de havens was het land in armoede gedompeld. De eerste maatregelen die Willem I nam waren gericht op het herstel van de economie. Hij gaf opdracht kanalen te graven, stimuleerde de opkomst van de industrie en zorgde voor de financiering door het oprichten van banken. De herstelde banden met de koloniën in de Oost en de West, waarvan het land was afgesneden geweest, droegen eveneens bij tot een economische opleving.
In het midden van de 19de eeuw kreeg nieuw gedachtegoed de kans zich te ontwikkelen. In deze periode werd de basis gelegd voor een zeer pluriforme samenleving. Een democratie waar de regering wordt gecontroleerd door een parlement waarin leden zitting hebben uit niet minder dan een tiental politieke partijen.

The Liberation from Spanish rule

On April 1, 1572, a group of rebels landed at the small city of Brielle and forced opened its gates. The flame was spreading. The city government met in Dordrecht on July 19 and declared freedom of religion. They chose William (Willem) of Orange as their governor or Stadhouder. Fredom of religion was an important impuse for the emigration of Spanish and Portuguese jews and protestants from the southern part of the Netherlands and France. The establishment of the United Republic of Seven Provinces was made formal in 1579 through the Treaty of Utrecht. Spain's King Philip II sent more mercenaries, placing them under the command of the Duke of Alva. Under succeeding Stadhouders, such as Maurits and Frederik Hendrik, the war moved more in favour of the Republic until in 1648 The Treaty of Munster put an end to the Eighty Year War.
The Republic was alternately ruled by a Stadhouder from the Orange family or by a Raadspensionaris, a government attorney. In the winter of 1795, French troops crossed the frozen rivers and establshed the Batavian Republic. Stadhouder Willem V escaped to England. In 1806, Napoleon appointed his brother Louis Napoleon as King, but this was not sufficient. In 1810, the Netherlands was taken over by France. After the Battle of Waterloo, the son of Willem V landed on the beach at Schevenigingen. Shortly afterwards, he was made King Willem I of the Netherlands.

The beginning of the parliamentary monarchy

Because of the blockade of the seaports during the French occupation, the country had plunged into poverty. Willem's first moves were aimed at the recovery of the economy. He ordered canals to be dug, stimulated the beginnings of the industrial revolution and took care of the financing of newly set up banks. The links with the colonies in the east and the west ,which had been cut, were restored and contributed to the recovery. Willem's successors had weaker personalities.

Under their governance, new ideas were given a chance to develop. Liberalism grew, the catholics could now leave their clandestine churches and the reformed, who were the overwhelming majority of the population, began to split into factions. The basis for the very pluriform political system which typlifies the Netherlands today was set in this period.

Befreiung von der spanischen Herrschaft

Am 1. April 1572 landete eine Gruppe Aufständischer nahe dem Städtchen Den Briel und eroberten die Stadt. Nun ging es hoch her. Die Stadtregierungen trafen sich am 19. Juli in Dordrecht und verkündeten die Religionsfreiheit. Sie ernannten Wilhelm von Oranien zu ihrem Statthalter.
Die Religionsfreiheit war ein wichtiger Impuls für die Zuwanderung von spanischen und portugiesischen Juden und Protestanten aus den südlichen Niederlanden und Frankreich. Die Gründung der Republik der sieben vereinigten Niederlande wurde mit der Union von Utrecht 1579 offiziell bekräftigt. Der spanische König Philipp II. schickte noch mehr Söldner; gefürchtet wurde vor allem ihr Heerführer, Herzog von Alba. Das Land wurde zum Schauplatz heftiger Kämpfe. Unter den folgenden Statthaltern Moritz und Friedrich Heinrich verlief der Kampf immer mehr zum Vorteil der Republik, bis 1648 der Friede von Münster diesem achtzig Jahre währenden Freiheitskampf ein Ende setzte. Bis zur französischen Revolution wurde die Republik abwechselnd von einem Statthalter aus dem Hause Oranien und von einem Ratspensionär oder Landesadvokat regiert. Dies hing davon ab, ob und in welchem Maße die "Staten", Oranien wohlgesonnen waren.
Im Winter 1795 zogen französische Truppen über die zugefrorenen Flüsse und errichteten hier nach dem Vorbild des französischen Zentralstaates die Batavische Republik. Statthalter Wilhelm V. mußte nach England fliehen. Nach dem Fall von Napoleon wurde der Sohn von Wilhelm V. am Strand bei Scheveningen feierlich empfangen und bald darauf von einer Gruppe weiser Männer zum König Wilhelm I. ausgerufen.

Die Anfänge der parlamentarischen Monarchie

Durch die Blockade der Häfen war das Land in Armut versunken. So zielten die ersten Maßnahmen, die Wilhelm I. ergriff, auf eine Wiederbelebung der Wirtschaft ab. Er ließ Kanäle bauen, förderte die Entwicklung der Industrie und sorgte durch die Gründung von Banken für die Finanzierung. Die Erneuerung der Bande mit den Kolonien in Ost und West, von denen das Land abgeschnitten gewesen war, trugen ebenfalls zum wirtschaftlichen Aufschwung bei.
Mitte des 19. Jahrhunderts erhielt neues Gedankengut die Chance zur Entfaltung. In dieser Zeit wurde der Grundstein für eine sehr vielgestaltige Gesellschaft gelegt. Eine Demokratie, in der die Regierung durch ein Parlament kontrolliert wird, in dem Mitglieder aus fast einem Dutzend Parteien ihren Sitz haben.

Le pays se libère de l'Espagne

Le 1er avril 1572, un groupe d'insurgés, les 'Gueux', débarqua à Brielle et força les portes. Ce fut le signal du soulèvement général. C'est à Dordrecht que se réunirent le 19 juillet les députés des villes confédérées. Guillaume d'Orange fut élu stathouder (gouverneur) et on proclama la liberté religieuse. Celle-ci donna une impulsion importante à l'immigration des juifs espagnols et portuguais, et des protestants venus des Pays-Bas du Sud et de France. L'Union d'Utrecht de 1579 fut à l'origine de la création de la République des sept Provinces-Unies. Philippe II, roi d'Espagne, envoya des renforts de mercenaires sous le commandement du redoutable duc d'Alba, et des combats acharnés éclatèrent. Ils se poursuivirent sous les stathouders Maurice et Frédéric-Henri, jusqu'au Traité de Münster, qui mit fin à cette guerre d'indépendance de quatre-vingt ans. Jusqu'à la Révolution française, la République fut dirigée en alternance par un stathouder de la Maison d'Orange et un 'grand pensionnaire'. Ceci dépendait des sympathies politiques des Etats-Généraux, l'assemblée des députés des provinces. Pendant l'hiver de 1795, les troupes françaises traversèrent les fleuves gelés et occupèrent le pays, qui fut constitué en république à la française : la République batave. Le stathouder Guillaume V s'exila en Angleterre. Après la chute de Napoléon, le fils de Guillaume V fut accueilli solennellement sur la plage de Scheveningue. Un peu plus tard, il fut proclamé roi par un comité de sages, sous le nom de Guillaume Ier.

Le début de la monarchie parlementaire

Les premières mesures prises par le roi concernaient le redressement de l'économie, le pays étant tombé dans la misère à cause du blocus des ports. Il ordonna le creusement de canaux, stimula l'industrie et restaura les finances par la création de banques. Les liens avec les colonies, qui avaient été coupés, furent rétablis, ce qui contribua également à la reprise économique.
Le milieu du 19e s. se caractérisa par un nouvel élan dans la pensée, le libéralisme se développa et les catholiques purent sortir de leurs églises clandestines. A l'intérieur de l'Eglise réformée, majoritaire dans le pays, des mouvements de séparation se multiplièrent. C'est à cette époque que furent établis les fondements d'une société pluriforme : une démocratie dans laquelle le gouvernement est contrôlé par un parlement constitué de députés, membres de pas moins d'une dizaine de partis politiques.

La liberación del dominio español

El 1 de abril de 1572 un grupo de rebeldes puso pie a tierra en la ciudad de Brielle y forzó la puerta de la ciudad. Este hecho fué el inicio de los acontecimientos futuros. El 19 de julio se reunieron los gobiernos municipales en Dordrecht y anunciaron la libertad religiosa al mismo tiempo que eligieron a Guillermo de Orange como estatúder. La libertad de religión fue una importante base para la estimulación de la emigración hacia Holanda de judíos españoles y portugueses asi como protestantes procedentes de Francia y de los Paises Bajos meridionales. La fundación de la República de los Siete Paises Bajos Unidos fue reafirmada en la Unión de Utrecht. En respuesta a ello, el rey español Felipe II mandó mas mercenarios asi como su capitán del ejercito el temido Duque de Alba. Al mando de los sucesivos estatúders Mauricio de Orange y Federico Enrique, la batalla se fué inclinando cada vez mas a favor de la Republica hasta que en 1648 se firmó la Paz de Westfalia poniendo fin a esta guerra de liberación que había durado 80 años.
Hasta la revolución francesa, la República fué gobernada alternativamente por un estatúder descendiente de la casa de Orange o por un concejal abogado del Estado. La designación del gobernante venía dada por la preferencia o no a la casa de Orange de los miembros que componían el Consejo de Estado que era la asamblea de los representantes de todas las comarcas.
Durante el invierno de 1795, las tropas francesas atravesaron los helados rios y establecieron la República bátava siguiendo el modelo francés huyendo el estatúder Guillermo V a Inglaterra. Despues de la caida de Napoleon se recibió solemnemente en la playa de Scheveningen al hijo de Guillermo V al que no mucho después un grupo de hombres justos le proclamó como rey Guillermo I.

El comienzo de la monarquía parlamentaria

A causa del bloqueo de los puertos, el pais se había visto sumergido en la pobreza. Las primeras medidas que tomó Guillermo fueron dirigidas a la recuperación económica. Dió orden de excavar canales, estimuló el inicio de la industria y cuidó el aspecto financiero constituyendo bancos. Restituyó los lazos con las colonias tanto del este como del oeste aspecto que contribuyó tambien al resurgimiento económico. A mitad del siglo XIX se propició el surgimiento de nuevas ideas. Durante esta fase se formó la base de una sociedad muy pluriforme. Una democracia en donde su gobierno es controlado por un parlamento ocupado por miembros de al menos diez diferentes partidos politicos.

Libertação do domínio da Espanha

Em 1 de Abril de 1572 atracou, próximo da vila de Brille, um grupo de rebeldes, que forçou as portas da vila. Agora é que a luta começou a sério. Os governos citadinos reuniram-se em 19 de Julho em Dordrecht e proclamaram a liberdade de religião. Eles elegeram Guilherme de Orange como o seu governador. A liberdade de religião foi um impulso importante para a imigração de judeus espanhois e portugueses e de protestantes das regiões do sul da Holanda e da França.
A fundação da República dos Setes Países Baixos Unidos foi ratificada formalmente em 1579, com a União de Utrecht. O rei espanhol Filipe II enviou mais mercenários e toda a gente temia o seu comandante, o duque de Alva. Sob diversos governadores, como Maurício e Frederico Henrique, a luta tornou-se cada vez mais a favor da República até que em 1648 o Tratado de Paz de Munster acabou com esta batalha de libertação que durou oitenta anos.
Até à Revolução Francesa a República foi dirigida alternadamente por um governador da geração dos Oranges ou por um Pensionário Conselheiro, um advogado do país. Isto dependia da medida em que os "Estados", a Assembleia dos Deputados Regionais, simpatizavam ou não com Orange.
No inverno de 1795 as tropas francesas atravessaram os rios congelados e estabeleceram aqui a República da Batávia, segundo o exemplo francês. O governador Guilherme V teve que fugir para a Inglaterra. Depois da queda de Napoleão, o filho de Guilherme V foi recebido festivamente na praia de Scheveningen e pouco tempo mais tarde foi proclamado, por um grupo de homens sensatos, Rei Guilherme I.

O início da monarquia parlamentar

Devido ao bloqueio dos portos o país caiu em miséria. A primeira medida que Guilherme I tomou foi dirigida ao restabelecimento da economia. Ele deu ordem para escavar canais, estimulou a introdução da indústria e cuidou do financiamento, por meio da fundação de bancos. Os laços reestabelecidos com as colónias no oriente e no ocidente, das quais o país esteve isolado, contribuiram também para um desenvolvimento económico.
Nos médios do século 19, um novo pensamento teve oportunidade de se desenvolver.
Neste período foi implantada a base para uma sociedade pluriforme. Uma democracia, onde o governo é controlado por um parlamento, no qual os membros se reunem, representando pelo menos uma dezena de partidos políticos.

De Middeleeuwen waren roerige tijden. Ten tijde van Karel V hadden de hertogen van Gelre een vermaard krijgsheer in dienst. Maarten van Rossem veroverde en plunderde met zijn legertje menige stad zelfs ver in het gebied van de graven van Holland. Zijn woonhuis te Arnhem (links) wordt nog steeds het Duivelshuis genoemd.
De Hollandse graaf Willem III verleende in 1328 Rotterdam het stadsrecht. Zijn standbeeld staat voor het Schielandhuis, waar eertijds het bestuur van het waterschap zetelde.
Burchten kenden vele vormen. De burcht in Leiden (rechts) was een ommuurde aarden heuvel en lag midden in de stad. Vaak een toevluchtsoord voor de bewoners in tijden van belegering, maar meestal bedoeld als dwangburcht om diezelfde bewoners onder de duim te houden.

The Middle Ages were turbulent.
During the reign of Charles V the Dukes of Gelre had a famous warrior in their service. Maarten van Rossum and his small army conquered and plundered many a town, even deep into the territory of the Counts of Holland. His house in Arnhem (left) is still referred to as the Devil's House.
Count William III of Holland granted Rotterdam its city charter in 1328. His statue stands in front of the Schielandhuis, where the executive of the district water board used to be housed.
There were many different castle designs. Leiden Castle (right) was a walled earth mound in the middle of the town. On occasion it was a refuge for the population when the town was under siege, but usually it was used as a prison to suppress that same population.

Das Mittelalter war eine unruhige Zeit. Zu Zeiten von Karl V. hatten die Herzöge von Geldern einen berühmten Kriegsherrn in ihren Diensten. Martin von Rossum eroberte und plünderte mit seiner Truppe so manche Stadt selbst im weit entfernten Reich der Grafen von Holland. Sein Wohnhaus in Arnheim (links) wird noch stets Teufelshaus genannt.
Der holländische Graf Wilhelm III. verlieh Rotterdam 1328 die Stadtrechte. Sein Standbild steht vor dem Schielandshuis, hier tagte einst der Rat der "Waterschap".
Burgen können viele Formen haben. Die Burg in Leiden (rechts) war ein von einer Mauer umgebener Erdhügel und lag mitten in der Stadt. Oft waren diese Burgen Zufluchtsorte für die Bewohner in Zeiten der Belagerung, meist jedoch dienten sie als Zwingburgen, um diese Bewohner klein zu halten.

Le moyen âge fut une période agitée. Du temps de Charles Quint, un général fameux était au service des ducs de Gueldre. Maarten van Rossum conquit et pilla maintes villes avec son armée. Il s'avança même profondément dans le territoire des ducs de Hollande. Sa demeure à Arnhem (g.) porte toujours le surnom de 'Maison du diable'. Guillaume III, comte de Hollande, accorda le statut de ville à Rotterdam en 1328. Sa statue se trouve devant la Maison de Schieland, où siègea jadis la direction du wateringue. Les châteaux-forts sont connus sous beaucoup de formes différentes. Le 'Burcht' (dr.) à Leiden était une colline artificielle cernée d'un rempart, située au centre de la ville. Bien que représentant un refuge pour les habitants en temps de siège, ces châteaux-forts eurent cependant le plus souvent une fonction de répression contre ces mêmes habitants.

La Edad Media fue una época muy turbulenta. En tiempos de Carlos V los duques de Gelre tuvieron un insigne militar a su servicio. Martín van Rossum conquistó y saqueó con su ejercito muchas ciudades dentro incluso de los territorios de los condes dc Holanda. Su casa en Arnhem (izquierda) es llamada aún la casa del diablo. El conde holandés Guillermo III concedió en 1328 los derechos de ciudad a Rotterdam. Su estatua se encuentra delante de la casa Schielandhuis que en su tiempo fue residencia del consejo del agua.
Los castillos fueron construidos de muchas formas. El castillo de Leiden (derecha) era un cerro amurallada en medio de la ciudad. Frecuentemente era el refugio de sus habitantes durante asedios pero normalmente servían estos castillos para tener sometidos a los propios habitantes de la ciudad.

A Idade Média foi um período turbulento. Nos tempos de Carlos V, os duques de Gelre tinham ao serviço um guerreiro muito famoso. Maarten van Rossum conquistou e saqueou com o seu pequeno exército várias cidades, mesmo afastadas no condado da Holanda. A sua moradia em Arnhem (à esquerda), tem ainda hoje o nome de "a Casa do Diabo". O conde holandês Guilherme III concedeu a Roterdão os direitos de cidade em 1328. A sua estátua encontra-se à frente da Casa de Schieland, nela esteve em tempos a Directoria da Instância de Protecção aos Pólders. Castelos havia-os de muitas formas. O castelo em Leiden (à direita) era um monte de terra com muralhas à volta e estava no meio da cidade. Muitas vezes era um refúgio para os moradores da cidade em casos de assédios, mas muitas vezes era usado como local de encerramento para subjugar os mesmos moradores.

Tolheffing op de rivieren was een belangrijke bron van inkomsten voor de middeleeuwse edelen. De meeste koopwaar werd per schip vervoerd. Het is niet verwonderlijk dat de meeste kastelen daarom aan rivieren en riviermondingen werden gebouwd. Op deze bladzijden drie robuuste kastelen uit de 13de eeuw van waaruit landheren elkaar bestreden: het Muiderslot te Muiden controleerde de scheepvaart over de Vecht naar Utrecht (links), kasteel Ammerzoyen ten noorden van Den Bosch domineerde de Maas (midden) en waar Maas en Waal samenvloeiden lag slot Loevestein (rechts).

Charging tolls on the rivers was an important source of income for the nobility in the Middle Ages. Most merchandise was transported by boat. It is therefore not surprising that most castles were built on rivers and estuaries. On these pages there are three formidable thirteenth-century castles, from where the local lords of the manor fought one another. The Muiderslot in Muiden controlled shipping on the River Vecht to Utrecht (left), Ammerzoyen Castle to the north of Den Bosch dominated the Maas (centre) and Loevestein Castle called the shots where the Maas and Waal converge (right).

Die Zollerhebung auf den Flüssen war eine wichtige Einkommensquelle der Adeligen im Mittelalter. Die meisten Handelswaren wurden per Schiff transportiert. So ist es nicht verwunderlich, daß die meisten Burgen an Flüssen und Flußmündungen gebaut wurden. Auf diesen Seiten sind drei robuste Burgen aus dem 13. Jahrhundert zu sehen, von denen aus sich die Landesherren gegenseitig bekämpften: Von der Burg Muiderslot in Muiden aus wurde die Schiffahrt auf der Vecht nach Utrecht kontrolliert (links), Burg Ammerzoyen im Norden von Den Bosch dominierte die Maas (Mitte), und am Zusammenfluß von Maas und Waal lag Burg Loevestein (rechts).

Les rivières à péage furent une source de revenus importants pour les nobles au moyen âge, les marchandises étant essentiellement transportées par bateau. Ce n'est donc pas étonnant si la plupart des châteaux furent dressés au bord de ces rivières et aux embouchures. Voici trois châteaux-forts du 13e s., depuis lesquels les seigneurs s'affrontaient. Le château de Muiden contrôlait l'embouchure de la Vecht (g.), le château Ammerzoyen au nord de Bois-le-Duc dominait la Meuse (milieu) et le château de Loevestein (dr.) se situait au confluent de la Meuse et du Waal.

El pago de los derechos de tránsito por los rios era un importante medio de riqueza de la nobleza de la Edad Media. La mayoria de las mercancias eran transportadas por barco. No es de extrañar por tanto que la mayoría de los castillos se construyeran en las orillas de los rios o en sus desembocaduras. En esta página podemos ver tres castillos del siglo XIII desde donde sus respectivos nobles guerrearon entre si: el castillo Muiderslot en Muiden controlaba la navegacion por el rio Vecht hacia Utrecht (izquierda), el castillo Ammerzoyen al norte de Bois le Duc dominaba el Mosa (medio) y donde el Mosa y el Waal se juntan, se encuentra el castillo Loevestein (derecha).

A cobrança de portagem nos rios foi uma importante fonte de receitas para os senhores nobres da Idade Média. A maioria dos produtos de comércio eram transportados por barco. Não é, portanto, de admirar que a maioria dos castelos tenham sido construídos à borda e na foz dos rios. Nestas páginas três castelos robustos que datam do século 13, a partir dos quais os senhores se combatiam: O Castelo de Muiden, em Muiden, controlava o tráfego fluvial pelo rio Vecht a caminho de Utreque (à esquerda), o Castelo de Ammerzoyen, a norte de Den Bosch dominava o Mosa (ao meio) e onde o Mosa e o Waal se juntavam encontrava-se o Castelo Loevestein (à direita).

Den Haag is de zetel van de regering alsmede de residentie van de koningin (zie blz. 60). In 1248 liet graaf Willem II hier een jachtslot bouwen. De voormalige feestzaal - de Ridderzaal - vormt na ingrijpende restauraties nog steeds het hart van het regeringscomplex aan het Binnenhof. Van hieruit bestuurden de stadhouders, raadpensionarissen en in later tijden minister-presidenten het land. Hiernaast enige standbeelden van markante bestuurders, drie raadpensionarissen en een minister-president:

Den Haag ist der Sitz der Regierung und die Residenz der Königin (siehe Seite 60). 1248 ließ Graf Wilhelm II. hier ein Jagdschloß erbauen. Der ehemalige Festsaal - der Rittersaal - ist auch nach umfangreichen Renovierungsarbeiten heute noch das Herz des Regierungskomplexes "Binnenhof". Von hier aus lenkten Statthalter, Ratspensionäre und in späteren Zeiten Ministerpräsidenten die Geschicke des Landes. Nebenstehend einige Standbilder herausragender Persönlichkeiten, drei Ratspensionäre und ein Ministerpräsident:

La Haya es la residencia oficial del gobierno asi como de la reina (ver pag.60). En 1248, el conde Guillermo II hizo construir un castillo de caza. La antigua sala de fiestas - la Ridderzaal - forma aún y a pesar de las reformas realizadas, el centro del complejo gubernamental que se encuentra en el Binnenhof. Desde aquí gobernaban el pais los estatúders, los consejeros y ya en tiempos posteriores el ministro-presidente. Aquí al lado algunas estátuas de gobernantes notables, tres consejeros y un ministro-presidente:

The Hague is the seat of government and also the residence of the Queen (see page 60). In 1248 Count William II had a hunting lodge built here. The former banqueting hall - the Ridderzaal - has been beautifully restored and still forms the heart of the government complex in the Binnenhof. It was from here that the Stadholders, Grand Pensionaries and later on Prime Ministers governed the country. Here are some statutes of prominent administrators, three Grand Pensionaries and one Prime Minister. :

La Haye est le siège du gouvernement et la résidence de la reine. (voir p.60). En 1248 le comte Guillaume II de Hollande y fit construire un pavillon de chasse. Son ancienne salle de fêtes, la 'Ridderzaal' (salle des chevaliers), se trouve aujourd'hui au coeur du centre politique au Binnenhof. D'ici, les stathouders, les pensionnaires et plus tard les 'Ministres-Présidents' (appellation du premier ministre néerlandais) dirigeaient le pays. A côté, quelques statues de dirigeants remarquables, trois grands pensionnaires et un premier ministre :

Haia é a sede do governo, e o lugar da residência da Raínha (veja a pag. 60).
Em 1248 o Conde Guilherme II mandou construir aqui um castelo para a caça. A antiga sala de festas - a Sala dos Cavaleiros - constitui ainda hoje, depois de uma importante restauração, o centro do complexo do governo, no Binnenhof (Paço Interior). A partir daqui os governadores e os pensionários-conselheiros e mais tarde o presidente do conselho de ministros, governavam o país. Ao lado algumas estátuas de governantes notáveis, três pensionários-conselheiros e um presidente do conselho de ministros:

Johan van Oldenbarnevelt (linksboven) was raadpensionaris aan het eind van de 16de eeuw. Johan de Witt (rechtsboven), hier samen met zijn broer Cornelis, werd in 1672 in dezelfde functie door het gewone volk vermoord omdat hij poogde het stadhouderschap af te schaffen. Jacob Cats (linksonder) ontleende meer bekendheid aan zijn dichterschap van moraliserende verzen. De liberale minister-president Thorbecke herzag in 1848 de Grondwet.

Johan van Oldenbarnevelt (links oben) war Ende des 16. Jahrhunderts Ratspensionär. Johan de Witt (rechts oben) wurde 1672 im selben Amt vom gemeinen Volk ermordet, weil er versuchte, die Statthalterschaft abzuschaffen. Jacob Cats (links unten) verdankte seine Bekanntheit eher seiner Eigenschaft als Dichter moralisierender Verse. Der liberale Ministerpräsident Thorbecke reformierte 1848 das Grundgesetz.

Juan van Oldenbarnevelt (izquierda arriba) fué consejero al final del siglo XVI. Juan de Witt (derecha arriba), aqui junto con su hermano Cornelio, fue asesinado por el pueblo siendo consejero por querer abolir el estatuderato. Jacobo Cats (izquierda abajo) que debió su fama mas que nada a sus versos de contenido moralizador. El ministro-presidente de tendencia liberal Thorbecke revisó en 1848 la Constitución.

Johan van Oldenbarnevelt (top left) was a Grand Pensionary at the end of the sixteenth century. Johan de Witt (top right), here together with his brother Cornelis, was murdered by the common people in 1672 because he tried to abolish the Stadholdership. Jacob Cats was a Grand Pensionary of Holland and also a poet who wrote well-known moralizing verses. Liberal Prime Minister Thorbecke revised the Constitution in 1848.

Johan van Oldebarnevelt (g. en haut) fut grand pensionnaire à la fin du 16e s. Johan de Witt (dr. en haut), ici avec son frère Cornelis, fut tué lors d'une émeute populaire, après sa tentation de supprimer le stadhoudérat. Jacob Cats fut grand pensionnaire de Hollande, mais surtout connu pour ses poèmes moralisateurs. Le premier ministre Thorbecke, chef des libéraux, réforma la Constitution en 1848.

Johan van Oldenbarnevelt (à esquerda acima) era o pensionário-conselheiro nos fins do século 16. Johan de Witt (à direita em cima), aqui com o seu irmão Cornelis, foi em 1672, quando tinha a mesma função, assassinado pelo povo, por ele ter tentado abolir a posição de governador. Jacob Cats (à esquerda em baixo) conquistou mais fama pela sua qualidade de poeta de versos moralizantes. O presidente do conselho de ministros liberal, Thorbecke reviu a lei da Constituição em 1848.

Toen eind 16de eeuw de Spaanse en Portugese joden wegens de godsdienstvrijheid naar Amsterdam kwamen kregen zij al spoedig toestemming tot het bouwen van een eigen synagoge. Later volgde de joodse begraafplaats in Ouderkerk. De rouwstoet kwam per boot naar de steiger met het rijkversierde toegangshek. Binnen de protestantse Kerk ontstond aan het begin van de 17de eeuw een schisma, de rekkelijken onder Arminius (hier zijn geboortehuis te Oudewater) legden het af tegen de lieden van de zware leer. In de Gouden Eeuw heerste rijkdom naast armoede. Oppassende armen konden op voorspraak van een welgestelde regent vaak een plaats verwerven in een hofje zoals dat in Breda (onder) of in een oude bessenhuis in Zutphen (boven).

When Spanish and Portuguese Jews came to Amsterdam at the end of sixteenth century because of the freedom of religion there, they were soon granted permission to build their own synagogue. This was followed later by the Jewish cemetery in Ouderkerk. The funeral procession travelled by boat to the jetty with its richly adorned entrance gate. A schism developed within the Dutch Reformed Church at the beginning of the seventeenth century. The moderates under Arminius (this is the house in Oudewater where he was born) were no match for the members of the orthodoxy. The Golden Age saw great wealth alongside poverty. Deserving poor people could often obtain a place in almshouses like these in Breda (below) or in the old women's home in Zutphen (top), on the recommendation of a prosperous local worthy.

Als die spanischen und portugiesischen Juden Ende des 16. Jahrhunderts wegen der Religionsfreiheit nach Amsterdam kamen, erhielten sie schon bald die Erlaubnis zum Bau einer eigenen Synagoge. Später folgte der jüdische Friedhof in Ouderkerk. Der Trauerzug kam per Boot zum Landungssteg mit dem reich verzierten Eingangstor. Unter den Reformierten kam es zu Beginn des 17. Jahrhunderts zu einer Spaltung, als sich die freisinnigen Calvinisten unter Arminius (hier sein Geburtshaus in Oudewater) gegen die Anhänger der orthodoxen Lehre auflehnten. Im Goldenen Jahrhundert herrschte neben dem Reichtum auch Armut. Tüchtige Arme konnten auf Fürsprache eines wohlmeinenden Regenten oft einen Platz in einem "Hofje" wie dem in Breda (unten) oder in einem alten Armenhaus wie dem in Zutphen (oben) erwerben.

La fin du 16e s. connut un afflux de juifs espagnols et portuguais, s'installant à Amsterdam pour la liberté religieuse. Les autorités leur accordèrent bientôt le droit de bâtir leur propre synagogue, suivie par le cimetière juif à Ouderkerk. Le cortège alla en bateau jusqu'à l'appontement, où se trouve la porte d'entrée richement décorée. Un schisme divisa l'Eglise réformée au début du 17e s. Les Remontrants, guidés par Arminius (voici sa maison natale à Oudewater) furent écartés par les partisans de la doctrine rigide. Au Siècle d'Or la richesse côtoyait la pauvreté. Grâce à l'intervention d'un régent fortuné, les pauvres de bonne conduite pouvaient souvent s'installer dans un 'hofje', sorte d'hospice ou béguinage (Zutphen, en haut et Breda, en bas).

Cuando al final del siglo XVI los judíos españoles y portgueses llegaron a Amsterdam, favorecidos por la libertad religiosa existente en el pais, obtuvieron rápidamente el beneplácito necesario para la construcción de su propia sinagoga. Poco despues siguió el cementerio judío de Ouderkerk. La procesión funeraria llegaba por barco al embarcadero en donde se encontraba la verja de entrada ricamente adornada. Dentro de los protestantes se dió un cisma al principio del siglo XVII, los transigentes bajo Arminius (aquí se ve su casa en Oudewater) perdieron la confrontación contra los partidarios de la intransigencia. Durante el siglo de oro convivieron juntos riqueza y pobreza. Algunos pobres necesitados, gracias a la intercesión de un regente acomodado, podían conseguir una plaza en un beguinaje como el de Breda (abajo) o en una vieja casa como ésta en Zutphen (arriba).

Quando no século 16 os judeus espanhois e portugueses vieram para Amesterdão, por causa da liberdade de religião, receberam eles pouco tempo depois autorização para construirem a sua própria sinagoga. Mais tarde seguiu-se o cimitério judeu em Ouderkerk. O funeral vinha de barco para o embarcadoiro, com um portão de entrada todo enfeitado.
Entre os protestantes deu-se no princípio do século 17 um cisma, os eclesiásticos sob Arminius (aqui a casa onde ele nasceu, em Oudewater), perderam contra os membros da doutrina mais severa. No Século Dourado havia riqueza a par de pobreza. Pobres cuidadosos conseguiam às vezes a pedido de um regente rico, receber um lugar num dos páteos da beguinaria, como este em Breda (em baixo) ou numa das casas para idosas, como esta em Zutphen (em cima).

Markante gebouwen uit het verleden. Hiernaast enige raadhuizen in diverse stijlen. Linksboven het gotische stadhuis van Middelburg. Het is tussen 1452 en 1520 gebouwd door de Vlaamse bouwmeesters van het geslacht Keldermans. De familie Keldermans tekende ook voor de bouw van het stadhuis van Gouda (1450, rechtsboven). De begane grond huisvestte vroeger de plaatselijke vleeshal. Het raadhuisje van De Rijp (1613, linksonder) was tevens in gebruik als waag. Tot de Franse tijd was het koninklijk paleis op de Dam in Amsterdam in gebruik als stadhuis. Bouwmeester Jacob van Campen kreeg in 1648 van de vroedschap een bijna onuitputtelijk budget. De rijke ornamenten en de timpanen aan de voor- en achterzijde zijn van de hand van de beeldhouwer Quellijn.

Prominent buildings from the past. Some town halls in varying styles. Top left is the Gothic town hall in Middelburg. It was built by Flemish master builders from the Keldermans family between 1452 and 1520. The Keldermans family also built Gouda town hall (1450, top right). The ground floor used to house the local meat market. De Rijp's diminutive town hall (1613, bottom left) was also used as a weigh house. Until the French era, the Royal Palace on the Dam in Amsterdam was the town hall. Master builder Jacob van Campen received an almost limitless budget from the city council in 1648. The rich ornamentation and the tympanums at the front and back are by the sculptor Quellijn

Markante Gebäude aus der Vergangenheit. Hier sind einige Rathäuser unterschiedlicher Stilrichtungen abgebildet. Links oben das gotische Rathaus von Middelburg. Es wurde zwischen 1452 und 1520 von den flämischen Baumeistern aus dem Hause Keldermans erbaut. Die Familie Keldermans zeichnete auch für den Bau des Rathauses von Gouda verantwortlich (1450, rechts oben). Im Erdgeschoß war früher die Fleischhalle des Ortes untergebracht. Das Rathaus von De Rijp (1613, links unten) wurde zugleich als Stadtwaage benutzt. Bis zur französischen Zeit diente der königliche Palast am Damm in Amsterdam zugleich als Rathaus. Dem Baumeister Jacob von Campen wurde 1648 vom Rat der Weisen ein beinahe unerschöpfliches Budget zur Verfügung gestellt. Die reichen Ornamente und die Giebelfelder an der Vorder- und Rückseite sind das Werk des Bildhauers Quellijn.

Des édifices remarquables du passé. A côté, quelques hôtels de ville de styles différents : l'hôtel de ville gothique de Middelburg (g. en haut), construit entre 1452 et 1520 par les architectes flamands membres de la famille Keldermans, qui a également oeuvré à l'hôtel de ville de Gouda (1450, dr. en haut). Son rez-de-chaussée hébergeait jadis la halle aux viandes. La petite mairie de De Rijp (1613, g. en bas) servit aussi de poids public. Le palais royal situé au Dam à Amsterdam, hôtel de ville jusqu'à la domination française, fut construit par Jacob van Campen en 1648, à qui la magistrature municipale accorda un budget presque illimité. Les façades avant et arrière sont surmontées de tympans et de riches ornements, de la main du sculpteur Quellin.

Notables edificios del pasado. Aqui al lado algunos ayuntamientos en variados estilos. Izquierda arriba el ayuntamiento gótico de Middelburg. Fué construido entre 1452 y 1520 por arquitectos flamencos de la familia Keldermans. Esta misma familia construyó tambien el ayuntamiento de Gouda en 1450 (derecha arriba). La planta baja albergaba en su tiempo el mercado de carne. El ayuntamiento de De Rijp de 1613 (izquierda abajo) se usaba al mismo tiempo como peso público. Hasta la época francesa, el palacio real del Dam en Amsterdam fue usado como ayuntamiento. El arquitecto Jacobo van Campen recibió en 1648 por parte de los consejeros del ayuntamiento un presupuesto inacabable para su construcción. Los ricos ornamentos y tímpanos de la parte delantera y trasera fueron realizados por el escultor Quellijn.

Edifícios notáveis do passado. Ao lado edifícios dos conselhos municipais em diversos estilos. À esquerda em cima a câmara municipal em estilo gótico de Middelburg. Foi construída entre 1452 e 1520, pelos constructores flamengos da geração Keldermans. A família Keldermans desenhou também para a construção do conselho municipal de Gouda (1450; à direita em cima). O rés-do-chão, em tempos, deu lugar à praça da carne local. A pequena câmara municipal de De Rijp (1613; à esquerda em baixo) foi usada ao mesmo tempo como salão da balança. Até ao tempo dos franceses o palácio real "de Dam" em Amesterdão serviu como conselho municipal.
O constructor Jacob van Campen recebeu em 1648 do Conselho um orçamento quase inesgotável. Os ornamentos e os tímpanos abundantes, nas traseiras e nas dianteiras são da autoria do escultor Quellijn.

Negen kerken in diverse stijlen uit uiteenlopende streken in Nederland (van links naar rechts en van boven naar onderen). De scheve toren Oldenhove te Leeuwarden resteert van de ooit afgebroken St.-Vituskerk. Kenmerkend voor het noorden van Nederland zijn de kerktorens met een zadeldak zoals deze in Anloo. De Martinitoren (96 meter) is de trots van iedere Groninger. Utrecht heeft met 110 meter de hoogste toren van het land. De St.-Janskerk in Den Bosch is een laat-gotische kruisbasiliek waarvan de oudste delen dateren uit 1280. In Zierikzee zijn de aspiraties nooit bewaarheid, in plaats van de geplande hoogte van 207 meter bleef de toren steken op 56 meter. De Munsterkerk in Roermond (1218) is gebouwd in een Rijnlandse variant op de laatromaanse stijl. Rond het jaar 1000 werd in Maastricht een begin gemaakt met deOnze Lieve Vrouwe Kerk, geheel in romaanse stijl. Tot slot het lieflijke kerkje van Asselt. Dit is gebouwd op een terp om het te beschermen tegen het hoge water van de Maas.

Nine churches in different styles from different parts of the Netherlands (from left to right and from top to bottom). The leaning Oldenhove Tower in Leeuwarden is a relic of the long since demolished St. Vituskerk. A characteristic of the north of the Netherlands is the church tower with a saddle roof, like this one in Anloo. The Martini Tower, 96 metres high, is the pride of everyone from Groningen. Utrecht has the tallest tower in the country, at 110 metres high. The St. Janskerk in Den Bosch is a late Gothic basilica on the cross plan. The oldest parts of the structure date from 1280. In Zierikzee, the aspirations of builders never materialized. The planned 207-metre-high tower got no further than 56 metres. The Munsterkerk in Roermond (1218) was built according to a Rhineland variation of the late Roman style. A start was made around the year 1000 on the Onze Lieve Vrouwe church in Maastricht, which is entirely in the Roman style. Finally, the charming little church in Asselt was built on a mound in order to protect it from high water levels in the Maas.

Neun Kirchen unterschiedlichster Stilrichtungen aus den verschiedenen Gegenden der Niederlande (von links nach rechts und von oben nach unten). Von der längst zerstörten St.-Vituskirche in Leeuwarden blieb nur der schiefe Turm Oldenhove erhalten. Typisch für den Norden der Niederlande sind die Kirchtürme mit Satteldach wie hier in Anloo. Auf den Martinsturm (96 Meter) ist ganz Groningen Stolz. Utrecht hat mit 110 Metern den höchsten Turm des Landes. Die St.-Janskirche in Den Bosch ist eine spätgotische Kreuzbasilika, deren älteste Teile bis ins Jahr 1280 zurückgehen. In Zierikzee wurde das ehrgeizige Projekt nie umgesetzt, statt der geplanten Höhe von 207 Metern erreichte der Turm nur 56 Meter. Die Münsterkirche in Roermond (1218) wurde in einer rheinländischen Variante des spätromanischen Stils erbaut. Um das Jahr 1000 begann man in Maastricht mit dem Bau der Liebfrauenkirche, ganz im romanischen Stil. Und zu guter Letzt die liebliche Kirche von Asselt, die zum Schutz vor dem Hochwasser der Maas auf einer Wurt errichtet wurde.

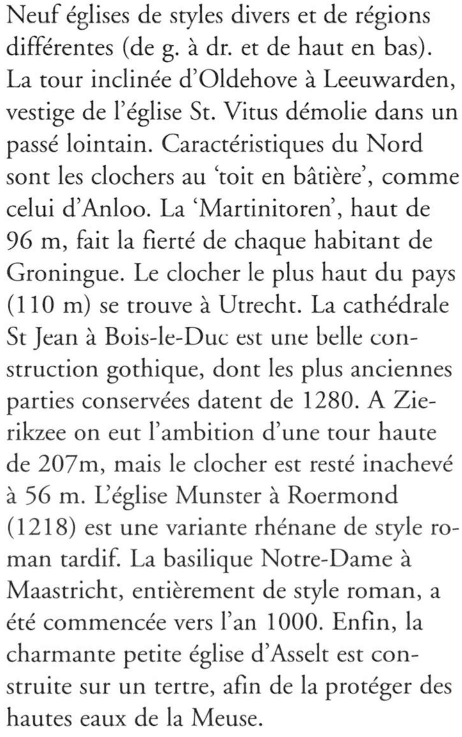

Neuf églises de styles divers et de régions différentes (de g. à dr. et de haut en bas). La tour inclinée d'Oldehove à Leeuwarden, vestige de l'église St. Vitus démolie dans un passé lointain. Caractéristiques du Nord sont les clochers au 'toit en bâtière', comme celui d'Anloo. La 'Martinitoren', haut de 96 m, fait la fierté de chaque habitant de Groningue. Le clocher le plus haut du pays (110 m) se trouve à Utrecht. La cathédrale St Jean à Bois-le-Duc est une belle construction gothique, dont les plus anciennes parties conservées datent de 1280. A Zierikzee on eut l'ambition d'une tour haute de 207m, mais le clocher est resté inachevé à 56 m. L'église Munster à Roermond (1218) est une variante rhénane de style roman tardif. La basilique Notre-Dame à Maastricht, entièrement de style roman, a été commencée vers l'an 1000. Enfin, la charmante petite église d'Asselt est construite sur un tertre, afin de la protéger des hautes eaux de la Meuse.

Nueve iglesias en diferentes estilos y situadas en diversas partes de Holanda (de izquierda a derecha y de arriba a abajo). La torre inclinada Oldenhove en Leeuwarden es un remanente de la iglesia de St.Vitus. Los techos de dos vertientes como este de Anloo son característicos en las torres del norte de Holanda. La torre Martini de 96 metros es el orgullo de la ciudad de Groninga. En Utrecht se encuentra la torre mas alta del pais con 110 metros. La basílica de St. Jans en Bois le Duc es del gótico posterior con su nave en forma de cruz y en la que las partes mas viejas datan del 1280. En Zierikzee no pudieron cumplir sus aspiraciones, en lugar de los 207 metros de altura planeados, la torre se quedó en 56 metros. La iglesia Munster de Roermond se construyó en 1218 en la variante renana del estilo romano posterior. Hacia el año 1000 se empezó la construcción en Maastricht de la iglesia Onze Lieve Vrouwe en estilo romano. Por último, la iglesita de Asselt fue construida sobre un cerro para salvarla de las subidas del agua del Mosa.

Nove igrejas em diversos estilos, em regiões diferentes da Holanda (da esquerda para a direita e de cima para baixo). A torre inclinada Oldenhove, em Leeuwarden, ficou ainda após a destruição da igreja de São Vito. Características para o norte da Holanda são as torres das igrejas, com um telhado em forma de selim, como esta em Anloo. A torre Martini (de 96 metros) é o orgulho de todos os habitantes de Groningen. Utrecht tem a torre mais alta do país, com os seus 110 metros. A igreja de São João em Den Bosch é uma basílica em cruz, do gótico tardio, da qual as partes mais velhas datam de 1820.
Em Zierikzee as aspirações de então nunca se realizaram: em vez dos 207 metros que se planeava, a torre ficou pelos 56 metros. A igreja de Munster, em Roermond (1218) foi construída numa variante do Rijnland, ao estilo romano tardio. À volta do ano 1000 iniciou-se em Maastricht a igreja da Nossa Senhora, toda em estilo romano. Finalmente a igrejinha de Asselt, que foi construída sobre um outeiro, para a proteger contra as águas do Maas.

Opkomst en bloei als handelsnatie

Development and growth as a trading nation

Aufstieg und Blüte einer Handelsnation

Essor d'une nation commerçante

Una nación comercial, su nacimiento y florecimiento

Proveniência e prosperidade como nação comercial

Nederland speelde door zijn ligging een centrale rol in de Duitse Hanze. De Hanze was een verbond van steden dat in de Middeleeuwen de handel in Noordwest-Europa niet alleen organiseerde maar ook beschermde. In de 14de eeuw werden de betrekkingen van de Hanze over land uitgebreid met Zuid-Duitsland en Italië. In Nederland waren het voornamelijk de steden in het oosten en noorden die officieel tot de Hanze waren toegelaten, in het noorden Groningen en Stavoren en in het oosten de steden langs de rivier de IJssel zoals Kampen, Zwolle, Deventer, Zutphen, en Arnhem en Nijmegen aan de Rijn. Over zee voerden de kooplieden hun waren aan met kleine koggeschepen. Het vervoer over land maakte gebruik van een stelsel van Hessenwegen, brede goed onderhouden zandwegen. Volgens overlevering danken zij hun naam aan de kooplieden uit de Duitse deelstaat Hessen. Hoogtepunten waren de jaarmarkten die soms wel een week of langer een stad in hun ban hadden.
In de 16de eeuw werden de koggen meer en meer vervangen door de grotere fluitschepen. Zij stelden de kooplieden in staat verdere reizen te ondernemen zoals naar de Portugese en Spaanse kusten. Omdat de fluitschepen moeilijk op de rivieren konden manoeuvreren werden de oorspronkelijke Hanzesteden overvleugeld door steden aan dieper water zoals Amsterdam, Hoorn en Enkhuizen aan de Zuiderzee en Rotterdam, Dordrecht en Vlissingen in het zuidwesten.

Due to its central geographic position, the Netherlands played a major role in the Hanseatic League of the Baltic states. The Hanseatic League was a bond of cities in the Middle Ages which organised and protected trade in northwest Europe. In the 14th century, the league was extended to cover the southern German states and Italy. In the Netherlands the Hanseatic members were confined largely to the east and north. Groningen and Stavoren in the north, and centres along the IJssel river such as Kampen, Zwolle, Deventer and Zutphen were members as were Arnhem and Nijmegen along the Rhine. Traders moved their goods overseas in small wooden sailing vessels known as koggesschepen. Transport over land was done by sets of Hesse waggons over broad sandy roads. By tradition, these waggons owed their name to the merchants of the German state of Hesse. The annual markets which went on for a week in each Hanseatic city were highpoints of the year. By the 16th century, the koggeschepen were replaced by larger fluitschepen. These enabled the merchants to take longer voyages with their goods to the Portuguese and Spanish coasts. But because it was difficult to manoeuvre the fluitschepen on the rivers, trade was moved to cities with deepwater access such aas Amsterdam, Hoorn, Enkhuizen on the Zuider Zee and Rotterdam, Dordrecht and Vlissingen in the southwest.

Aufgrund ihrer Lage spielten die Niederlande in der deutschen Hanse eine bedeutende Rolle. Die Hanse war ein Städtebund, der im Mittelalter den Handel im nordwestlichen Europa nicht nur organisierte, sondern auch schützte. Im 14. Jahrhundert wurden die Beziehungen der Hanse auf dem Landweg mit Süddeutschland und Italien ausgebaut. In den Niederlanden waren vor allem die Städte im Osten und Norden der Hanse angeschlossen, im Norden Groningen und Stavoren und im Osten die Städte entlang der IJssel wie Kampen, Zwolle, Deventer und Zutphen sowie Arnheim und Nimwegen am Rhein. Auf dem Seeweg lieferten die Kaufleute ihre Waren mit kleinen Koggen an. Zu Lande fand der Handel über ein Netz von Hessenwegen - breiten, gut ausgebauten Sandstraßen - statt. Der Überlieferung zufolge verdanken sie ihren Namen den Kaufleuten des deutschen Teilstaats Hessen. Höhepunkte waren die Jahrmärkte, die oft eine Woche oder länger eine Stadt in ihrem Bann hielten. Im 16. Jahrhundert wurden die Koggen nach und nach durch größere langgezogene Schiffe, die sogenannten Fleuten, ersetzt. Mit ihnen war es den Kaufleuten möglich, längere Reisen bis an die Küsten Portugals und Spaniens zu unternehmen. Da die Fleuten nur schwer auf den niederländischen Flüssen manövriert werden konnten, verloren die ursprünglichen Hansestädte im Landesinneren an Bedeutung, wohingegen die an tieferen Gewässern gelegenen Städte wie Amsterdam, Hoorn und Enkhuizen an der Zuiderzee und Rotterdam, Dordrecht und Vlissingen im Südwesten aufblühten.

C'est par leur situation géographique que les Pays-Bas ont joué un rôle central dans la ligue hanséatique. La Hanse était une association de villes du Nord de l'Europe, détenant le monopole du commerce par eau au moyen âge. Dès le 14e s. les relations furent élargies sur terre jusqu'à l'Allemagne du Sud et l'Italie. Les villes hollandaises affiliées à la Hanse étaient Groningue et Stavoren dans le Nord, Kampen, Zwolle, Deventer et Zutphen sur les rives de l'IJssel dans l'Est, et Arnhem et Nimègue au bord du Rhin. Le trafic par mer se faisait avec des petits navires, appelés 'kogge', le transport par terre utilisait un réseau de chemins, dits de la Hesse, rappelant les commerçants de cette région allemande.
Un événement important était la foire annuelle, mettant en fête toute une ville, parfois pendant une semaine ou plus.
Dès le 16e s. les navires hanséatiques furent remplacés par les caravelles plus grandes permettant le commerce avec des destinations plus éloignées comme les côtes espagnoles et portuguaises. Ces navires étant difficilement manoeuvrables sur les rivières, les premières villes hanséatiques furent donc éclipsées par celles situées en bordure d'eaux plus profondes comme Amsterdam, Hoorn et Enkhuizen sur le Zuiderzee, et Rotterdam, Dordrecht et Vlissingen dans le Sud-ouest.

Debido a su posición geográfica Holando jugó un importante papel para la confederación anseática alemana. El Ansa fué una alianza de ciudades en la Edad Media encaminada no solo a la relación comercial con el noroeste de Europa sino tambien a su protección. Durante el siglo XIV la relación de los anseáticos se extendió hacia la Alemania meridional e Italia.Las ciudades que en Holanda formaban parte de la liga anseática estaban oficialmente en el norte y este del pais; en el norte las ciudades de Groninga y Stavoren y en el este las ciudades a orilla del Ijssel como son Kampen Zwolle, Deventer Zutphen y Arnhem asi como Nimega a orillas del Rin. Los comerciantes transportaban sus mercancías por mar en pequeñas naves. El transporte terrestre usaba la red de carreteras de Hessen, caminos anchos y bien cuidados. Según cuenta la tradición, este nombre provenía de comerciantes alemanes de la región de Hessen. Puntos culminantes del comercio eran los mercados anuales que solían organizar las ciudades y que solían durar una semana aunque en algunos casos incluso la sobrepasaban. En el siglo XVI las pequeñas naves marinas fueron sustituidas por naves de mayor embargadura. Con ello se posibilitaban los viajes mas lejanos como por ejemplo a las costas portugesa y española. Dado que para estas grandes naves suponía mucha dificultad su maniobrabilidad dentro de los rios, las ciudades anseáticas se vieron paulatinamente superadas por las ciudades que disponían de aguas mas profundas como eran Amsterdam, Hoorn y Enkhuizen en el Zuiderzee y Rotterdam, Dordrecht y Vlissingen en el suroeste.

A Holanda desempenhava, graças à sua situação, um papel primordial na União Hansa Alemã. A Hansa era uma união de cidades que na Idade Média não só organizava o comércio no noroeste da Europa, como também o protegia. No século 14 as relações das cidades 'hansas' foram ampliadas por terra com a Alemanha e a Itália. Na Holanda eram em especial as cidades no oriente e no norte que eram admitidas oficialmente à União Hansa. No norte Groningen e Stavoren e no oriente eram as cidades ao longo do rio IJssel, como por exemplo, Kampen, Zwolle, Deventer, Zutphen, Arnhem e Nijmegen aan de Rijn. Os negociantes transportavam as suas mercadorias pelo mar com pequenos barcos comerciais (Koggeschepen). O transporte por terra servia-se do sistema dos caminhos Hessen: caminhos de areia em boas condições. Segundo a tradição eles receberam este nome dos comerciantes da província alemã Hessen. Tópicos eram os mercados anuais, os quais às vezes, dominavam uma cidade durante uma semana ou mais.
No século 16 os pequenos barcos comerciais foram substituídos, a pouco e pouco por barcos de carga com três mastros, maiores. Estes davam aos mercadores a oportunidade de fazer viagens mais longas, como por exemplo, até à costa de Portugal e da Espanha. Como com estes barcos maiores era difícil de manobrar nos rios, as cidades de Hansa foram ultra-passadas em favor de cidades junto a águas mais profundas, tais como Amesterdão, Hoorn e Enkhuizen no Zuiderzee e Roterdão, Dordrecht e Vlissingen no sudeste.

Hoorn was een van de steden die opbloeiden nadat de Hanzesteden aan belang moesten inboeten. De ligging aan het ruime water van de Zuiderzee waarborgde een ideale uitvalsbasis voor de schepen met verre bestemmingen (rechts). In Zierikzee konden schepen met een kostbare lading veilig afmeren achter de Zuidhavenpoort.

Hoorn was one of the cities which flourished when the Hanseatic cities lost lst their power. Its position on the broad waters of the Zuider Zee made it an ideal home port for ships which sailed long distances. (right) In Zierikzee ships with valuable cargoes could moor safely behind the Zuidhavenpoort.

Hoorn war eine der Städte, die aufblühten, als die Hansestädte an Bedeutung verloren. Die Lage am Ufer der großen Zuiderzee war eine ideale Ausgangsbasis für Schiffe mit fernen Zielen. (rechts) In Zierikzee konnten Schiffe mit kostbarer Ladung hinter der 'Zuidhavenpoort' sicher anlegen.

Hoorn connaît son épanouissement après le déclin des villes hanséatiques. Sa situation au bord des eaux profondes du Zuiderzee garantit la navigation maritime à destination lointaine (dr.). Derrière la Zuidhavenpoort, à Zierikzee, les bateaux à cargaison précieuse pouvaient s'amarrer en toute sécurité.

La prosperidad de Hoorn fué consecuencia de la perdida de importancia de las ciudades anseáticas. Su situación y profundidad de agua del Zuiderzee hacían de esta ciudad una base ideal para los barcos con destinos lejanos. (derecha) En Zierikzee los barcos que transportaban mercancías valiosas podían atracar tras la puerta Zuidhavenpoort.

Hoorn foi uma das cidades que progrediu, depois das cidades da Hansa terem perdido o seu valor. A sua posição nas amplas águas do Zuiderzee, garantiam-lhe uma base de acção ideal, para barcos com destinos longínquos (à direita). Em Zierikzee os navios com cargas valiosas podiam atracar sem perigo, detrás do Portal do Zuidhaven.

De handel op de Oostzee bleef jarenlang verreweg het belangrijkst. Rond het jaar 1600 voerde een vloot van zeshonderd schepen zoveel graan aan dat niet minder dan vier vijfde van de Amsterdamse pakhuizen nodig was om het op te slaan. De handel op de Middellandse Zee werd Straatvaart genoemd. Hierbij waren doorgaans 250 à 300 schepen betrokken. Samen met de kustvaart op Engeland en de riviervaart naar Midden-Europa waren dit grote pijlers onder de bloei van een economie van een land in oorlog. Dit laatste aspect werkte in het voordeel van de noordelijke Nederlanden. De Spaanse troepen kregen de zuidelijke Nederlanden steeds meer in hun greep en veel hervormden namen de wijk naar het noorden. In 1585 moest Antwerpen zich overgeven en veel welgestelde hervormde kooplieden die de stad ontvluchtten vestigden zich in de Hollandse handelssteden. De republikeinse troepen sloten de Schelde af en daarmee werd een belangrijke concurrent voor lange tijd uitgeschakeld.
In dezelfde periode kwam de immigratie van Franse Hugenoten en Spaanse joden opgang. Zij werden vanwege hun afwijkende godsdienst in hun eigen land steeds meer onderdrukt en zochten hun toevlucht in het, voor die tijd, ruimdenkende Nederland.

In navolging van de Portugezen werd in 1595 de eerste expeditie naar de Oost uitgestuurd. De missie verliep niet naar tevredenheid. Vier schepen verlieten de haven van Amsterdam met een bemanning van 250 koppen. Na twee jaar keerden zij terug met slechts een bescheiden lading specerijen en hadden onderweg niet minder dan 160 bemanningsleden verloren. Desondanks werd dit de aanleiding de vaart op Indië grootschalig aan te pakken.

Trade around the Baltic was the most important for years. Around 1600, a fleet of 600 vessels delivered enough grain that no less than 80% of Amsterdam's warehouses were needed to store it. Trade to the Mediterranean was known as street trade, involving 250 to 300 ships. Together with the coastal trade to England and the river shipping to middle Europe, these were the pillars of the economy of a country at war. This last aspect favoured the northern part of the Netherlands. Spanish troops had increasingly more grip on the southern part of the country and many reformed citizens fled to the north. In 1585 Antwerp was captured, and many of its reformed fled the city to settle in the Dutch merchant centres. The republican troops closed the access to the Schelde estuary leading to Antwerp and an important rival was out of the competition for some time.

In the same period, French Hugenots and Spanish jews immigrated to the northern part of the Netherlands. Because of their religion, they were persecuted in their native lands and moved to what was, for the time, the broad-thinking Netherlands.

After the Portuguese, the first expedition to the Far East took place in 1595. But the mission led to disappointment. Four ships left the Port of Amsterdam with a total crew of 250 men. The vessels returned two years later with a small cargo of spices, but had lost no less than 160 members of the crew en route. Nevertheless, this led to large-scale trade with the East.

Viele Jahre lang nahm der Ostseehandel eine zentrale Bedeutung ein. Um das Jahr 1600 lieferte eine Flotte von sechshundert Schiffen soviel Getreide an, daß vier Fünftel aller Amsterdamer Lagerhäuser gebraucht wurden, um diese Mengen unterzubringen. Der Handel übers Mittelmeer wurde "Straßenschiffahrt" genannt und umfaßte 250 bis 300 Schiffe. Zusammen mit der Küstenschiffahrt nach England und der Flußschiffahrt nach Mitteleuropa bildeten sie einen der Pfeiler für die florierende Wirtschaft eines Landes im Kriegszustand. Letzteres wirkte sich übrigens für die nördlichen Niederlande positiv aus. Als die spanischen Truppen in den südlichen Niederlanden immer mehr an Boden gewannen, wichen unzählige Reformierte nach Norden aus. 1585 mußte sich Antwerpen ergeben, und viele wohlhabende reformierte Kaufleute, die aus der Stadt flüchteten, ließen sich in den holländischen Handelsstädten nieder. Die republikanischen Truppen schlossen die Schelde ab und schalteten damit einen mächtigen Konkurrenten für lange Zeit aus.
In dieser Zeit begann die Immigration französischer Hugenotten und spanischer Juden. Sie wurden wegen ihres Glaubens in ihrer Heimat immer stärker unterdrückt und suchten Zuflucht in den für damalige Zeiten freigeistigen Niederlanden.

Nach dem Vorbild der Portugiesen wurde 1595 die erste Expedition nach Osten ausgesandt. Die Mission verlief allerdings nicht zufriedenstellend: Vier Schiffe mit einer Besatzung von 250 Mann liefen aus dem Amsterdamer Hafen aus. Nach zwei Jahren kehrten sie zurück, an Bord lediglich eine bescheidene Ladung Gewürze, wobei sie unterwegs 160 Besatzungsmitglieder eingebüßt hatten. Nichtsdestotrotz wurde daraufhin die Schiffahrt nach Indien in größerem Maßstab angepackt.

Le commerce sur la mer baltique demeura longtemps le plus important. Vers 1600 une flotte de 600 navires transporta vers Amsterdam une telle quantité de blé, qu'il nécessitait pas moins de 4/5 des entrepôts disponibles pour le stockage. On appellait le commerce sur la Méditerranée la 'navigation du détroit'. 250 à 300 bateaux y participaient. En outre, le cabotage vers l'Angleterre et le trafic fluvial vers l'Europe centrale se développa. L'ensemble fut un pilier solide au service de l'épanouissement d'une économie d'un pays en guerre. Ce dernier fait avantagea les Pays-Bas du Nord. Les troupes espagnoles s'emparèrent petit à petit des Pays-Bas du Sud, et les protestants s'enfuirent au Nord. En 1585, Anvers dut se rendre et beaucoup de riches commerçants réformés se réfugièrent dans les villes marchandes de Hollande. La fermeture des bouches de l'Escaut par les troupes républicaines élimina pour longtemps un concurrent important.
En même temps débuta l'immigration des huguenots français et des juifs espagnols. Persécutés dans leurs propres pays à cause de leur religion divergente, ils cherchèrent un refuge dans le pays réputé pour son esprit de tolérance qu'était la Hollande.

Dans le sillage des portuguais, une première expédition en Orient fut entreprise en 1595. Elle ne fut guère satisfaisante. Quatre navires quittèrent le port d'Amsterdam, équipés de 250 hommes, pour revenir deux ans plus tard, chargés d'une modeste cargaison d'épices, et ayant perdu en route 160 personnes. Ceci dit, ce fut le début du développement à grande échelle de la navigation vers les Indes .

Durante muchos años, el comercio con el mar Báltico fué el mas importante. Alrededor del año 1.600, una flota de 600 barcos transportaba tanto grano que llenaban el 80% de los almacenes de Amsterdam. El comercio con el mar Mediterráneo era llamado el de la navegación del Estrecho. Entre 250 y 300 barcos estaban involucrados en la misma. Junto con la navegación a la costa inglesa y la fluvial hacia el centro de Europa, constituyeron los grandes pilares que hicieron florecer la economía de un pais en guerra. Bajo este aspecto, el comercio se decantaba del lado de la Holanda septentrional. Las tropas españolas tenían cada vez mas en su poder a la Holanda meridional y muchos protestantes huyeron hacia el norte. En 1.585 se rindió Amberes a las tropas españolas y muchos comerciantes protestantes que habían huido de la ciudad se establecieron en las ciudades mercantiles holandesas. Las tropas republicanas cerraron el Escalda consiguiendo con ello poner fuera de circulación un importante competidor.
En ese mismo periodo empezó a tomar forma la inmigración de calvinistas franceses y judíos españoles. Debido a su creencia eran perseguidos en sus paises de origen y buscaban refugio en Holanda que para su tiempo era un pais de ideas muy liberales.

Siguiendo a los portugueses, en 1.595 se mandó la primera expedición hacia las Indias con un resultado poco satisfactorio. Cuatro navíos partieron del puerto de Amsterdam con 250 marinos a bordo. Al cabo de dos años volvieron con un pequeño asortimiento de especies y habiendo perdido 160 tripulantes. A pesar de ello fué éste el inicio de la navegación a gran escala hacia las Indias.

O comércio no Mar Báltico manteve-se, o mais importante, durante muitos anos. Por volta do ano de 1600 uma frota de seiscentos barcos transportou tanto cereal, que foram precisas quatro quintas partes dos armazéns de Amesterdão para o armazenar todo. O comércio no Mar Mediterrâneo passou a chamar-se a navegação do Estreito. Nesta navegação serviam normalmente à volta de 250 a 300 barcos. Com a navegação costeira para a Inglaterra e a navegação fluvial na Europa Central elas formavam os grandes pilares que sustentavam a prosperidade da economia de um país em guerra.
Este último aspecto favorecia os Países Baixos no norte. As tropas espanholas subjugavam cada vez mais os Países Baixos no sul e muitos protestantes fugiram para o norte. Em 1585 Antuérpia teve que se render e muitos comerciantes protestantes ricos, que fugiram da cidade fixaram-se nas cidades comerciais holandesas.
As tropas republicanas encerraram o Escalda e assim foi eliminado por longo tempo, um importante concorrente.
No mesmo período começou a imigração dos Huguenotes franceses e dos Judeus espanhóis. Devido à sua religião divergente, estes eram subjugados cada vez mais no seu próprio país e procuraram asilo na Holanda, que naquele tempo era um país com bastante liberdade de pensamento.

A exemplo dos portugueses, foi enviada em 1595 a primeira expedição em direcção ao Oriente. A missão não decorreu satisfatoriamente. Quatro navios saíram do porto de Amesterdão com uma tripulação total de 250 homens. No fim de dois anos voltaram com apenas uma pequena carga de especiarias e tinham perdido no caminho um total de 160 tripulantes. Contudo, isto foi o motivo para pôr mãos à obra para uma viagem mais ampla à Índia.

Twee handelscentra aan het begin van de 16de eeuw. Op de vogelvluchtkaart van Amsterdam van Cornelis Anthonisz. uit 1538 is het aantal zeeschepen nu veruit in de minderheid bij het aantal kleinere veelal binnenschepen of kustvaartuigen. Uit dezelfde periode dateert het gezicht op de lakenmarkt van 's-Hertogenbosch. Het is geschilderd in opdracht van het gilde van lakenkooplieden.

Two trading centres in the beginning of the 16th century. In Cornelisz. Anthonisz.'s birds-eye-view of Amsterdam in 1538, the number of sailing vessels is far less than the total number of the largely river and coastal vessels then in service. The view of the cloth market in 's-Hertogenbosch dates from the same period. It was commissioned by the cloth merchants' guild.

Zwei Handelszentren zu Beginn des 16. Jahrhunderts. Auf der Darstellung von Amsterdam aus der Vogelperspektive von Cornelisz. Anthonisz. aus dem Jahre 1538 sind die Hochseeschiffe bei weitem in der Minderheit angesichts der unzähligen kleineren Schiffe, die meist für die Binnen- oder Küstenschifffahrt gebaut sind. Aus derselben Zeit stammt der Blick auf den Tuchmarkt von s'-Hertogenbosch. Das Gemälde wurde von der Tuchhändler-Gilde in Auftrag gegeben.

Deux centres commerciaux au début du 16e s. La carte d'Amsterdam faite par Cornelis Anthonisz en 1538 montre un nombre de navires maritimes inférieur à celui des navires fluviaux ou caboteurs plus petits. De cette même époque date la vue sur le marché aux draps de Bois-le-Duc, une peinture commandée par la guilde des marchands drapiers.

Dos centros comerciales al principio del siglo XVI. En el mapa panorámico de Amsterdam realizado por Cornelisz. Anthonisz. en 1.538 se aprecia que los barcos de mar se encontraban en gran minoría con respecto a los pequeños barcos de navegación interior y costera. Del mismo periodo es esta vista del mercado de paños de Bois le Duc. Esta pintada por orden del gremiode mercaderes de paños.

Dois centros de comércio no princípio do século 16. No mapa de supervisão de Amesterdão feito por Cornelisz. Anthonisz., em 1538, a quantidade de navios marítimos é já uma grande minoria em relação aos barcos fluviais ou costeiros. Do mesmo período data a vista sobre o mercado dos panos em 's-Hertogenbosch. Pintado por encargo da confraria dos negociantes de panos.

Het was de gegoede burgerij die de dienst uitmaakte. Zij waren lid van de vroedschappen en van de schutterijen. Onderling werden niet alleen de bestuurlijke functies maar ook de belangen in de financiële consortia geregeld. Sommigen gingen hun eigen weg zoals Lodewijk de Geer. Afkomstig uit een adellijke familie in Luik vestigde hij zich in 1611 in Amsterdam als zelfstandig koopman in ijzer. Al snel exploiteerde hij ertsmijnen in eigen beheer in Zweden en niet veel later ontwikkelde hij zich tot de belangrijkste wapenfabrikant in een Europa waar alom oorlog werd gevoerd. Bij een geschil om de doorvaart in de Sont ruste hij zijn eigen vloot uit. Hij woonde in het zgn. 'Huis met de Hoofden' te Amsterdam (rechts).

The rich citizens made up the top of society. They were members of the corporation and the militia. Subordinates not only took over the management functions but they had interests in the financial consortia. Some of them, like Lodewijk de Geer, made their own way. A member of a noble family from Liege, he settled in Amsterdam in 1611 as an independent iron merchant. He rapidly became an iron mine operator in Sweden and not soon afterwards he was the most important weapons manufacturer in Europe where war was almost continuous. He operated his own fleet after a dispute over shipping in the Sont river. He resided in the so-called 'House with the heads' in Amsterdam.

Das Großbürgertum hatte das Sagen. Sie saßen im Rat der Weisen und waren Mitglieder der Bürgerwehr. Sie regelten nicht nur alle Verwaltungsangelegenheiten untereinander, sondern auch die Interessen in finanziellen Konsortien. Manche gingen jedoch ihre eigenen Wege: einer davon war Lodewijk de Geer. Der gebürtige Adelige aus Lüttich ließ sich 1611 in Amsterdam als selbständiger Eisenhändler nieder. Schon bald baute er in eigener Regie Erz in schwedischen Bergwerken ab und entwickelte sich wenig später zum bedeutendsten Waffenfabrikanten Europas, wo allenthalben Krieg geführt wurde. Bei einem Streit um die Durchfahrt durch den Sund rüstete er eine eigene Flotte auf. Er wohnte im sogenannten 'Huis met de Hoofden' in Amsterdam (rechts).

La bourgeoisie aisée tirait les ficelles. Elle faisait partie de la magistrature municipale et de la garde civique. On règlait entre soi les affaires financières et de gestion. Mais certains suivirent leur propre chemin. Ce fut le cas de Lodewijk de Geer. Issu d'une famille noble liégeoise, il s'établit en 1911 à Amsterdam en tant que marchand en fer indépendant. Bientôt, il exploîta en régie propre des mines de fer en Suède, et devint l'armurier le plus important de l'Europe, où la guerre sévissait partout. Lors d'un différend concernant le passage sur le Sont, il arma sa propre flotte. Il habitait la 'Maison aux têtes' à Amsterdam.

Los ciudadanos acomodados eran los que mandaban. Formaban parte de los cabildos del ayuntamiento y de las milícias urbanas. Entre ellos se repartían, no solo las funciones gubernamentales sino tambien se regulaban los intereses en consorcios financieros. Algunos de estos ciudadanos sin embargo seguían su propio camino, como en el caso de Lodewijk de Geer. Descendiente de una familia noble de Lieja, se estableció en 1.611 en Amsterdam como comerciante independiente en hierro. Muy rapidamente empezó a explotar minas minerales en Suecia y poco mas tarde se convirtió en el mas importante fabricante de armas de Europa en donde por todas partes se libraban guerras. Debido a unas diferencias sobre la travesía por el Oresund, armó su propia flota. Vivió en la llamada "Casa de las Cabezas" en Amsterdam (derecha).

A burguesia rica é que punha e dispunha. Os seus membros participavam nos Conselhos Citadinos da República e nas Milícias da Cidade. Entre e por eles eram reguladas não só as funçocs directivas, mas também os interesses nos consórcios financeiros. Alguns deles escolhiam o seu próprio destino, como Lodewijk de Geer. Originário de uma família nobre de Liége, ele estabeleceu-se em 1611 em Amesterdão, como negociante independente em ferro. Brevemente começou ele a explorar minas de ferro na Suécia, por conta própria, e dentro de pouco tempo revelou-se como o mais importante fabricante de armas numa Europa, onde sempre algures havia guerra. Num conflito sobre a passagem pelo rio Sont, armou ele a sua própria frota. Ele habitava no casarão conhecido como a 'Casa das Cabeças', em Amesterdão (à direita).

In meerdere steden verenigden zich kooplieden om het Amsterdamse initiatief na te volgen. In 1602 drongen de Staten-Generaal aan op samenwerking en werd de Verenigde Oost-Indische Compagnie (VOC) opgericht.
Deze kreeg als enige het octrooi om in de Aziatische wateren handel te drijven. Het stichtingskapitaal bedroeg 6,5 miljoen gulden en was bijeengebracht door aandeelhouders uit alle lagen van de bevolking: kooplieden zowel als werklieden. De VOC had naast Amsterdam als voornaamste zetel vestigingen in vijf andere handelssteden. In de bloeiperiode die ongeveer 200 jaar heeft geduurd was de VOC dermate invloedrijk dat zij gemachtigd was verdragen te sluiten, forten te bouwen en bovendien militair op te treden.
Het succes van de VOC was in 1621 aanleiding tot de oprichting van een West-Indische Compagnie, de WIC. Zij verkreeg het octrooi op de handel en scheepvaart op de westkust van Afrika tot aan Kaap de Goede Hoop en op het Amerikaanse continent. Omdat de Republiek in oorlog was met Spanje was tot de vrede van Münster (1648) de kaapvaart in de door Spanje gedomineerde gebieden een lucratieve activiteit. In de periode van 1622 tot 1636 bedroeg deze buit maar liefst 36 miljoen gulden. Zo overviel een vloot onder aanvoering van Piet Heyn bij Cuba in 1628 een complete Spaanse zilvervloot. De landhonger van de compagnie kwam tot uiting door het in bezit nemen van Nieuw-Amsterdam (het latere New York), de Nederlandse Antillen, Guyana, delen van Brazilië en talrijke handelsposten aan de Afrikaanse kust.
Na de vrede in 1648 leed de WIC aanzienlijke verliezen en gingen de bezittingen in Brazilië en Noord-Amerika verloren. In haar nadagen tot de ontbinding in 1691 vormde de slavenhandel nog de enige bron van inkomsten.
De vooraanstaande rol die de Nederlandse zeevaart in de wereld vervulde werd enorm ondersteund door de opkomst en bloei van de cartografie. Beroemde namen uit die tijd waren: Mercator, Plancius en Waghenaer. De precisie die zij in hun kaarten konden aanbrengen was te danken aan de verbetering van de navigatiemiddelen en de uitvinding van het slingeruurwerk door Huygens.

Merchants in other cities soon followed the lead of Amsterdam. In 1602, the States-General of the Dutch Republic forced them to cooperate and the United East Indies Company (VOC) was formed.

The VOC had the monopoly on trade in Asian waters. The VOC had equity of 6.5 million guilders raised by shareholders from all levels of society. In addition to Amsterdam, the VOC had seats in five other trading cities. In its prime which lasted for nearly 200 years, the VOC was so influential that it was empowered to negotiate treaties, build forts and to raise an army.

Following the success of the VOC, the West Indies Company (WIC) was formed in 1621. It obtained the monopoly on trade and shipping to the West coast of Africa to the Cape of Good Hope as well as to the continent of North America. Because the Dutch Republic was at war with Spain until the Treaty of Munster in 1648, privateering in Spanish-dominated regions was an extremely lucrative activity. The spoils amounted to at least 36 million guilders between 1622 and 1638. A fleet f ships under the command of Piet Heyn captured the complete Spanish silver fleet off Cuba in 1628. The VOC's hunger for land was seen in its settlement of Nieuw Amsterdam (later New York), the Netherlands Antilles, Guyana, parts of Brazil and numerous trading posts on the African coast.
The prominent role of Dutch shipping all over the globe was supported enormously by the rise and flowering of cartography. Famous names at the time were Mercator, Placius and Waghenaer. The precision they brought to their maps was due in part to improved navigation and the invention of the pendulum clock by Huygens.

In mehreren Städten schlossen sich Kaufleute zusammen, um die Amsterdamer Initiative nachzuahmen. 1602 drängten die Ständeversammlungen, die sogenannten Generalstaaten, auf Zusammenarbeit, und so wurde die Vereinigte Ostindische Compagnie (VOC) gegründet.
Diese erhielt als einzige das Patent für den Handel in asiatischen Gewässern. Das Gründungskapital belief sich auf 6,5 Millionen Gulden und wurde von Anteilseignern aus allen Bevölkerungsschichten zusammengetragen: Kaufleuten ebenso wie Arbeitern. Die VOC hatte neben ihrem Hauptsitz in Amsterdam noch Niederlassungen in fünf anderen Handelsstädten. In ihrer Blütezeit, die etwa 200 Jahre andauerte, war die VOC so einflußreich, daß sie zum Abschluß von Verträgen, zum Bau von Befestigungsanlagen und sogar zu militärischen Eingriffen berechtigt war.
Der Erfolg der VOC war 1621 Anlaß für die Gründung einer Westindischen Compagnie, der WIC. Sie erhielt das Handels- und Schiffahrtspatent für die Westküste Afrikas bis hinunter zum Kap der Guten Hoffnung und für den amerikanischen Kontinent. Da die niederländische Republik mit Spanien im Krieg lag, war die Kapschiffahrt in den spanisch beherrschten Gebieten bis zum Frieden von Münster (1648) ein lukratives Unterfangen. In der Zeit von 1622 bis 1636 betrug die Beute gut und gerne 36 Millionen Gulden. So überfiel eine Flotte unter der Führung von Piet Heyn im Jahre 1628 bei Kuba eine komplette spanische Silberflotte. Der Landhunger der WIC äußerte sich in der Besitznahme von Neu-Amsterdam (dem späteren New York), der niederländischen Antillen, Guyana, Teilen Brasiliens und zahlreicher Handelsposten an der afrikanischen Küste.
Nach dem Frieden von 1648 erlitt die WIC beträchtliche Verluste, und die Besitzungen in Brasilien und Nordamerika gingen verloren. In den Jahren des Niedergangs bis zu ihrer Auflösung im Jahr 1691 war der Sklavenhandel die letzte noch verbleibende Einnahmequelle.
Die herausragende Rolle der niederländischen Schiffahrt in der Welt wurde durch das Aufkommen und die Verbreitung der Kartographie stark unterstützt. Berühmte Namen dieser Zeit sind: Mercator, Placius und Waghenaer. Die Präzision, mit der sie ihre Karten erstellen konnten, war der Verbesserung der Navigationsinstrumente und der Erfindung der Pendeluhr durch Huygens zu verdanken.

L'expérience fut suivie par des marchands d'autres villes. Les Etats-Généraux insistèrent sur une coopération, ce qui eut pour résultat la fondation de la Compagnie Réunie des Indes orientales (VOC) en 1602. Celle-ci obtint le monopole de la navigation et du commerce avec l'Extrême Orient. Le capital initial de 6,5 millions de florins fut apporté par des actionnaires appartenant à toutes les classes de la société. La Compagnie avait son siège principal à Amsterdam et des succursales dans cinq autres villes commerçantes. Elle connut une période de prospérité d'à peu près 200 ans, pendant laquelle sa puissance était telle, qu'elle fut mandatée pour conclure des accords, construire des forteresses et conduire des actions militaires.
Le succès de la VOC fut à l'origine de la création de la Compagnie des Indes Occidentales, la WIC, qui couvrait à la fois la côte ouest de l'Afrique jusqu'au Cap de Bonne Espérance, et l'Amérique. La République étant en guerre avec l'Espagne, la course dans les territoires espagnols s'avéra une activité lucrative, jusqu'à la Paix de Münster (1648). En quatorze ans, de 1622 à 1636 le butin s'éleva à 36 millions de florins. Ainsi, à Cuba, en 1628, l'amiral Piet Heyn s'empara dans sa totalité d'une flotte espagnole de transport d'argent. La Compagnie démontra son esprit de conquête par l'établissement de la Nouvelle Amsterdam, aujourd'hui New York, à travers l'occupation des Antilles, de la Guyane, du Nord est du Brésil, et par la création de nombreux comptoirs commerciaux sur les côtes africaines. Dès la paix de 1648, cependant, la WIC subit de grosses pertes et dut renoncer à ses possessions au Brésil et en Amérique du Nord. Jusqu'à sa liquidation en 1691, la traite des esclaves devint sa seule source de profits.
La prépondérance de la navigation hollandaise dans le monde fut fortement aidée par le développement de la cartographie. Mercator, Placius et Waghenaer sont des noms réputés de cette époque. Leurs cartes font preuve d'une grande précision, due à l'amélioration des outils de navigation, et à la découverte par Huygens de l'horloge à balancier.

Los comerciantes de otras ciudades se unieron tambien para seguir la iniciativa de Amsterdam. En 1602 los Estados Generales promovieron la cooperación entre estos comerciantes y fundaron la Compañía de las Indias orientales (VOC).
A esta compañía se le dió la concesión para navegar y ejercer el comercio en las aguas asiáticas. Su capital fundacional fué de 6,5 millones de florines y sus accionistas salieron de todas las capas de la sociedad, de comerciantes a trabajadores. La VOC tuvo ademas de su importante residencia en Amsterdam, establecimientos en cinco otras ciudades mercantiles.Durante su periodo de florecimiento que duró aproximadamente 200 años, la VOC tuvo tal influencia e importancia que estuvo incluso capacitada para la construcción de fuertes y ademas para intervenir militarmente.
El éxito de la VOC fue la causa de que en el 1621 se fundara la compañía de las Indias occidentales (WIC). Esta compañía obtuvo la concesión comercial de la costa occidental de Africa hasta el cabo de Buena Esperanza asi como la del continente americano. Por causa de la guerra existente, entre la República y España que duró hasta la Paz de Westfalia en 1648, la piratería por los territorios de dominación española fue de gran lucro. Entre los años 1622 y 1636 se consiguió un botín de 36 millones de florines. Una flota de barcos al mando de Piet Heyn asaltó en 1628 cerca de Cuba toda una armada de plata española. El anexionismo de la Compañía tuvo su expresión mas relevante con la toma en posesión de Nueva-Amsterdam (llamada posteriormente New York), las Antillas holandesas, Guayana, partes de Brasil y numerosas colonias comerciales a lo largo de toda la costa africana.
Despues de la paz de 1648, la compañía WIC sufrió perdidas economicas de importancia y perdió sus propiedades en Brasil y Norte America. En su época posterior hasta su desaparición en 1691, su única fuente de ingresos fué el resultado del tráfico de esclavos.
El gran protagonismo de la navegación marítima holandesa en el mundo fué debido al desarrollo y florecimiento de la cartografía. Podemos citar personajes importantes en este aspecto como Mercator, Placius y Waghenaer. La precisión con que desarrollaron sus mapas se debió tanto a la mejora de los medios de navegación como al descubrimiento por Huygens del reloj de péndola.

Em diversas outras cidades reuniram-se os negociantes para seguir a iniciativa de Amesterdão. Em 1602 os Estados Gerais insistiram em colaboração e foi fundada a Companhia Unida da Índia Oriental (em holandês conhecida como: VOC). Esta recebeu como única, licença para fazer negócios nas águas asiáticas. O capital de fundação somou a 6,5 milhões de florins, e foi junto por accionistas de todas as camadas do povo: tanto negociantes como trabalhadores. A VOC tinha além de Amesterdão, como sede principal, sucursais em cinco outras cidades comerciais. No período de prosperidade, que durou à volta de 200 anos a VOC tinha uma tal influência que ela era autorizada a fazer pactos, a construir fortes e, além disso, a intervir militarmente.
O êxito da VOC foi em 1621 a razão para a fundação da Companhia da Índia Ocidental, (em holandês West-Indische Compagnie = WIC). Ela recebeu licença para negociar e fazer viagens marítimas para a costa ocidental da África até ao Cabo da Boa Esperança e para o continente americano. Como a República estava em guerra com a Espanha, até ao Tratado de Paz de Munique (1648), a navegação para o Cabo nas regiões dominadas pelos espanhóis, era uma actividade bastante lucrativa. No período de 1622 até 1636 os despojos adquiridos subiram a 36 milhões de florins. Desta maneira uma frota comandada por Piet Heyn, atacou próximo de Cuba, em 1628 uma esquadra da prata completa espanhola. O desejo de conquista de terras da Companhia demonstrou-se pela invasão de Nova Amesterdão (mais tarde: Nova Iorque), as Antilhas Holandesas, Guiana, partes do Brasil e inúmeros postos comerciais na costa ocidental da África.
Depois da paz em 1648 a WIC sofreu enormes perdas e perdeu os territórios no Brasil e na América do Norte. Nos seus últimos dias, até à sua dissolução em 1691, o comércio de escravos era a sua única fonte de receitas.
O papel eminente que a navegação holandesa desempenhava no mundo foi apoiado imensamente pelo aparecimento e a prosperidade da cartografia. Nomes famosos desse tempo são: Mercator, Placius e Waghenaer. A precisão que eles podiam aplicar nos seus mapas foi adquirida graças a um aperfeiçoamento nos meios de navegação e pela invenção do relógio de pêndula feita por Huygens.

In opdracht van de VOC maakte Jan Pietersz. Coen vanuit zijn geboortestad Hoorn in 1607 zijn eerste reis naar Oost-Indië. Hij was de stichter van de hoofdstad Batavia, het huidige Jakarta.
In de 17de eeuw raakte de jonge Republiek driemaal in oorlog met rivaal Engeland. Michiel de Ruyter geboren te Vlissingen, besliste als admiraal door zijn kunde menige zeeslag. Tot zijn grootste wapenfeiten behoort de tocht naar Chatham, waar zijn goedgetrainde vloot een ijzeren verdedigingsketting in de Theems-monding stuk voer.

Jan Pietersz. Coen made his first trip to the East Indies in 1607 from his home town of Hoorn, commissioned by the VOC. He founded the capital, Batavia, which is the present Jakarta. In the 17th century, the young Republic was at war with England three times. As admiral, Vlissingen-born Michiel de Ruyter, decided many naval battles. His greatest feat took place in Chatham where his well-trained fleet placed a chain across the mouth of the Thames.

Im Auftrag der VOC machte Jan Pietersz. Coen sich von seiner Geburtsstadt Hoorn aus 1607 auf seine erste Reise nach Ostindien. Er gründete die Hauptstadt Batavia, das heutige Jakarta. Im 17. Jahrhundert führte die junge Republik dreimal Krieg gegen den Rivalen England. Michiel de Ruyter, geboren in Vlissingen, entschied als Admiral mit seinem Können so manche Seeschlacht zu seinen Gunsten. Zu seinen größten Ruhmestaten gehört die Fahrt nach Chatham, wo seine gut ausgebildete Flotte eine eiserne Verteidigungskette in der Themse-Mündung sprengte.

Sur commande de la VOC, Jan Pietersz. Coen partit de sa ville natale Hoorn pour sa première expédition aux Indes orientales. Il y fonda Batavia, aujourd'hui Djakarta. Au 17e s. la jeune République entra trois fois en guerre avec son concurrent l'Angleterre. Amiral compétent, natif de Vlissingen, Michiel de Ruyter emporta plus d'une bataille navale. Un de ses exploits mémorables fut l'attaque de Chatham, où sa flotte bien entraînée brisa une chaîne de protection en fer posée à travers de l'embouchure de la Tamise.

Bajo el mandato de la compañía VOC, Jan Piertersz. Coen, saliendo de su ciudad natal Hoorn, realizó en 1.607 su primer viaje a las Indias orientales. Fué el fundador de su capital Batavia, la actual Jacarta. En el siglo XVII la naciente República se vió envuelta en tres guerras contra su rival Inglaterra. Michiel de Ruyter, nacido en Vlissingen y debido a su gran maestría, ganó diversas batallas navales. Una de sus grandes hazañas fué su expedición a Chatham donde su experimentada flota destrozó las cadenas defensivas de la desembocadura del Támesis.

Por ordem da VOC fez o Jan Pietesz. Coen, partindo da sua terra de nascimento Hoorn, em 1607, a sua primeira viagem à Índia Oriental. Ele foi o fundador da capital Batávia, a actual Jacarta.
No século 17, a jovem República esteve três vezes em guerra com a rival Inglaterra. Michiel de Ruyter, nascido em Vlissingen, resolveu como almirante, várias batalhas navais, graças à sua perícia. Às suas maiores façanhas pertence a passagem para Chatham, onde a sua frota bem treinada rebentou uma corrente de defesa na foz do Tamisa.

De sfeer van de zeventiende eeuw is nog op veel plaatsen in Nederland aanwezig. Door het gehele land staan huizen met kenmerkende trap-, klok- en halsgevels. Het ministadje Sloten in Friesland staat slechts wat betreft schaalgrootte in contrast met Amsterdam.

The sphere of the 17th century is still to be seen in many parts of the Netherlands. Throughout the country, there are many houses with the typical stair, clock and collar gables. The mini-city of Sloten in Friesland differs from Amsterdam only in scale.

Die Atmosphäre des 17. Jahrhunderts ist an vielen Orten in den Niederlanden noch spürbar. Im ganzen Land stehen Häuser mit den typischen Treppen-, Glocken- und Halsgiebeln. Die Kleinstadt Sloten in Friesland steht Amsterdam dabei höchstens im Maßstab nach.

On retrouve l'ambiance du 17e s. un peu partout. Typiques sont les façades des maisons à pignon de formes différentes : à redans, en 'cloche' ou en 'cou'. La ville miniature de Sloten en Frise ne se distingue d'Amsterdam que par son échelle réduite.

En muchos lugares de Holanda se aprecia aún el ambiente del siglo XVII. Por toda Holanda encontramos casas con frontispicios en forma de campana, escalera y de cuello. La mini ciudad de Sloten en Frisia contrasta, por lo que respecta en dimension, con Amsterdam.

O ambiente do século dezassete está ainda bem patente em muitos locais da Holanda. Por todo o país há casas com as fachadas características em forma de escada, de sino e de gargalo. A cidade em ponto pequeno Sloten na Frísia, está em contraste com Amesterdão apenas pelo seu tamanho.

De Amsterdam, een replica van een 17deeeuws koopvaardijschip, ligt hier afgemeerd bij het voormalige 's Land Zeemagazijn. Het was het enterpot voor de uitrusting van de schepen. Nu dient het als scheepvaartmuseum. De wereldkaart van Ortelius uit 1570 geeft een beeld van de kennis die men op dat tijdstip van de wereld had. Als enig Europees land had de Republiek het privilege om met Japan handel te drijven. Nederland had er een eigen handelspost bij de stad Nagasaki Decima genaamd.

The Amsterdam, a replica of a 17th century merchant ship, is berthed near the former national naval depot.
The impressive depot was used for ships' stores, and now serves as the national maritime museum. Orteluis' map of the world illustrates the knowledge of the world at that period of time. The Republic was the only European power to have trading privileges with Japan. The Netherlands maintained its own trading port on the island of Decima, near Nagasaki.

Die Amsterdam, eine Nachbildung eines Handelsschiffs aus dem 17. Jahrhundert, liegt hier angedockt am ehemaligen 's Land Zeemagazijn. Das ehemalige Depot für die Ausstattung der Schiffe dient heute als Schiffahrtsmuseum. Die Weltkarte von Ortelius aus dem Jahre 1570 zeigt, wieviel man damals von der Erde kannte. Als einziges europäisches Land hatte die niederländische Republik das Privileg, mit Japan Handel zu treiben. Dort hatten die Niederlande nahe der Stadt Nagasaki einen eigenen Handelsposten namens Decima.

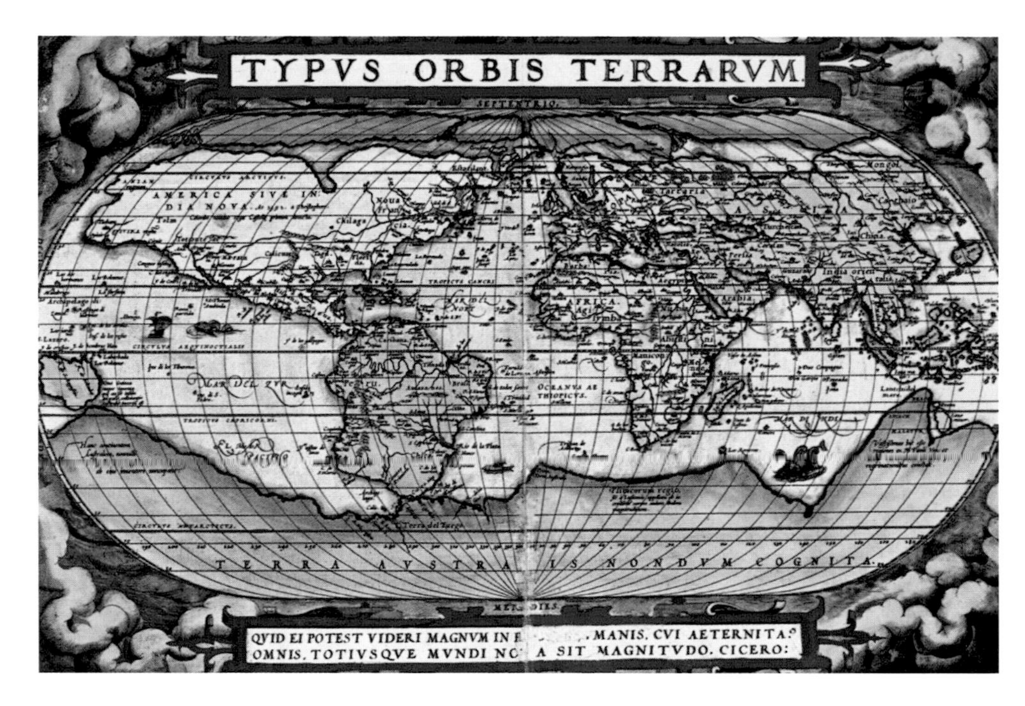

L' 'Amsterdam', réplique d'un navire marchand traditionnel du 17e s., est amarré en face de l'ancien arsenal, où fut installé un vaste entrepôt maritime, aujourd'hui Musée d'Histoire maritime. Le mappemonde d'Ortelius de 1570 représente l'image du monde à cette époque. La République fut le seul pays européen à détenir le privilège du commerce avec le Japon. Elle y avait établi un comptoir commercial près de Nagasaki, appelé Decima.

La Bolsa de Amsterdam (aquí arriba) era el corazón del comercio en Holanda. El mapa mundi de Ortelius de 1.570 nos muestra el conocimiento que en dicha época se tenía del mundo. La República, como único país europeo, tuvo el privilegio de comerciar con Japon. Holanda tuvo su propia colonia comercial, llamada Decima, en la ciudad de Nagasaki.

O "Amsterdam", uma réplica de um navio comercial do século 17, encontra-se aqui junto ao Armazém Marítimo Nacional. Aqui era o entreposto para o equipamento dos navios. Agora faz serviço como Museu da Navegação. O mapa do mundo de Ortelius, de 1570 dá uma impressão dos conhecimentos que se tinha do mundo naquele tempo. A República tinha, como único país europeu, o privilegio de negociar com o Japão. A Holanda tinha lá um posto comercial próximo da cidade Nagasaki, com o nome de "Decima".

De Beurs in Amsterdam, afgebeeld door de schilder De Witte, was het trefpunt voor kooplieden uit vele windstreken. Op regionaal niveau troffen de kooplieden elkaar meestal bij het waaggebouw. In de prachtige Waag te Gouda (1668, midden) ging het meestal om de Goudse kaas. De Waag te Deventer (rechts) dateert uit 1528. Deventer vervulde een doorvoer functie tussen Rijnland-Westfalen en het westen van de Republiek.

A version of the Amsterdam stock exchange by the painter De Witte. The bourse was the meeting point of traders from all parts of the world. On a regional level, merchants met mostly at the weighing houses. In the splendid weighing house in Gouda (1668, centre), trade was largely in local Gouda cheese. The Deventer weighing house (right) dates from 1528. Deventer was a transit point between Rhineland-Westphalia and the western part of the Republic.

Die Amsterdamer Börse, künstlerisch festgehalten von dem Maler De Witte, war Treffpunkt für Kaufleute aus allen Himmelsrichtungen. Die regionalen Händler trafen sich meist bei der Stadtwaage. In der prächtigen 'Waag' in Gouda (1668, Mitte) ging es meistens um Gouda-Käse. Die 'Waag' von Deventer (rechts) stammt aus dem Jahre 1528. Deventer war eine wichtige Zwischenstation auf dem Weg zwischen dem westfälischen Rheinland und dem Westen der niederländischen Republik.

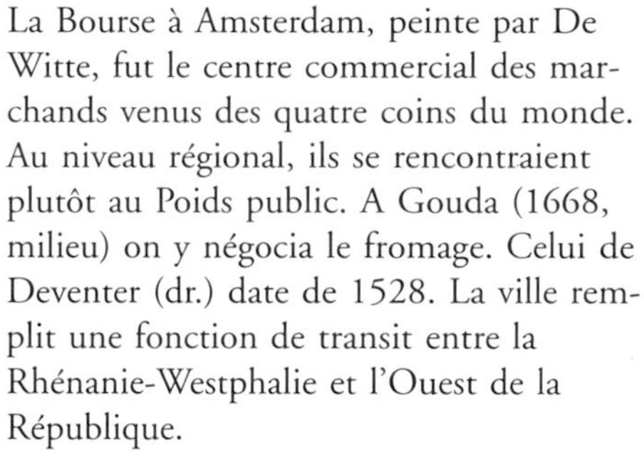

La Bourse à Amsterdam, peinte par De Witte, fut le centre commercial des marchands venus des quatre coins du monde. Au niveau régional, ils se rencontraient plutôt au Poids public. A Gouda (1668, milieu) on y négocia le fromage. Celui de Deventer (dr.) date de 1528. La ville remplit une fonction de transit entre la Rhénanie-Westphalie et l'Ouest de la République.

La Bolsa de Amsterdam (aquí arriba) era el corazón del comercio en Holanda. El mapa mundi de Ortelius de 1.570 nos muestra el conocimiento que en dicha época se tenía del mundo. La República, como único país europeo, tuvo el privilegio de comerciar con Japon. Holanda tuvo su propia colonia comercial, llamada Decima, en la ciudad de Nagasaki.

A Bolsa de Amesterdão, aqui pintada pelo pintor De Witte, era o ponto de encontro dos negociantes de muitas regiões. A nível regional os negociantes encontravam-se, em geral, junto ao Edifício da Balança (Waaggebouw). Na magnífica "de Waag" de Gouda (1668) (ao meio) negociava-se em especial o queijo de Gouda. A balança de Deventer (à direita) data de 1528. Deventer desempenhava uma função de tráfego entre Rijland-Westfalen e o ocidente da República.

Er werd in de Gouden Eeuw veel geld verdiend. Veel kooplieden en regenten schroomden niet hun welstand te tonen. De meeste Amsterdamse welgestelden lieten een buitenplaats aan de Vecht bouwen. Door hun inspanningen is de Vechtstreek veranderd in een waar lustoord. Kosten noch moeite werden gespaard om met name de waterzijde van de kleine paleizen een zo fraai mogelijk uiterlijk te verschaffen. Even verderop in het dorp 's-Graveland liet admiraal Tromp zijn buitenplaats verrijzen. Het vertoont grote gelijkenis met een schip. (bladzijde 84.)

A lot of money was earned during the Golden Age. Many merchants and regents of the VOC were not afraid to display their wealth. Many of the well-to-do in Amsterdam built country houses along the Vecht river. They transformed the region into an idyllic spot. No costs were spared, particularly on the waterside of the minor palaces. Further along the river in 's-Gravesand, Admiral Tromp built his country estate. In many ways, it resembles a ship.

Im Goldenen Zeitalter wurde viel Geld verdient. Unzählige Kaufleute und Regenten scheuten sich nicht, ihren Reichtum zur Schau zu stellen. Die meisten reichen Amsterdamer errichteten sich Landhäuser an der Vecht. Durch ihre Aufwendungen verwandelte sich der Landstrich entlang der Vecht in ein wahres Paradies. Weder Kosten noch Mühen wurden gescheut, um vor allem die Uferfront der kleinen Paläste so prachtvoll wie möglich zu gestalten. Etwas weiter flußaufwärts im Dorf 's-Graveland ließ Admiral Tromp seinen Landsitz erbauen. Das Gebäude hat großeÄhnlichkeit mit einem Schiff (Seite 84).

Au Siècle d'Or, on gagnait beaucoup d'argent. Les marchands et régents d'Amsterdam n'hésitaient pas à faire montre de leurs richesses, ils construisirent leurs gentilhommières au bord de la Vecht, ainsi transformant cette région en véritable paradis. Sans épargner leur peine, ils firent embellir leurs petits châteaux, surtout les façades côté rivière. Dans le bourg de 's-Gravenland, l'amiral Tromp dressa son manoir, qui ressemble beaucoup à un bateau (p. 84)

Durante el Siglo de Oro hubo grandes beneficios ecomómicos. Los comerciantes y regentes no se abstenían en mostrar sus riquezas. La mayoría de la gente rica de Amsterdam construyeron sus casas solariegas a orillas del Vecht transformando así a esta región en un lugar idílico. Encaminaron todos sus esfuerzos en construir estos pequeños palacios con las mas hermosas fachadas en su parte correspondiente al rio. El almirante Tromp construyó tambien su mansión en 's-Graveland dándole una forma muy parecida a una nave. (pagina 84).

No Século Áureo ganhou-se muito dinheiro. Muitos negociantes e regentes não se envergonhavam de demonstrar a sua riqueza. A maioria dos ricos em Amesterdão adquiriam uma moradia no exterior junto ao rio Vecht. Graças à sua dedicação a região do Vecht tornou-se um verdadeiro paraíso. Nada se poupou, nem custos nem esforços, para dar, em especial, ao lado dos palacetes virado para o rio, um aspecto o mais formoso possível. Um pouco mais adiante, na aldeia 's-Gravenland, o almirante Tromp mandou construir o seu palacete no campo. Este tem uma enorme parecença com um navio (página 84).

Welvaart stimuleert kunst en wetenschap

Prosperity stimulates the arts and science

Kulturelle Blüte

Prospérité, arts et sciences

La prosperidad como estímulo del arte y la ciencia

Desenvolvimento cultural

De economische welvaart betekende voor de Nederlanden een hechte waarborg voor culturele bloei. In geen enkel tijdperk bleek dit duidelijker dan in de Gouden Eeuw. Dit gold voor de beeldende kunsten, maar ook voor de andere uitingen van de cultuur zoals letterkunde en wetenschap.

Schilderkunst

In het buitenland is de schilderkunst uit deze periode het meest bekend. De Nederlanders onderscheidden zich door hun hoge graad van realisme en zij behandelden de achtergrond even gelijkwaardig als het hoofdgegeven. Licht en perspectief speelden bij alle schilders een dominerende rol. De Nederlandse landschapschilders legden de horizon laag en vulden de lucht met licht. Ook bij een schilderij van een sober Hollands binnenhuis draagt licht bij aan een heel bijzondere stemming. Het realisme vond weerklank bij brede lagen van de bevolking. De breedste laag was de gegoede burgerij, die in de bloeitijd van de handel ruimschoots over middelen beschikte om kunstwerken aan te kopen. Hun overheersende smaak dwong de schilders min of meer een tastbare werkelijkheid weer te geven. Kenmerkend is tevens het ontbreken van hofschilderkunst. De stadhouders, met uitzondering van Frederik Hendrik, waren niet scheutig met het geven van opdrachten. Opmerkelijk in dit opzicht is de anekdote dat de Staten-Generaal aan de zeeschilders vader en zoon Van de Velde een scheepje ter beschikking stelden om de zeeslagen van de Hollandse vloot met de Engelsen zo natuurgetrouw weer te kunnen geven.
Grootmeesters als Rembrandt en Frans Hals daargelaten, konden de schilders maar amper van hun doeken leven. Jan Steen was naast schilder ook herbergier en Meindert Hobbema, de schilder van het beroemde schilderij 'Het laantje van Middelharnis', was controleur van geïmporteerde wijn.

Bouwkunst

De bouwkunst van de Gouden Eeuw werd bepaald door het classicisme. De meer speelse renaissancebouw van beroemde architecten als Lieven de Key en Hendrick de Keyser werd overvleugeld door de wens naar deftige soberheid. Een zeer goed voorbeeld is het Paleis op de Dam te Amsterdam. Het werd in 1638 gebouwd als stadhuis door de bouwmeester Jacob van Campen. De bouw duurde zeven jaar. Bepalend voor de schoonheid van het gebouw is het beeldhouwwerk dat werd uitgevoerd door Artus Quellijn. De broers Philips en Justus Vingboons waren meer gespecialiseerd in huizenbouw. Kenmerkend voor hun stijl is

For the Netherlands, economic prosperity represented a real guarantee of blossoming culture. This was never more clearly demonstrated than during the Golden Age – not just in the fine arts, but in other cultural expressions such as literature and science.

Painting

People in other countries are most familiar with Dutch paintings from this era. Dutch artists excelled in the degree of realism they achieved, and they treated the background as being as important as the central subject. Light and perspective played a dominant role in the work of all the painters of this period. Dutch landscape artists put the horizon low and flooded the sky with light. Even a painting of a sombre Dutch house interior uses light to create a very special atmosphere. This realism caught the imagination of large sectors of the population. The largest group was made up of the well-to-do middle class who, with trade booming, had plenty of money to buy works of art. Their prevailing taste compelled the painters to produce an almost tangible realism. Another feature is the absence of court paintings. With the exception of Frederick Henry, the Stadholders were not generous when it came to commissioning works of art. An interesting anecdote in this regard is that the States General made a ship available to the Van de Veldes, father and son, who were marine painters, so that they could make their paintings of sea battles between the Dutch and British fleets as authentic as possible.
With the exception of the great masters like Rembrandt and Frans Hals, most painters were barely able to scrape a living from their canvasses. Jan Steen was an innkeeper as well as a painter, and Meindert Hobbema, who painted the famous work The Avenue at Middelharnis, was controller of imported wine.

Architecture

Architecture in the Golden Age was defined by classicism. The more lively Renaissance style of famous architects like Lieven de Key and Hendrick de Keyser was eclipsed by the desire for dignified sobriety. A very good example of this is the Palace on the Dam in Amsterdam. It was built as the Town Hall in 1638 by master builder Jacob van Campen. Construction took seven years. The beauty of the building is due to the sculpture by Artus Quellijn. The Vinboons brothers, Philips and Justus, tended to specialize in building houses. Their style is typified by a mixed form of classicism and baroque. Another famous architect of

Der wirtschaftliche Wohlstand bedeutete für die Niederlande auch die Grundlage einer kulturellen Blütezeit. In keiner Epoche wurde dies deutlicher als im Goldenen Jahrhundert. Und dies galt sowohl für die bildende Kunst als auch für andere kulturelle Ausdrucksformen wie Literatur und Wissenschaft.

Malerei

Im Ausland ist die Malerei aus dieser Zeit am bekanntesten. Die niederländischen Meister differenzierten sich durch ihren ausgeprägten Wirklichkeitssinn und behandelten den Hintergrund als ebenso wichtig wie das zentrale Motiv. Licht und Perspektive spielten bei allen Malern eine dominierende Rolle. Die niederländischen Landschaftsmaler setzten den Horizont tief an und füllten die Luft mit Licht. Auch auf dem Bild eines Zimmers in einem einfachen holländischen Haus sorgt das Licht für eine ganz besondere Stimmung. Der Realismus fand in breiten Bevölkerungskreisen Anklang, wobei das Bürgertum einen besonders wichtigen Platz einnahm. Während der Blütezeit des Handels verfügten die Bürger über genug Mittel und Geld, um Bilder zu kaufen. Ihr vorwiegender Geschmack zwang die Maler mehr oder weniger dazu, eine greifbare Wirklichkeit abzubilden. Kennzeichnend ist auch das Fehlen der Hofmalerei. Mit Ausnahme von Frederik Hendrik waren die Statthalter nicht gerade großzügig im Erteilen von Aufträgen. Interessant ist in diesem Zusammenhang auch eine Anekdote: Die Generalstaaten stellten den Marinemalern Van de Velde Vater und Sohn ein kleines Schiff zur Verfügung, damit sie die Seeschlachten der holländischen Flotte gegen die Engländer so naturgetreu wie möglich wiedergeben konnten.
Von den großen Meistern wie Rembrandt und Frans Hals abgesehen, konnten die Maler jedoch kaum von ihren Gemälden leben. Jan Steen arbeitete neben seiner Malerei als Wirt, und Meindert Hobbema, der Maler des berühmten Gemäldes "Die Allee von Middelharnis" war Kontrolleur für Importwein.

Architektur

Die Architektur wurde im Goldenen Zeitalter durch den Klassizismus bestimmt, der eher spielerische Renaissancestil berühmter Architekten wie Lieven de Key und Hendrick de Keyser wurde vom Wunsch nach vornehmer Schlichtheit abgelöst. Ein hervorragendes Beispiel dafür ist das 'Paleis' auf dem Damm in Amsterdam. Es wurde 1638 von dem Architekten Jacob van Campen als Rathaus errichtet. Die Bauarbeiten

La prospérité économique fut une solide garantie pour l'essor culturel des Pays-Bas. Le Siècle d'Or l'a confirmé de façon très nette : aucune autre période n'a connu un tel épanouissement des arts plastiques, mais aussi des autres domaines culturels comme la littérature et les sciences.

Peinture
A l'étranger, c'est la peinture de cette époque qui est la plus remarquée. Les artistes hollandais se distinguaient par la recherche du réalisme, et ils attachaient la même importance au devant de la scène qu'à l'arrière-plan. Lumière et perspective jouaient un rôle prépondérant. Les paysagistes peignirent de larges horizons et remplirent le ciel de lumière. On retrouve cette même luminosité dans un tableau représentant une simple scène d'intérieur, où elle contribue à créer une atmosphère particulière.
Le réalisme reçut un accueil favorable auprès de larges couches de la population. Mais ce fut surtout la bourgeoisie aisée, disposant de moyens considérables dans cette période de prospérité commerciale, qui commanda des oeuvres d'art. Aussi, les peintres durent plus au moins obéir à son goût et représenter la réalité tangible.
On peut constater également qu'il n'exista pas de 'peinture courtisane' : les stathouders n'étaient guère enclins à stimuler les arts, et peu généreux dans leurs commandes, à l'exception du stathouder Frédéric Henri. A ce propos, il est à noter la petite histoire qui raconte que les Etats-Généraux mirent un petit bateau à la disposition des peintres de marines Van de Velde, père et fils, afin qu'ils puissent représenter le plus fidèlement possible les batailles navales entre la flotte hollandaise et les anglais.
A l'exception des grands maîtres comme Rembrandt et Frans Hals, les peintres avaient du mal à vivre de leurs tableaux. Outre son activité de peintre, Jan Steen était aussi aubergiste, et Meindert Hobbema, auteur du célèbre tableau 'L'allée à Middelharnis', était inspecteur des vins importés.

Architecture
Le style dominant de l'architecture du Siècle d'Or est qualifié de classique. La légèreté gracieuse de la Renaissance, que l'on retrouve dans les oeuvres d'architectes réputés comme Lieven de Key et Hendrick de Keyser, fut supplantée par une attirance pour une sobriété distinguée. Un bon exemple se révèle être le Palais royal, situé au Dam à Amsterdam. L'ancien hôtel de ville fut construit par Jacob van Campen et sa construction dura sept ans. Les sculptures de la main d'Artus Quellin contribuent large-

La prosperidad económica de Holanda fué la garantía de su florecimiento cultural. El Siglo de Oro es la expresión mas real de esta premisa. Este florecimiento se dió no solo en las bellas artes sino tambien en otras expresiones culturales como la literatura y la ciencia.

La Pintura.
La pintura de esta época es la más conocida fuera de Holanda. Se caracterizaba por su gran realismo al mismo tiempo que trataba con igual importancia el motivo principal del cuadro y su entorno. La perspectiva y la luz eran las características mas importantes de todos los pintores de esta época. Los paisajistas holandeses situaban el horizonte mu bajo llenando el resto del cuadro con cielo y luz. Tambien en sus interiores la luz contribuía de forma prominente a dar al cuadro una armonía muy característica.Este realismo tuvo su repercusión en los mas amplios sectores de la población. Uno de los mas amplios sectores de la población era el formado por los ciudadanos acomodados los que, en el periodo de florecimiento comercial, poseían suficientes medios para la adquisición de obras de arte. Su dominante gusto obligó a los pintores a expresar en sus obras una realidad mas o menos palpable. Típico de esta época es la falta de pintores cortesanos.Los estatúders, a excepción de Frederik Hendrik, no fueron demasiado generosos encargando obras de arte. Caracterizando este estilo de pintura, es notable la anecdota que cuenta que los Estados Generales dieron un barco a los pintores de marinas Van de Velde, padre e hijo, para que de la manera mas fiel posible reprodujeran las batallas naveles entre las flotas inglesa y holandesa. A excepción de los grandes maestros como Rembrandt y Frans Hals, los demás pintores no podían vivr del arte. Jan Steen, ademas de pintor, era mesonero y Meindert Hobbema, el pintor del conocido cuadro "La avenida de Middelharnis", era controlador de la importación de vino.

La Arquitectura
El clasicismo caracterizó la arquitectura del Siglo de Oro. La mas coqueta construcción renacentista de famosos arquitectos como Lieven de Key y Hendrik de Keyser, se vió superada por los deseos de un estilo de moderada gravedad. Buen ejemplo de ello es el Palacio Real de la plaza del Dam en Amsterdam. Fué construido en 1.638 por Jacob van Campen como ayuntamiento y se tardaron siete años en terminar la construcción. Caracteristicas de la hermosura de este edificio son sus obras escultóricas realizadas por Artus Quellijn.

O bem-estar económico significava para os Países Baixos a garantia de um desenvolvimento cultural. Em nenhum período isto se demonstrou tanto como na Época Áurea. Isto era tanto para as artes decorativas, como para as outras expressões de cultura, como seja a literatura e a ciência.

Pintura
No estrangeiro a pintura deste período é a mais conhecida. Os holandeses distinguiam-se pelo seu alto grau de realismo e eles elaboravam os fundos com a mesma minuciosidade que o temas principais.
A luz e a perspectiva desempenhavam em todos os pintores um papel predominante. Os pintores holandeses de panoramas colocavam o horizonte baixo e preenchiam o céu com muita luz. Até mesmo numa pintura do interior de uma casa holandesa humilde a luz contribuía para um ambiente bastante claro. O realismo encontrava repercussão numa grande camada do povo. A camada mais ampla era a burguesia rica a qual, na floração do comércio, dispunha de meios suficientes para comprar obras de arte.
O seu gosto dominante obrigou, assim se pode dizer, os pintores a exprimirem uma realidade palpável. Característica é também, a ausência de pintores da corte. Os governadores, com excepção de Frederik Hendrik, não eram poupados em fazer encomendas.
Notável neste sentido é a anedota em que o Estados Gerais puseram um barco à disposição do pai e filho Van de Velde, pintores de temas marítimos, para que eles exprimissem, o mais real possível, as batalhas de mar da armada holandesa com os ingleses.
Grão-mestres da pintura, à excepção de Rembrandt e Frans Hals, não podiam viver dos seus trabalhos. Jan Steen era, além de pintor, estalajadeiro e Meindert Hobbema, o pintor da famosa pintura "A avenida de Middelharnis", era inspector de vinho importado.

Arquitectura
A arquitectura da Época Áurea foi determinada pelo classicismo. A construção mais lúdica da Renascença de famosos arquitectos como Lieven de Key e Hendrick de Keyser foi superada pelo desejo de sobriedade distinta. Um bom exemplo é o Palácio na Dam, em Amsterdão. Foi construído em 1688, como Câmara Municipal, pelo arquitecto Jacob van Campen. A construção durou sete anos. Determinante para a beleza do edifício são as esculturas executadas por Artus Quellijn. Os irmãos Philips e Justus Vingboons eram mais especializadas na

Rembrandt van Rijn werd in 1606 te Leiden geboren. Hij bezocht de Latijnse school en schreef zich hierna in aan de universiteit. Over zijn studie is weinig bekend. Wel dat hij al spoedig in de leer ging bij de kunstschilder Pieter Lastman. In 1631 vestigde Rembrandt zich definitief in Amsterdam als kunstschilder. In zijn vroege tijd zocht hij het vooral in bijbelse taferelen. Naast het schilderen handelde hij in kunst en stichtte hij een schilderschool. Het aantal opdrachten nam toe. In een akte uit 1638 was te lezen dat hij 'buitengewoon welgesteld' was. Dit blijkt ook uit de portretten die hij maakte van zijn echtgenote Saskia. Haar dood in 1642 greep hem aan en maakte hem eenzelvig. Toch schilderde hij in deze periode enkele van zijn belangrijkste werken. Zijn laatste zelfportret uit 1661, het jaar van zijn overlijden, toont een vermoeid en eenzaam mens. Boven: zelfportret als apostel, rechts: De Staalmeesters.

Rembrandt van Rijn was born in Leiden in 1606. He attended the Latin School and was then registered at the university. Little is known about his studies, but we know that he soon became a pupil of the painter Pieter Lastman. In 1631 Rembrandt settled permanently in Amsterdam as a painter. During his early career he concentrated primarily on biblical scenes. He traded in art and set up a school of painting in addition to his work as an artist. The number of commissions increased. A deed dating from 1638 refers to him as being `extremely prosperous'. This can also be seen from the portraits he painted of his wife Saskia. Her death in 1642 was a devastating blow and he withdrew within himself. Nevertheless it was during this period that he produced some of his most important works. In 1661, the year before his death, he painted his last self-portrait, which depicts a tired and lonely person. Above: Self-portrait as an Apostle, right: The Syndics.

Rembrandt van Rijn wurde 1606 in Leiden geboren. Er besuchte die Lateinschule und schrieb sich danach an der Universität ein. Über sein Studium ist wenig bekannt. Schon bald jedoch ging er bei dem Kunstmaler Pieter Lastman in die Lehre. 1631 ließ sich Rembrandt definitiv in Amsterdam als Kunstmaler nieder. In seiner Frühzeit beschäftigte er sich hauptsächlich mit Bibelszenen. Neben der Malerei handelte er mit Kunst und gründete eine Malerschule. Die Zahl seiner Aufträge nahm zu. In einer Urkunde aus dem Jahr 1638 ist zu lesen, daß er 'außergewöhnlich wohlhabend' war. Dies zeigt sich auch in den Porträts seiner Frau Saskia. Deren Tod im Jahre 1642 machte ihm schwer zu schaffen und ließ ihn einsilbig werden. Dennoch schuf er in dieser Zeit einige seiner bedeutendsten Werke. Sein letztes Selbstporträt aus dem Jahre 1661, seinem Todesjahr, zeigt einen abgespannten und einsamen Menschen. Oben: Selbstbildnis als Apostel, rechts: Die Staalmeesters.

Rembrandt van Rijn naquit en 1606 à Leiden. Il fréquenta l'école latine, puis fut inscrit à l'université. Ce que l'on sait de ses études, c'est qu'il entra bientôt en apprentissage chez le peintre Pieter Lastman. En 1631, Rembrandt se fixa définitivement à Amsterdam. Dès ses débuts il montra un penchant pour les scènes bibliques. A côté de son activité d'artiste, il était également négociant d'oeuvres d'art, et il fonda un atelier de peinture. Les commandes affluèrent. On lit dans un document de 1638, qu'il était 'très aisé'. Les portraits qu'il peignit de son épouse Saskia, en témoignent. La mort de sa femme en 1642 le bouleversa, et il se replia sur lui-même. Cependant, il peignit dans cette période quelques oeuvres considérées comme les plus importantes. Son dernier autoportrait de 1669 montre un homme fatigué et solitaire. En haut : Autoportrait en apôtre, à droite : Les Syndics des Drapiers.

Rembrandt van Rijn nació en Leiden el año 1.606. Estudió en la Escuela Latina y se inscribió en la universidad. Hay muy poco conocido sobre los estudios que realizó. Desde muy pronto fué ya alumno del pintor Pieter Lastman. En 1.631 se estableció definitivamente como pintor en Amsterdam. Durante su primera época pintó sobretodo temas bíblicos. Al mismo tiempo que pintaba, fué comerciante de arte y fundó una escuela para pintores. Los encargos que le hacían iban aumentando y ya en 1.638 se podía leer sobre él que tenía una posición bien acomodada, cosa que se puede observar también en los retratos que hizo de su esposa Saskia.
El fallecimiento de su esposa en 1.642 le volvió huraño y a pesar de ello pintó en dicha época sus mas importantes trabajos. Su último autoretrato en 1.661, el año de su muerte, le muestra ya como una persona cansada y solitaria. Arriba: autoretrato como apóstol; derecha: Los Síndicos de los Pañeros.

Rembrandt van Rijn nasceu em Leiden em 1606. Ele frequentou a Escola Latina e depois disso inscreveu-se na universidade. Sobre os seus estudos pouco se sabe. Sabe-se sim que ele brevemente começou a aprender com o pintor artístico Pieter Lastman. Em 1631 Rembrandt fixou-se definitivamente em Amsterdão como pintor. No seu período inicial dedicou-se ele em especial a cenas da Bíblia. Paralelamente com os trabalhos de pintura, ele negociava em objectos de arte e fundou uma escola de pintura. As encomendas aumentaram. Numa acta que data de 1638 podia-se ler que ele era 'extraordinariamente rico'. Isto constatava-se também nos retratos que ele fez da sua esposa Saskia. A morte dela em 1642 causou-lhe muito desgosto e ele tornou-se insociável. No entanto, neste período pintou ele alguns dos seus trabalhos mais importantes. O seu último auto-retrato de 1661, ano do seu falecimento, mostra um homem fatigado e solitário.Em cima: auto-retrato como apóstolo; à direita: Os Síndicos dos Fanqueiros.

de mengvorm tussen classicisme en barok. Andere beroemde architecten als Pieter Post tekenden voor bijvoorbeeld de Waag te Leiden of het stadhuis te Maastricht. Het fraaie Mauritshuis te Den Haag is totstandgekomen door samenwerking van Post en Van Campen.

Wetenschap

De vrijheid van drukpers gaf wetenschappers de ruimte om nieuwe inzichten wereldkundig te maken. De universiteiten trokken veel studenten uit alle landen van Europa. Jaren van tweeduizend studenten waren voor de Leidse universiteit geen uitzondering. Het waren niet alleen wijsgerige denkers als onder anderen Descartes, Spinoza, Comenius en Locke, maar ook de beoefenaars van de exacte wetenschappen als de natuurkundigen 's-Gravesande en Van Musschenbroek en de arts/botanicus Boerhaave.
Hun boeken werden verspreid door een groot aantal uitgevers. Onder hen leden van het geslacht Elsevier, die op hun beurt de Zuidelijke Nederlanden waren ontvlucht om hier in vrijheid te kunnen publiceren.

this period was Pieter Post, who designed the Waag (Weigh House) in Leiden and Maastricht Town Hall. The beautiful Mauritshuis in The Hague was the result of collaboration between Post and van Campen.

Science

Freedom of the press gave scientists the scope to publish their new knowledge.
The universities attracted large numbers of students from all over Europe. Years when there were two thousand students enrolled at the University of Leiden were by no means exceptional. They were philosophers, such as Descartes, Spinoza, Comenius and Locke, and also scientists like the physicists 's-Gravesande and van Musschenbroek and the physician and botanist Boerhaave.
Their books were distributed by a large number of publishers. They included members of the Elsevier family who had fled from the Southern Low Countries in order to publish freely in the north.

dauerten sieben Jahre. Ausschlaggebend für die Schönheit dieses Gebäudes ist die Bildhauerei von Artus Quellijn. Die Gebrüder Philips und Justus Vingboons hatten sich eher auf den Häuserbau spezialisiert. Ihren Stil kennzeichnet eine Mischung aus Klassizismus und Barock. Andere berühmte Architekten wie Pieter Post entwarfen beispielsweise die Stadtwaage in Leiden oder das Maastrichter Rathaus. Das herrliche 'Mauritshuis' in Den Haag entstand durch eine Zusammenarbeit von Post und Van Campen.

Wissenschaft

Die Freiheit des Buchdrucks ermöglichte den Wissenschaftlern die Bekanntmachung ihrer neugewonnenen Erkenntnisse. An die Universitäten strömten viele Studenten aus allen Ländern Europas. Jahrgänge mit zweitausend Studenten waren für die Leidener Universität keine Ausnahme. Darunter befanden sich nicht nur wißbegierige Denker wie Descartes, Spinoza, Comenius und Locke, sondern auch Mathematiker und Naturwissenschaftler wie 's-Gravesande und Van Musschenbroek oder der Arzt und Botaniker Boerhaave.
Ihre Bücher wurden von zahlreichen Verlägen verbreitet, darunter auch Angehörigen der Familie Elsevier, die aus den südlichen Niederlanden geflüchtet waren, um hier in aller Freiheit publizieren zu können.

ment à la splendeur de l'édifice. Les frères Philips et Justus Vingboons s'intéressaient plutôt à la construction de maisons, caractérisées par un style mêlant le classicisme et le baroque. On doit le poids public de Leiden et l'hôtel de ville de Maastricht au célèbre architecte Pieter Post. A la Haye, il a édifié le très beau Mauritshuis, réalisé en coopération avec Van Campen.

Sciences

La liberté de la presse permit aux scientifiques de publier leurs nouvelles idées et découvertes. Les universités accueillirent des étudiants des quatre coins de l'Europe. Que l'université de Leiden comptât 2000 étudiants inscrits pour une seule année, n'était pas un fait exceptionnel. Des oeuvres parurent non seulement dans le domaine de la philosophie, représentée par des penseurs comme Descartes, Spinoza, Comenius et Locke, mais aussi de la main des hommes de science comme les physiciens 's-Gravensande et Van Musschenbroek, et le médecin-botaniste Boerhaave. Leurs livres furent diffusés par un grand nombre d'éditeurs, dont la famille Elsevier, qui avait fui les Pays-Bas du Sud, afin de pouvoir publier en liberté.

Los hermanos Philips y Justus Vingboons estuvieron mas especializados en la construcción de viviendas. Su característica más notable fué el uso mezclado de los estilos del clasicismo del barróco. Otro famoso arquitecto, Pietr Post, construyó el edificio de la balanza municipal de Leiden y el ayuntamiento de Maastricht. La bella casa Mauritshuis en La Haya fué realizada por el trabajo conjunto de Post y Van Campen.

La Ciencia

La libertad de imprenta dió la posibilidad a los científicos de dar a conocer al mundo sus nuevas ideas. Las universidades atrajeron estudiantes de toda Europa. La universidad de Leiden tuvo con frecuencia años de mas de dos mil estudiantes en sus aulas. Fueron no solo filósofos como Descartes, Spinoza, Comenius o Locke, sino tambien adeptos a las ciencias exactas como los físicos 's-Gravesande y Van Musschenbroek y el médico/botánico Boerhaave. Un gran número de ditores divulgó sus libros. Uno de estos editores fué la familia Elsevier que en su momento huyeron de la Holanda meridional para poder publicar sus libros aquí con toda libertad.

construção de casas. Característica para o seu estilo é a mistura entre o classicismo e o barroco. Outros arquitectos famosos, como Pieter Post, construíram, por exemplo, 'de Waag' (a Balança), em Leiden e a Câmara Municipal de Maastricht. A linda 'Mauritshuis' (a Casa de Maurício) em Haia foi executada numa colaboração entre Post e Van Campen.

Ciência

A liberdade de imprensa deu aos cientistas a oportunidade de tornar públicas novas visões. As universidades atraíram muitos estudantes de todos os países da Europa. 2000 Estudantes por ano lectivo não eram excepção para a universidade de Leiden. Não eram apenas pensadores-filósofos, como Descartes, Spinoza, Comenius e Locke, mas também praticantes de ciências exactas, como o físico 's-Gravensande e Van Musschenbroek e o botânico-médico Boerhaave.
Os seus livros foram dispersos por uma grande quantidade de editores. Entre eles membros da geração Elsevier que, por sua vez, fugiram dos Países Baixos do Sul para poderem publicar livremente na Holanda do Norte.

Twee grootmeesters in Hollandse luchten. Links: gezicht op Dordrecht (1640) van Jan van Goyen en rechts: De molen bij Wijk bij Duurstede (1672) van Jacob van Ruysdael.
Als kunstschilder werd Van Goyen bij zijn leven niet altijd even gewaardeerd. Men kon immers buiten zien wat hij op het doek bracht? Toch blijkt dat hij fantasie en werkelijkheid kundig met elkaar combineerde.
De romanticus Ruysdael behoort tot de vernieuwers in de landschapschilderkunst. Hij schilderde met een gevoel voor drama. De Molen bij Wijk bij Duurstede met de dreigende wolkenpartijen behoort tot zijn beste werken. De figuren op de voorgrond zijn het werk van een collega. Dit gebeurde vaker in de 17de eeuw.

Two great masters of Dutch skies.
Left: View of Dordrecht (1640) by Jan van Goyen and right: The Windmill at Wijk (1672) by Jacob van Ruisdael.
While he was alive, van Goyen was not particularly highly thought of as a painter. After all, why bother to paint what you can see out the window? However, he could combine imagination and reality with great skill.
The romantic Ruisdael is one of the innovators of landscape painting. He painted with a sense of drama. The Windmill at Wijk, with its threatening clouds, is among his best known works. The figures in the foreground were painted by a colleague. This was not uncommon in the seventeenth century.

Zwei Großmeister der holländischen Lüfte.
Links: Ansicht auf Dordrecht (1640) von Jan van Goyen und rechts: Windmühle bei Wijk bij Duurstede (1672) von Jacob van Ruysdael.
Als Kunstmaler wurde Van Goyen bei Lebzeiten nicht immer gebührend gewürdigt. Was er malte, konnte man ja schließlich auch draußen sehen. Doch konnte er offensichtlich Phantasie und Realität geschickt miteinander verbinden.
Der Romantiker Ruysdael gehörte zu den Erneuerern der Landschaftsmalerei. Er malte besonders dramatische Szenen. Die Windmühle bei Wijk bij Duurstede mit den bedrohlichen Wolken gehört zu seinen besten Werken. Die Figuren im Vordergrund sind das Werk eines Kollegen, was im 17. Jahrhundert nicht unüblich war.

Deux maîtres des ciels hollandais. A gauche : Vue sur Dordrecht (1640) de Jan van Goyen et à droite : Le moulin à Wijk bij Duurstede (1672) de Jacob van Ruysdael. De son vivant, l'artiste Van Goyen ne fut pas toujours apprécié. Ce qu'il représentait sur ses toiles, ne pouvait-on pas simplement le regarder au dehors? Toutefois, il savait combiner fantaisie et réalisme avec habileté. Le romantique Ruysdael fait partie des rénovateurs dans l'art des paysagistes. Ses oeuvres expriment un sens dramatique. Le Moulin à Wijk bij Duurstede, avec son ciel menacé par l'orage, est l'un de ses meilleurs tableaux. Les figures sur le devant de la scène sont de la main d'un collaborateur. Cette pratique fut fréquente au 17e s.

Dos grandes maestros de los cielos holandeses. Izquierda: Vista de Dordrecht (1.640) de Jan van Goyen; y derecha: Los molinos de Wijk bij Duurstede (1.672) de Jacob van Ruysdael.
Durante su vida como pintor Van Goyen no fué siempre apreciado como tal. Saliendo al exterior la gente podía ver lo que él pintaba. De todas maneras fué un artista en combinar la realidad con la fantasía.
El romántico Ruysdael forma parte de los innovadores de la pintura paisajista. Pinta con un sentido dramático. El cuadro "Los molinos de Wijk bij Duurstede" con sus amenazantes nubes, forma parte de sus mejores trabajos. Los personajes de primer plano fueron realizados por un colega pintor cosa que sucedía frecuentemente en el siglo XVII.

Dois grão-mestres em "céus holandeses". À esquerda: vista sobre Dordrecht (1640) de Jan van Goyen e à direita: O moinho em Wijk bij Duurestede (1672) de Jacob van Ruysdael.
O pintor Van Goyen não foi muito apreciado em vida. Toda a gente podia, pois, ver lá fora aquilo que ele pintava. Contudo, chegou-se à conclusão de que ele combinava fantasia com realidade.
O romântico Ruysdael faz parte dos renovadores na arte da pintura de paisagens. Ele pintava com sensibilidade para o drama. O Moinho em Wijk bij Duurstede com as nuvens ameaçadoras faz parte das suas melhores obras. As figuras no primeiro plano foram pintadas por um colega. Isso acontecia muitas vezes no século 17.

Heroïek en symboliek. Schuttersstukken bleven gedurende de gehele 17de eeuw een gewild genre. Hierboven een detail van 'De Officieren en onderofficieren van de St.-Jorisdoelen door de Haarlemse schilder Frans Hals (1580-1666).
Op het schilderij 'Vrolijk gezelschap' van de schilder/herbergier Jan Steen (1626-1679) werd voor tijdgenoten veel meer afgebeeld dan slechts een voorstelling van een gezellige bijeenkomst. Papegaai en kooitje hun hebben zo een eigen moraliserende betekenis.

Heroism and symbolism. Paintings of militias continued to be popular throughout the whole of the seventeenth century. Above: a detail from The Banquet of the Officers of the St. George Militia Company by the Haarlem painter Frans Hals (1580-1666).
The painting The Parrot Cage by painter and innkeeper Jan Steen (1626-79) meant much more to his contemporaries than just a depiction of an enjoyable get-together. The parrot and cage have their own moralizing significance.

Heldenhaft und symbolträchtig. Schützenstücke waren während des gesamten 17. Jahrhunderts ein beliebtes Genre. Hier ein Ausschnitt aus den "Offizieren und Unteroffizieren des St. Jorisdoels" des Haarlemer Malers Frans Hals (1580 - 1666).
Das Gemälde "Fröhliche Gesellschaft" des Malers und Wirts Jan Steen (1626 - 1679) stellte für seine Zeitgenossen sehr viel mehr dar, als nur ein geselliges Beisammensein. Papagei und Käfig haben eine eigene, moralisierende Bedeutung.

Héroïsme et symbolisme. Les tableaux corporatifs des gardes civiques furent en vogue pendant tout le 17e s. En haut un détail du tableau 'Le Dîner des officiers du corps des archers de Saint-Georges' par Frans Hals, peintre à Haarlem (1580 - 1666).
Le tableau ' Une joyeuse compagnie' du peintre/aubergiste Jan Steen (1626 - 1679) représenta, pour ses contemporains, beaucoup plus que l'image d'une réunion conviviale. Le perroquet et sa cage ont une certaine signification moralisatrice.

Heroísmo y simbolísmo. El cuerpo de tiradores fué durante el siglo XVII uno de los temas mas apreciados y queridos. Arriba un detalle del cuadro del pintor de Haarlem Frans Hals (1.580-1.666) llamado"Los oficiales y suboficiales de St. Jorisdoelen".
En el cuadro "Compañía alegre" del pintor/posadero Jan Steen (1.626-1.679) se plasma para sus contemporáneos mucho mas que una reunión bulliciosa. El papagayo y la jaula tienen de esta manera su moral significado.

Heroísmo e simbolismo. As peças sobre a infantaria foram durante todo o século 17 um género muito apreciado. Acima um detalhe de "Os oficiais e suboficiais dos objectivos de São Jorge", do pintor de Haarlem Frans Hals (1580-1666).
No quadro 'Companhia alegre" do pintor/estalajadeiro Jan Stein (1626-1679) mostrou aos seus contemporâneos mais do que um encontro alegre. O papagaio e a gaiola têm um significado moralizador.

Paleis Het Loo te Apeldoorn is een van de meest prestigieuze bouwwerken uit deze periode. Stadhouder Willen III, die door zijn huwelijk met Maria Stuart tevens koning van Engeland was geworden, kocht in 1684 hier een klein kasteeltje. Hij bezat reeds jachtterreinen in de omgeving. Hij gaf de stadhouderlijke architect Jacob Roman de opdracht hier een paleis te bouw dat door zijn uitstraling zich moest kunnen meten met de paleizen van Versailles. Ook de tuinen werden door Daniël Marot geheel in Franse stijl aangelegd. Sinds 1972 is het als Rijksmuseum Paleis Het Loo opengesteld voor het publiek.

Het Loo Palace in Apeldoorn is one of the most prestigious buildings dating from this period. Stadholder William III, who also became King of England through his marriage to Mary Stuart, bought a small castle here in 1684. He already owned hunting estates in the region. He gave the Stadholder's architect Jacob Roman the job of building a palace with such radiance that it could measure up to the Palace of Versailles. The gardens were also laid out in the French style by Daniël Marot. Het Loo Palace, now a museum, has been open to the public since 1972.

Das 'Paleis Het Loo' in Apeldoorn ist einer der prächtigsten Bauten aus dieser Zeit. Statthalter Wilhelm III., der durch seine Heirat mit Maria Stuart auch König von England wurde, kaufte hier im Jahre 1684 ein kleines Schloß. Er besaß bereits Jagdreviere in der Umgebung. Dem statthalterlichen Architekten Jacob Roman erteilte er den Auftrag, hier ein Lustschloß zu bauen, das von seinem Flair her mit dem Schloß von Versailles mithalten können sollte. Auch die Gärten wurden von Daniel Marot ganz im französischen Stil angelegt. Seit 1972 ist es als Reichsmuseum Paleis Het Loo für die Öffentlichkeit zugänglich.

Le Palais Het Loo à Apeldoorn est un des édifices les plus prestigieux de cette époque. Le stathouder Guillaume III, devenu Roi d'Angleterre par son mariage avec Marie Stuart, acheta ici en 1684 un petit château. Il possédait déjà des domaines de chasse dans les environs. L'architecte des stathouders, Jacob Roman, reçut la commande de construire un palais à côté du premier, qui devrait, par sa magnificence, pouvoir rivaliser avec ceux de Versailles. La création des jardins, entièrement à la française, fut alors confiée à Daniel Marot. Devenu musée national en 1972, le palais est ouvert au public.

El palacio Het Loo en Apeldoorn es uno de los edificios arquitectónicos mas prestigiosos de este periodo. El estatúder Willem III, que a su vez por su matrimonio con Maria Estuardo era rey de Inglaterra, compró en 1.684 este pequeño castillo. Ya era propietario de diferentes cotos de caza en esta región. Ordenó al arquitecto estatal Jacob Roman que construyera un palacio que por sus características se pudiera medir con el de Versalles. Sus jardines en el mas puro estilo francés fueron diseñados por Daniël Marot. En 1.972 se abrió al público este palacio en su función de museo real Het Loo.

O Palácio 'Het Loo', em Apeldoorn é uma das obras mais prestigiosas deste período. O Governador Willem III, o qual por meio do seu casamento com Maria Stuart passou a ser também rei da Inglaterra, comprou aqui em 1684 um pequeno palacete. Ele já possuía terrenos de caça nas proximidades. Ele deu ao arquitecto do governador Jacob Roman ordem para construir aqui um palácio que pelo seu esplendor se deveria poder comparar com os palácios de Versalhes.Também os jardins foram plantados por Daniel Marot, segundo o estilo francês. Desde 1972 o Museu Imperial "Paleis Het Loo" está aberto ao público.

De uitvinding van de boekdrukkunst vond al zeer snel ingang in de Nederlanden. Naast Amsterdam dat zich ontwikkelde als het centrum van deze nieuwe nijverheid, vestigden zich drukkers in een groot aantal steden door het gehele land In de Gouda herinnert dit beeld aan de zestiende eeuwse boekdrukker Gheeraaert Leu. Het lezen van boeken raakte populair bij grote groepen van de burgerij. Reisverslagen van ontdekkingstochten maar ook stichtelijke werken verheugden zich in een grote belangstelling. Tot de meest gewilde auteurs uit die tijd behoorden: de dichters en toneelschrijvers Vondel en Bredero.
Jacob Cats combineerde zijn dichterschap met de functie van staatsman. Zijn werk muntte uit door opvoedkundige vermaningen.

The invention of printing was adopted very quickly in the Netherlands. Amsterdam developed as the centre of this new industry, but printers set up shop in many other towns and cities throughout the country. This picture in Gouda depicts the sixteenth century book printer Gheeraaert Leu. Reading books became popular with large sections of the public. Travel books describing expeditions and pious works enjoyed equal interest. The top authors of the era included the poets and dramatists Vondel and Bredero.
Jacob Cats combined his work as a poet with the position of statesman. His work stood out because of its educational exhortations.

Die Erfindung der Buchdruckkunst fand schon bald Eingang in den Niederlanden. Neben Amsterdam, das sich zum Zentrum dieses neuen Gewerbes entwickelte, entstanden zahlreiche Druckereien in vielen Städten des gesamten Landes. In Gouda erinnert diese Skulptur an den Buchdrucker Gheeraaert Leu, der im 16. Jahrhundert lebte. Das Lesen von Büchern wurde in vielen bürgerlichen Kreisen beliebt. Reiseberichte von Entdeckungsfahrten, aber auch erbauliche Lektüre erfreuten sich großen Interesses. Zu den beliebtesten Autoren jenes Jahrhunderts gehören die Dichter und Theaterschriftsteller Vondel und Bredero.
Jacob Cats verband seine Dichtkunst mit seiner Funktion als Staatsmann. Sein Werk zeichnet sich durch pädagogische Ermahnungen aus.

L'invention de l'imprimerie n'est pas restée sans écho aux Pays-Bas. Amsterdam devint le centre de cette nouvelle activité, et bientôt des imprimeurs s'établirent dans un grand nombre de villes de tout le pays. A Gouda fut érigé ce monument à la mémoire de l'imprimeur Gheeraert Leu, qui vécut au 16e s. La lecture des livres se vulgarisait auprès d'une grande partie de la population. Les récits de voyage, mais aussi les oeuvres édifiantes jouirent d'un intérêt grandissant. Les poètes et dramaturges Vondel et Bredero furent des auteurs très demandés. Jacob Cats associa le génie poétique à sa fonction d'homme d'état.

El descubrimiento de la imprenta tuvo una rápida introducción en Holanda. Ademas de Amsterdam que se desarrolló como el centro de esta nueva industria, se establecieron imprentas en una gran número de ciudades de todo el país. Este monumento nos recuerda en Gouda al impresor Gheeraaert Leu. La lectura de libros se fué cogiendo adeptos en gran parte de la población. Populares fueron en este tiempo los libros de reportajes de viajes y también los de temas religiosos. Los poetas y dramaturgos Vondel y Bredero fueron de los autores mas populares de su época. Jacob Cats combinaba su poesía con sus funciones estatales. Sus obras rebosan de contenido educacional.

A descoberta da imprensa foi introduzida rapidamente nos Países Baixos. Além de em Amsterdão, que se desenvolveu como um centro desta indústria, fixaram-se muitos tipógrafos por todo o país. Em Gouda esta estátua faz-nos lembrar o tipógrafo do século 16, Gheeraaert Leu. A leitura de livros tornou-se muito popular em grandes grupos de cidadãos. Descrições de viagens de descobertas, mas também obras educativas gozavam de um grande interesse. Aos autores mais preferidos daquele tempo pertencem os poetas e escritores de peças de teatro Vondel e Bredero. Jacob Cats combinou a sua qualidade de poeta com a função de estadista. A sua obra sublima de repreensões educativas.

Na het beleg van Leiden en de daarop getoonde moed van de stad schonk prins Willen van Oranje de stad in 1575 de eerste Noordnederlandse universiteit. Het Academiegebouw, het hoofdgebouw van de Universiteit, is in het begin van de zestiende eeuw gebouwd als kapel van een dominicanessenklooster.
Het heeft veel beroemdheden onder zijn dak gehad zoals Boerhave, 's-Gravesande Lorentz, e.v.a. Momenteel telt Nederland 10 universiteiten.
De kleine stad Franeker kreeg haar universiteit van de Staten van Friesland in 1585. Er is gedoceerd tot de opheffing door Napoleon in 1811.
Er werd onderwijs gegeven in het Fries. In Friesland is deze taal nog steeds de voertaal. Het bord aan de muur van de voormalige studentensociëteit herinnert aan deze periode. Volgende bladzijde: In 1884 schilderde Vincent van Gogh het kerkje te Nuenen. De vader van Van Gogh was er predikant. Het kerkje staat en nog precies zo.

After the siege of Leiden and the courage demonstrated by the city, in 1575 Prince William of Orange endowed it with the first Dutch university. The Academie building, the main building of the university, was constructed at the beginning of the sixteenth century as the chapel of a Dominican nunnery. Many famous figures have been in this building at one time or another, including Boerhaave, 's-Gravesande and Lorentz. There are presently ten universities in the Netherlands. The small town of Franeker was granted its university by the States of Friesland in 1585. Students were taught there until Napoleon closed it down in 1811.
Students were taught in Fries. This language is still spoken daily in Friesland. The board on the wall of the former student society is a memento of this period. Following page: in 1884 Vincent van Gogh painted the church in Nuenen, where van Gogh's father was pastor. The church is exactly the same today.

Nach der Belagerung Leidens und nachdem die Stadt soviel Mut bewiesen hatte, schenkte Prinz Wilhelm von Oranien der Stadt im Jahr 1575 die erste nordniederländische Universität. Der Academiegebouw, das Hauptgebäude der Universität, wurde zu Beginn des 16. Jahrhunderts als Kapelle eines Dominikanerklosters errichtet.
Viele Berühmtheiten verweilten hier wie Boerhaave, 's-Gravesande Lorentz u.v.m. Derzeit gibt es in den Niederlanden 10 Universitäten. Die kleine Stadt Franeker erhielt ihre Universität 1585 von der friesischen Ständeversammlung. Dort wurde bis zur Auflösung durch Napoleon im Jahre 1811 gelehrt.
Der Unterricht erfolgte in Friesisch. In Friesland ist diese Sprache immer noch Verkehrssprache. Das Schild an der Mauer der ehemaligen Studentenverbindung erinnert an diese Zeit. Folgende Seite: 1884 malte Vincent van Gogh die kleine Kirche von Nuenen. Der Vater von Van Gogh war in diesem Ort Prediger. Die Kirche steht noch immer dort.

Après sa courageuse résistance pendant le siège espagnol, la ville de Leiden fut récompensée par le prince Guillaume d'Orange, par la fondation de la première université des Pays-Bas du Nord en 1575. Le siège de l'université, l' 'Academie', fut installé dans la chapelle d'un ancien couvent de dominicaines datant du début du 16e s. Elle a hébergé un grand nombre de célébrités, comme Boerhaave, 's-Gravesande, Lorentz et beaucoup d'autres. Aujourd'hui les Pays-Bas comptent dix universités.
La petite ville de Franeker reçut une université des Etats de Frise en 1585. Elle fut supprimée en 1811 par Napoléon. L'enseignement se faisait en frison, langue encore utilisée aujourd'hui dans la province de Frise. La plaque fixée au mur de l'ancien foyer des étudiants rappelle cette période.
Page suivante : En 1884, Vincent van Gogh peignit la petite église de Nuenen. Son père y fut pasteur. L'église n'a absolument pas changé.

Despues del sitio de Leiden y como recompensa por el valor mostrado por esta ciudad, el príncipe Guillermo de Orange le concedió la primera universidad de la Holanda septentrional en 1.575. El edificio académico de la universidad, su edificio principal, fué construido al principio del siglo XVI como capilla de un monasterio dominicano. Bajo su techo se han cobijado personalidades famosas como Boerhave, 's-Gravesande y Lorentz entre otros. Actualmente hay diez universidades en Holanda.
La pequeña ciudad de Franeker obtuvo su universidad de los Estados de Frisia en 1.585. Estuvo repartiendo enseñanza hasta que en 1.811 fué clausurada por Napoleón. La enseñanza se realizaba en lengua frisona que actualmente es aún la usada en Frisia. La placa en la pared de la sociedad estudiantil nos recuerda dicha época. Pagina siguiente: En 1.884 Vincent van Gogh pintó la iglesia de Nuenen que se encuentra aún igual que entonces. El padre de Van Gogh fue predicador.

Depois do cerco de Leiden e da coragem demonstrada pela cidade nessa altura, o príncipe Willem van Oranje ofereceu à cidade em 1575 a primeira universidade dos Países Baixos do Norte. O Edifício da Academia, o edifício principal da Universidade, foi construído no início do século 16 como capela de um mosteiro de dominicanas. Teve muita gente famosa sob o seu teto, como por exemplo, Boerhave, 's-Gravesande e muitos outros. Presentemente a Holanda possui 10 Universidades. A vila Franaker recebeu a sua Universidade dos Estados da Frísia, em 1585. Lá foram dadas lições até à sua liquidação por Napoleão em 1811. As lições eram na língua frísia. Esta língua é ainda uma língua vernácula na Frísia. A tabuleta na parede da antiga sociedade de estudantes faz-nos recordar este período.
Na página seguinte: Em 1884 pintou Vincent van Gogh a pequena igreja de Nuenen. O pai de van Gogh era lá o pastor protestante. A igreja encontra-se ainda no mesmo estado.

Land in beweging

Country on the move

Ein Land im Wandel

Un pays en mouvement

La convivencia con el agua

País em andamento

In het begin van de 19de eeuw veranderde het aanzien van Europa. De Franse Revolutie had een eind gemaakt aan het feodale tijdperk. De Verenigde Staten werden door velen beschouwd als het toonbeeld van een vrije natie. Veranderingen volgden elkaar op. Er kwam ruimte voor de ontwikkeling van nieuwe vindingen als stoom en electriciteit. Ondernemers zagen de nieuwe mogelijkheden en gaven hiermee de aanzet tot de Industriële Revolutie.

Nederland was economisch vrijwel te gronde gericht door de afsluiting van zijn zeehavens als gevolg van het continentaal stelsel. Toen de Nederlanders in 1816 de macht over hun koloniën herkregen hadden zij een achterstand op andere landen met koloniën, zoals Engeland. Hun overzeese bezittingen hadden een dubbele economische betekenis gekregen: enerzijds voorzagen zij het moederland van grondstoffen maar anderzijds fungeerden zij als een extra afzetgebied voor de industriële producten.
Als een van de maatregelen werd, mede door koning Willem I, de Nederlandsche Handel-Maatschappij opgericht om de handel zowel te financieren als zelf te organiseren. Hiernaast stelde de staat eenzijdig de prijzen voor de exportgewassen vast, het cultuurstelsel. De opbrengsten namen met sprongen toe, maar het systeem was uiteraard niet echt profijtelijk voor de inlandse bevolking.
Met deze inkomsten werden activiteiten in het moederland gestimuleerd: spoorwegen werden aangelegd, de bedrijvigheid in algemene zin nam toe en, conform de Engelse situatie, ontwikkelde zich ook hier textielindustrie. De IndustriëleRevolutie kwam hier navenant later opgang.
Door al deze maatregelen breidde de Nederlandse vloot zich sterk uit. Binnen een tiental jaren na de invoering van het cultuurstelsel voeren er reeds zo'n 150 koopvaarders op Indië. De stoomvaart begon terrein te winnen op de zeilvaart en de havenfaciliteiten schreeuwden om uitbreiding. Het was in 1863 dat Rotterdam zijn gegraven verbinding met de zee kreeg in de vorm van de Nieuwe Waterweg. De directe verbinding voor Amsterdam, het Noordzeekanaal met zeesluizen te IJmuiden, kwam in 1876 gereed.

Het was voor de economie van Nederland bijzonder gunstig neutraal te blijven in de Frans-Duitse oorlog en in het bijzonder in de Eerste Wereldoorlog. De reeds bestaande industrieën konden, zij het op beperkte schaal, doorgaan met produceren.
Na de Tweede Wereldoorlog kreeg het leven een hoger tempo. Het aangeslagen Eu-

The face of Europe changed at the beginning of the nineteenth century. The French Revolution had brought the feudal age to a close. The United States was considered by many to be the model of a free nation. Changes followed hard on one another's heels. There was scope for the development of new discoveries like steam and electricity. Businessmen saw new opportunities and in so doing they laid the foundations of the industrial revolution.

In economic terms the Netherlands was virtually brought to its knees through the closing of the its sea ports as a result of the Continental System. When the Dutch regained power over their colonies in 1816, they found themselves lagging behind other colonial powers, for example the British. Their overseas possessions had developed dual economic significance: on the one hand they provided the mother country with raw materials, and on the other they were an additional market for industrial products.
The Nederlandsche Handelsmaatschappij was set up by King William I and others as one of the measures to finance and even organize trade. The government also unilaterally set the prices for crops exported from colonies – the system of forced farming. Yields grew rapidly, but naturally the system was not really profitable for the native populations. This income was used to stimulate activities in the mother country. Railways were built, industry as a whole grew and, just as in Britain, the textile industry in the Netherlands also prospered. Compared with other countries, however, the industrial revolution in the Netherlands started relatively late.
As a result of all these measures the Dutch fleet expanded dramatically. Within ten years of the introduction of the forced farming system there were some 150 merchantmen on the East Indies route. Steam navigation began to take over from sail and port facilities were in dire need of expansion. It was in 1863 that Rotterdam achieved its man-made link to the sea in the form of the New Waterway. The direct route to Amsterdam, the North Sea Canal with sea locks at IJmuiden, was completed in 1876. The neutrality of the Netherlands during the Franco-Prussian War and in particular during the First World War was particularly lucrative for the Dutch economy.
Existing industries could continue to produce, albeit on a limited scale.

After the Second World War the tempo of life increased. A Europe ravaged by six years of war was able to recover reasonably

Zu Beginn des 19. Jahrhunderts änderte sich das Gesicht Europas. Die französische Revolution hatte der Feudalherrschaft ein Ende gesetzt. Die Vereinigten Staaten wurden von vielen als Inbegriff einer freien Nation betrachtet. Veränderungen folgten einander auf raschem Fuße. Neue Erfindungen wie Strom und Elektrizität konnten entwickelt werden. Unternehmer erkannten die neuen Möglichkeiten und gaben so den Anstoß zur industriellen Revolution.

Die Niederlande waren wirtschaftlich so gut wie zugrundegerichtet, nachdem aufgrund der Kontinentalsperre ihre Seehäfen abgetrennt waren. Als die Niederländer im Jahre 1816 die Macht über ihre Kolonien wieder erhielten, waren sie, verglichen mit anderen Kolonialmächten wie England, ins Hintertreffen geraten. Ihre überseeischen Besitze hatten eine doppelte wirtschaftliche Bedeutung erlangt: Einerseits versorgten sie das Mutterland mit Rohstoffen, andererseits dienten sie jedoch auch als Absatzmärkte für die industriell hergestellten Produkte.
Eine der Reaktionen auf diese Situation bestand in der Errichtung der Niederländischen Handelsgesellschaft mit tatkräftiger Unterstützung von König Wilhelm I., die sowohl die Finanzierung als auch die eigentliche Durchführung des Handels sichern sollte. Daneben setzte der Staat mit dem sog. 'Cultuurstelsel' einseitig die Preise für Exportpflanzen fest. Die Erträge nahmen sprunghaft zu, doch profitierte natürlich nicht die einheimische Bevölkerung davon. Mit diesen Einnahmen wurden Aktivitäten im Mutterland angeregt: Eisenbahngleise wurden verlegt, die Wirtschaftsaktivität nahm generell zu, und ähnlich wie in England entwickelte sich auch hier die Textilindustrie. Die industrielle Revolution erfolgte hier entsprechend später.
All diese Maßnahmen führten zu einem raschen Anwachsen der niederländischen Flotte. Innerhalb von etwa 10 Jahren nach Einführung des Cultuurstelsels fuhren bereits rund 150 Handelsschiffe Indien an. Die Dampfschiffahrt gewann gegenüber der Segelschiffahrt an Boden, und die Hafenanlagen mußten dringend ausgebaut werden. 1863 schließlich erhielt Rotterdam mit dem Nieuwe Waterweg eine Wasserstraße zum Meer. Die Direktverbindung für Amsterdam, der Nordseekanal mit Schleusen bei IJmuiden, wurde 1876 fertiggestellt.
Besonders positiv wirkte es sich auf die niederländische Wirtschaft aus, daß die Niederlande während des deutsch-französischen Krieges und insbesondere während des 1. Weltkriegs neutral blieben.

Au début de 19e s. l'Europe changea de visage. La Révolution française avait mis fin à l'époque féodale. Beaucoup de gens considéraient les Etats Unis comme l'exemple d'une nation libre. Les changements se succédaient les uns aux autres, et le siècle s'ouvrit aux nouvelles inventions comme la vapeur et l'électricité. Les entrepreneurs s'aperçurent du progrès possible : l'impulsion à la révolution industrielle était donnée.

L'économie des Pays-Bas était pratiquement ruinée par la fermeture de ses ports, due au Blocus continental. Après le rétablissement du pouvoir sur leurs colonies, en 1816, les néerlandais durent rattraper le retard pris vis à vis d'autres pays détenant des colonies, comme l'Angleterre. Leurs possessions d'outre-mer avaient acquis une fonction économique à double sens : d'une part elles approvisionnaient la métropole en matières premières, d'autre part elles servaient de débouché supplémentaire pour les produits industriels.
Une des mesures prises à l'instigation du roi Guillaume II, fut la création de la Compagnie Commerciale Néerlandaise, organisme de financement et d'organisation du commerce avec les colonies. En outre, l'Etat développa le système dit des 'cultures forcées', qui fixa unilatéralement les prix de la production destinée à l'exportation. Les profits se multiplièrent, mais le système ne fut guère profitable à la population indigène.
En métropole, cette source de revenus stimula les activités, axées sur la construction des chemins de fer, le développement de l'industrie textile, à l'instar de l'Angleterre, et l'extension de l'industrie en général.
La prise de toutes ces dispositions fit que la flotte néerlandaise s'étendit fortement. Une dizaine d'années après l'instauration du système des cultures forcées, 150 navires marchands prenaient déjà la route des Indes. Les bateaux à vapeur gagnaient du terrain sur la navigation à voile, et les ports souffraient d'un besoin criant d'extension. En 1863, Rotterdam fut relié à la mer par le creusement du Nieuwe Waterweg. Amsterdam suivit en 1876, l'année où fut achevé le canal de la Mer du nord, avec ses écluses à IJmuiden.
La neutralité conservée dans le conflit franco-allemand de 1870, et surtout pendant la Première Guerre Mondiale, a profité à l'économie néerlandaise. Les industries déjà existantes continuèrent à produire, bien qu'à échelle réduite.

Après la Deuxième Guerre Mondiale, la vie prit un élan supplémentaire. L'Europe ravagée se rétablit relativement vite à l'aide du

El aspecto de Europa cambió al principio del siglo XIX. La revolución francesa puso punto final a la época feudal. Muchos fueron los que consideraron a los Estados Unidos como el ejemplo de nación libre. Fué un tiempo de cambios contínuos. Se desarrollaron nuevos inventos como el vapor y la electricidad. Los empresarios vieron las posibilidades económicas de dichos descubrimientos y ello dió lugar a la revolución industrial.

La economía de Holanda se vió casi arruinada por el cierre de sus puertos marítimos como consecuencia del Bloque Continental. Cuando en el 1.816, Holanda recobró el poder sobre sus colonias, llevaban ya un retraso en su desarrollo con respecto a otros paises dominadores de colonias como Inglaterra. Sus propiedades de ultramar tenían un doble significado económico: Por un lado proveían al pais madre de materias primas y por otro lado eran un mercado consumidor de sus productos industriales.
Una de las primeras medidas que se tomaron, sustentada por el rey Guillermo I, fué la creación de la compañía holandesa del comercio con el objetivo de organizar y financiar el comercio. Otra de las medidas adoptadas por el Estado fue la de dictar unilateralmente los precios para las cosechas dirigidas a la exportación. Con todo ello se logró el aumentó constante de los ingresos del Estado pero este sistema no era ventajoso para la poblacion propia del pais. Con esta recaudación se estimularon actividades en el pais madre: se construyeron ferrocarriles, la actividad industrial en general aumentó y, conforme a la situación inglesa, se desarrolló tambien aquí la industria textil. De un modo análogo, la revolución industrial llegó a Holanda con retraso. Otra consecuencia de estas medidas fué el fuerte aumento sufrido por la flota holandesa. En los 10 años siguientes a la introducción del precio fijo para las exportaciones, había ya 150 buques mercantes haciendo el trayecto con las Indias.En 1.863 Rotterdam abrió su conexion excavada hacia el mar llamada Nieuwe Waterweg. La salida directa de Amsterdam se acabó en 1.876 y se realizaba por el Canal del Mar del Norte que terminaba en las esclusas de Ijmuiden. Para la economía de Holanda fue de vital importancia el permanecer neutral en la guerra franco-alemana y especialmente durante la Primera Guerra Mundial. La primitiva industria que se habia creado pudo de esta manera, aunque de forma limitada, continuar produciendo.

Acabada la Segunda Guerra Mundial la vida tomó un ritmo trepitante. La derruida

No princípio do século 19 o aspecto da França mudou-se muito. A Revolução Francesa tinha posto termo à era feudal. Os Estados Unidos eram considerados por muitos como o exemplo de uma nação livre. Modificações deram-se umas após outras. Criou-se a oportunidade para o desenvolvimento de novas descobertas como o vapor e a electricidade. Empresários previram novas possibilidades e com elas realizaram a revolução industrial.

A Holanda estava quase arruinada devido ao fecho dos seus portos marítimos, por consequência do Sistema Continental. Quando os holandeses, em 1816, receberam novamente o poder sobre as suas colónias, tinham eles um atraso em relação a outros países com colónias, como a Inglaterra. As suas colónias ultramarinas receberam um duplo significado económico: por um lado proviam a pátria de matérias primas, mas por outro lado tinham a função de novos campos de venda dos produtos industriais.
Como uma das medidas para esse fim foi fundada, graças também ao rei Willem I, a Companhia Comercial Holandesa, tanto para financiar o comércio, como mesmo para o organizar. Paralelamente o Estado fixou unilateralmente o preço dos produtos agrícolas para exportação: o Sistema da (agri)Cultura. As receitas aumentaram enormemente, mas o sistema não favorecia, evidentemente, a população campesina. Com estas receitas foram estimuladas actividades no território nacional:
Foram construídas linhas ferroviárias, a actividade geral aumentou e, conforme a situação inglesa, desenvolveu-se também a indústria têxtil. A revolução industrial propagou-se aqui, em seguida, proporcionalmente.
Graças a todas estas medidas a frota holandesa ampliou-se imensamente. Dentro de uma dezena de anos, após a introdução do Sistema da Cultura navegavam já à volta de 150 navios para a Índia. A navegação a vapor ganhou terreno à navegação à vela e as instalações portuárias necessitavam de ampliações. Foi em 1863 que em Roterdão foi escavada uma ligação com o mar, a que se deu o nome 'Nieuwe Waterweg' (Nova Via Fluvial).
A ligação directa de Amsterdão com o mar, o Canal ao Mar do Norte, com eclusas em IJmuiden, foi concluída em 1876.
Foi uma grande vantagem para a economia da Holanda, ela ter ficado neutra na Guerra da França e a Alemanha e em especial na Primeira Guerra Mundial.
As indústrias já existentes puderam continuar

Welbeschouwd heeft Nederland een hoofdstad die niet als zodanig in de atlassen vermeld staat: de Randstad. In het zeer dichtbevolkte westen van het land groeien de steden naar elkaar toe. De bebouwing van Rotterdam is Den Haag, via Delft, zeer dicht genaderd; tussen Den Haag, Leiden en Haarlem liggen de bollenvelden als kleurige open vlakten. Langs het Noordzeekanaal groeit de Amsterdamse haven op zijn beurt in de richting van Haarlem.
Dit neemt niet weg dat de formele hoofdstad, Amsterdam, deze benaming meer dan waard is. De fraaie binnenstad volgt het patroon van de 17de-eeuwse grachtengordel die in het noorden wordt begrensd door het IJ. Het Centraal Station (links) is aangelegd op een kunstmatig eiland in het IJ. Rechts van het station is in een hypermodern gebouw New Metropolis gevestigd. Het is een museum waar voorlichting over wetenschap en techniek interactief wordt gepresenteerd. Het stadhuis van Amsterdam is gecombineerd met het muziektheater (onder).

The capital of the Netherlands for all practical purposes is not shown in the atlases. This is the Randstad – the name given to the conurbation that includes Amsterdam, Utrecht, The Hague and Rotterdam. In this very densely populated area in the west of the country the cities are expanding towards one another. The edges of Rotterdam and The Hague, via Delft, are not far apart. There is a small, richly coloured area of bulb fields between The Hague, Leiden and Haarlem. The port of Amsterdam in its turn is growing in the direction of Haarlem along the North Sea Canal. However, the official capital continues to be Amsterdam, and it certainly deserves to be. The beautiful city centre is based on the seventeenth century rings of canals, which are bordered to the north by the River IJ. The Central Station (left) stands on an artificial island in the IJ. To the right of the station is the ultramodern newMetropolis building – an interactive science and technology museum. Amsterdam City Hall is housed together with the music theatre (below).

Genau gesehen haben die Niederlande eine Hauptstadt, die als solche auf keiner Karte zu finden ist: das Ballungsgebiet Randstad. Im äußerst dichtbevölkerten Westen des Landes wachsen die Städte zusammen. Die Bebauung von Rotterdam hat sich über Delft schon stark bis an Den Haag herangeschlichen; zwischen Den Haag, Leiden und Haarlem liegen die Tulpenfelder als bunte offene Flächen. Entlang des Nordseekanals wächst der Amsterdamer Hafen in Richtung Haarlem.
Das verhindert jedoch nicht, daß die offizielle Hauptstadt Amsterdam diesem Namen mehr als gerecht wird. Die hübsche Innenstadt verläuft entlang der Grachtengürtel aus dem 17. Jahrhundert, die im Norden von dem Fluß Het IJ begrenzt wird. Der Hauptbahnhof befindet sich auf einer künstlich errichteten Insel in Het IJ. Rechts vom Bahnhof befindet sich das New Metropolis, ein hypermodernes Gebäude, in dem ein Museum für Technik und Wissenschaft mit interaktiven Präsentationen untergebracht ist. Das Amsterdamer Rathaus ist mit dem Musiktheater kombiniert (unten).

En fait, les Pays-Bas possèdent une capitale, qui n'est pas marquée sur les atlas à ce titre. Il s'agit de la 'Randstad', vaste conurbation située dans l'Ouest, à forte densité démographique, où les villes se soudent entr'elles. Rotterdam se rapproche, via Delft, de la Haye. La Haye forme avec Leiden et Haarlem un triangle, où les champs de bulbes à fleurs s'étendent en espaces multicolores. Le long du canal de la mer du Nord, le port d'Amsterdam s'accroît à son tour dans la direction de Haarlem. Néanmoins, la capitale officielle est Amsterdam, et elle mérite bien cette appellation. Le beau centre-ville suit le dessin de la ceinture des canaux du 17e s., limitée au Nord par l'IJ (golfe du lac d'IJssel). La gare centrale (gauche) est construite sur une île artificielle. A droite de la gare se dresse un bâtiment ultramoderne, qui abrite le Musée New Metropolis. Ici, sciences et techniques sont présentées de façon interactive. L'hôtel de ville d'Amsterdam est accolé au Muziektheater (en bas).

Si lo observaramos detenidamente, Holanda tiene una capital que no viene mencionada en ningún atlas: la llamada Randstad (ciudad periférica). En el Oeste del pais, de gran densidad de población, las ciudades crecen hasta juntarse. La zona urbana de Rotterdam se extiende a través de Delft hasta casi La Haya; entre La Haya, Leiden y Haarlem se encuentran los campos de bulbos formando una colorida planície. A lo largo del canal del Mar del Norte crece el puerto de Amsterdam en dirección a Haarlem. A pesar de ello, la ciudad de Amsterdam continúa siendo la capital por excelencia. Sus hermosos barrios céntricos siguen el modelo de canales del siglo XVII, limitando por el norte con el IJ. La estación central (izquierda) está situado sobre una isla artificial situada en el IJ. A la derecha de la estación se encuentra el modernísimo edificio New Metropolis. Se trata de un museo donde se ofrece información sobre la ciencia y la técnica de una forma interactiva. El edificio del ayuntamiento de Amsterdam acoge tambien el teatro de la música (abajo).

Considerando bem a Holanda tem uma capital que não está citada nos atlas como tal: Randstad (aglomerado citadino ao longo da costa). No ocidente muito populoso as cidades crescem em direcção umas às outras. As construções de Roterdão, passando Delft, aproximam-se de Haia; entre Haia, Leiden e Haarlem encontram-se os campos dos bulbos de flores, como espaços coloridos. Ao longo do Canal do Norte o porto de Amsterdão, por sua vez, desenvolve-se em direcção a Haarlem. Isto não quer dizer que a verdadeira capital, Amsterdão, não mereça esse nome. O interior da cidade, de grande beleza, acompanha o padrão da cintura de canais, típico para o século 17, ao norte limitado pelo rio IJ. A Estação Central (à esquerda) foi construída numa ilha artificial no rio IJ. À direita da estação encontra-se o edifício hipermoderno New Metropolis. Trata-se de um museu, onde são dados esclarecimentos sobre ciência e técnica, duma maneira interactiva.
A Câmara Municipal de Amsterdão combina-se com um teatro/sala de concertos (abaixo).

ropa kon door de financiële injectie van de Marshall-hulp weer redelijk snel op orde worden gebracht. De economische ontwikkeling werd gestoeld op verder gaande mechanisatie en schaalvergroting.
Vooral de grote concerns grepen hun kans om zich breder internationaal te ontplooien. Vanuit Nederland waren dat o.a. Philips, Shell, Unilever, etc.
Om het bedrijfsleven verder te stimuleren nam de Nederlandse overheid doeltreffende maatregelen om de infrastructuur te verbeteren.
Nederland heeft zich ontwikkeld tot een van de grootste distributeurs van Europa met niet alleen Rotterdam als grootste haven en Schiphol als vooraanstaande luchthaven, maar ook met een ondernemende transportsector die een derde van de Europese vracht vervoert.

quickly thanks to the financial injection of the Marshall Plan. Economic growth was based on far-reaching mechanization and increases in scale.
Large corporations, in particular, seized their opportunity to develop their international operations. Dutch players in this global arena included Philips, Shell and Unilever. The Dutch government took effective measures to improve the infrastructure in order to stimulate the private sector. The Netherlands has grown to become one of the largest distributors in Europe. This is not just because of Rotterdam, the world's largest port, and Schiphol, a leading airport, but also because of an enterprising transport sector which carries one third of Europe's freight.

Die bereits bestehenden Industrien konnte so in begrenztem Umfang weiterproduzieren.

Nach dem zweiten Weltkrieg beschleunigte der Alltag seinen Rhythmus. Das angeschlagene Europa kam durch die Finanzspritzen aus dem Marshall-Plan ziemlich schnell wieder auf die Beine. Die Wirtschaftsentwicklung beruhte auf einer weiteren Mechanisierung und der Produktion großer Mengen.
Insbesondere Großkonzerne ergriffen die Chance zur Entfaltung auf internationaler Ebene. In den Niederlanden waren dies u.a. Philips, Shell und Unilever. Zur weiteren Anregung der Wirtschaft ergriff die niederländische Regierung entsprechende Maßnahmen zur Verbesserung der Infrastruktur.
Die Niederlande entwickelten sich zu einem der größten Verteilerzentren in Europa, nicht nur mit Rotterdam als größtem Hafen und Schipol als wichtigem Flughafen, sondern auch mit einem unternehmensstarken Transportsektor, der ein Drittel des europäischen Frachtaufkommens befördert.

Plan Marshall. Le développement économique reposait sur une mécanisation poussée et sur une concentration des structures.
En particulier, les grands groupes s'ouvrirent au déploiement international. Aux Pays-Bas il s'agit entre autres de Philips, Shell, Unilever, etc.
Dans un souci d'encourager la vie économique, le gouvernement néerlandais prit des mesures efficaces afin d'améliorer les infrastructures. Les Pays-Bas sont devenus un des plus importants pays de transit, non seulement parce que le pays bénéficie du plus grand port du monde qu'est Rotterdam, et d'un aéroport de premier plan, Schiphol, mais également grâce à un secteur des transports entreprenant, acheminant un tiers du fret européen.

Europa, por medio de la injección financiera que le supuso el Plan Marshall, pudo recomponerse en un tiempo bastante rápido. El desarrollo económico se vió favorecido por el avance de la mecanización y la masificación. Las grandes empresas en especial aprovecharon esta oportunidad para su desarrollo internacional. Fueron éstas las empresas holandesas como Philips, Shell y Unilever entre otras.
Para estimular el sector industrial, el gobierno holandes tomó las medidas oportunas para crear y mejorar la infraestructura del pais. Holanda se ha convertido en uno de los mayores paises distribuidores de Europa, no solo por la grandeza del puerto de Rotterdam o su avanzado aeropuerto Schiphol, sino tambien con un sector de transporte terrestre que llega a transportar una tercera parte de las mercancías europeas.

a sua produção, embora isso fosse numa escala reduzida.

Depois da Segunda Guerra Mundial a vida tomou um ritmo mais rápido. A Europa empobrecida pôde ser restabelecida relativamente rápido, graças ao Auxílio do Plano Marshall. O desenvolvimento económico apoiou-se na mecanização já adiantada e numa ampliação da escala de produção. Nomeadamente, as grandes companhias agarraram o oportunidade de se desenvolverem internacionalmente. Na Holanda foram elas, a Philips, a Shell, a Unilever, etc. Para estimular mais a economia as autoridades holandesas tomaram medidas eficazes, para melhorar a infra-estrutura. A Holanda desenvolveu-se a um dos maiores países de transportes distributivos da Europa com, não só Roterdão como o maior porto do mundo e Schiphol como aeroporto eminente, mas também com um sector de transporte activo, que transporta uma terça parte da carga europeia.

Buiten het centrum van Amsterdam verrijzen moderne kantoortorens. De multifunctionele Arena fungeert als stadion van de voetbalclub Ajax en er worden (pop-)concerten gegeven (links). De meeste steden kunnen bogen op fraaie architectonische overblijfselen uit vroeger eeuwen. Rechts: het stadhuis van Haarlem en de Korenmarkt te Leiden.

Surrounding the centre of Amsterdam is a forest of modern office blocks. The multifunctional Arena is the home of Ajax football club and it also plays host to pop concerts (left). Most Dutch cities have stunning examples of architecture from bygone ages. Right: Haarlem Town Hall and the Corn Market in Leiden.

Außerhalb des Zentrums von Amsterdam ragen moderne Bürotürme empor. Die multifunktionale Arena dient als Stadion für den Fußballclub Ajax und als Veranstaltungsort für (Pop-)Konzerte (links). Die meisten Städte können sich schöner architektonischer Bauwerke aus früheren Jahrhunderten rühmen. Rechts: das Haarlemer Rathaus und der Kornmarkt in Leiden.

A l'extérieur du centre-ville se dressent des tours de bureaux modernes. L'Arena, à usage multiple, fait fonction de stade pour le club de football d'Ajax et de lieu de concert (g.). La plupart des villes peuvent se vanter de vestiges d'architecture d'antan. A droite : l'hôtel de ville de Haarlem et le Korenmarkt à Leiden.

Fuera del centro de Amsterdam crecen los modernos edificios de oficinas. El estadio multifuncional Arena acoge de igual manera partidos del Ajax como conciertos tanto de música moderna como clásica (izquierda). La mayoria de las ciudades se ven enriquecidas por edificios provenientes de los siglos pasados. Derecha: el ayuntamiento de Haarlem y el mercado Korenmarkt de Leiden.

Fora do centro de Amsterdão elevam-se modernas torres de escritórios. A Arena multifuncional, serve de estádio de futebol do Ajax e lá são dados também concertos (de Pop) (à esquerda). A maioria das cidades regozijam-se de ter belos restos arquitectónicos dos séculos passados. À direita: a Câmara Municipal de Haarlem e o Mercado dos Cereais em Leiden.

Overal ter wereld verplaatsen de activiteiten van havensteden zich steeds meer naar buiten en steeds dichter naar zee. De Zandhoek geeft nog een beeld van vroeger. Elke vijf jaar organiseert Amsterdam het evenement Sail. Aan de kaden van de oude havens liggen de windjammers als vanouds weer afgemeerd. Rechts: een zeeschip passeert de sluizen van IJmuiden. Door de aanleg van nieuwe faciliteiten ontwikkelt het gebied zich als de voorhaven van Amsterdam.

All over the world the activities of ports are moving away from the city centre towards the sea. The Zandhoek still reflects the way things used to be. Once every five years Amsterdam organizes the Sail event. Tall ships are moored along the jetties of the old docks. Right: an ocean-going vessel passes through the locks at IJmuiden. This area is developing into the outport of Amsterdam thanks to the construction of new facilities.

Überall auf der Welt verlagern sich die Aktivitäten von Hafenstädten weiter nach außen und dichter an die See. De Zandhoek zeigt, wie es früher aussah. Alle fünf Jahre organisiert Amsterdam die Veranstaltung Sail. An den Kaden der alten Häfen liegen die Windjammer wie von alters her vertäut. Rechts: Ein Hochseeschiff passiert die Schleuse von IJmuiden. Durch den Bau der neuen Anlagen entwickelt sich das Gebiet zum Vorhafen von Amsterdam.

Partout dans le monde, les activités des ports se déplacent vers l'extérieur, et toujours plus près de la mer. Le Zandhoek donne encore une image du passé. Tous les cinq ans, Amsterdam organise l'événement 'Sail'. Aux quais des vieux ports sont amarrés les bateaux de l'époque. A droite : Un navire passe les écluses d'IJmuiden, devenu avant-port d'Amsterdam par l'aménagement de ses espaces portuaires.

En todo el mundo, las actividades portuarias se van trasladando cada vez más hacia el exterior de los puertos más cerca del mar. El Zandhoek nos ofrece aún una visión del pasado.
Cada cinco años Amsterdam organiza la concentración marina llamada Sail. Al igual que antaño, los grandes veleros se encuentran atracados en el viejo puerto. Derecha: un velero pasando las esclusas de Ijmuiden. Mediante la construcción de nuevas y mejores facilidades, esta demarcación se esta desarrollando de forma prominente como la avanzadilla del puerto de Amsterdam.

Em todo o mundo, as actividades das cidades portuárias deslocam-se para fora e cada vez mais próximo do mar. O Zandhoek tem ainda a imagem dos tempos passados. De cinco em cinco anos Amsterdão organiza o evento Sail. Nos cais do porto antigo atracam os barcos à vela do alto-mar, como antigamente. À direita: um navio passa a eclusa de IJmuiden. Graças à construção das novas instalações esta região desenvolve-se como um "porto avançado" de Amsterdão.

Linkerbladzijde: Amsterdam is sinds mensen heugenis het internationale centrum van de handel in cacaobonen. De cacao komt voornamelijk uit Afrika en wordt daar niet gemechaniseerd geladen. Het lossen van de zeeschepen is daarom een arbeidsintensief karwei. De lading van elk binnenkomend schip wordt minutieus door een expert gecontroleerd. Rechterbladzijde: de Amsterdamse haven verwerkt ook containerschepen. Met grote regelmaat lopen luxecruiseschepen de haven binnen. Om de passagiers te verwelkomen is er vlak bij het centrum een moderne passengers-terminal aangelegd. Op de foto rechtsonder passeert een modern cruiseschip het westelijk deel van het centrum.

Left-hand page: Amsterdam has been the international centre of the cocoa bean trade for as long as people can remember. The cocoa comes primarily from Africa and it is not loaded mechanically. Unloading the ocean-going freighters is therefore a labour-intensive activity. The cargo of every incoming vessel is thoroughly checked by a loss adjuster. Right-hand page: the port of Amsterdam also handles container carriers. Luxury cruise ships are frequent visitors to the port. Close to the city centre a modern terminal has been built to welcome passengers. On the photograph, below right, a modern cruise ship passes through the western part of the city centre.

Linke Seite: Amsterdam ist seit jeher internationales Handelszentrum für den An- und Verkauf von Kakaobohnen. Der Kakao kommt in erster Linie aus Afrika, und die Verladung erfolgt dort nicht mechanisch. Das Löschen der Schiffe ist deshalb sehr arbeitsintensiv. Die Ladung jedes einlaufenden Schiffes wird minutiös von einem Experten geprüft. Rechte Seite: Der Amsterdamer Hafen bedient auch Containerschiffe. Mit großer Regelmäßigkeit laufen Luxuskreuzschiffe in den Hafen ein. Zur Begrüßung der Passagiere wurde ganz in der Nähe der Innenstadt ein modernes Passagierterminal gebaut. Auf dem Foto rechts unten passiert ein modernes Kreuzschiff den westlichen Teil des Stadtzentrums.

Page de gauche : Amsterdam est depuis toujours le centre international du commerce des fèves de cacao. Le cacao arrive essentiellement d'Afrique, où il est chargé de façon manuelle. C'est pourquoi le déchargement des navires est une activité à fort coefficient de travail. La cargaison de chaque bateau entrant est minutieusement contrôlée par un expert. Page de droite : Le port d'Amsterdam traite également des porte-conteneurs. Régulièrement, des paquebots de croisière de luxe s'amarrent aux quais. Pour accueillir les passagers, un terminal moderne a été aménagé à proximité du centre-ville. La photo à droite en bas montre le passage d'un paquebot à l'ouest du centre.

Página izquierda: desde tiempo inmemorial, Amsterdam es el centro internacional del comercio de cacao. El cacao procede en su mayoría de Africa donde no es cargado de forma maquinal. Su descarga por tanto requiere un gran esfuerzo manual. Cada carga traída por un barco es controlada minuciosamente por un experto. Página derecha: El puerto de Amsterdam es tambien una terminal de contenedores. Regularmente hacen escala en Amsterdam los grandes cruceros. Para dar una cordial bienvenida a estos visitantes se ha construido cerca del centro de la ciudad una moderna terminal de pasajeros. En la foto abajo a la derecha un moderno crucero atraviesa la parte occidental del centro.

Página esquerda: Amsterdão é desde tempos imemoráveis um centro internacional do comércio de cacau em grão. O cacau é proveniente, especialmente, da África e lá não é carregado mecanicamente. A descarga dos barcos que vêm de lá é, por isso, um trabalho muito intensivo. A carga de todos os barcos que chegam é controlada minuciosamente por um perito. Página à direita: O porto de Amsterdão serve também navios de contentores. Com grande regularidade entram no porto barcos cruzeiros de luxo. Para dar as boas-vindas aos passageiros foi instalado próximo do centro da cidade um moderno terminal de passageiros. Na fotografia em baixo à direita passa um navio moderno de cruzeiro a parte ocidental do centro.

Schiphol verbindt Nederland door de lucht met meer dan 250 steden in meer dan 100 landen. De luchthaven is door jaren van spectaculaire groei opgeklommen tot een van de belangrijkste van Europa. Dit geldt niet alleen voor het aantal passagiers, maar in toenemende mate ook voor vracht. Van de ongeveer 50.000 personen die werkzaam zijn op of om Schiphol houdt 25% zich bezig met vracht. Schiphol, in 1916 begonnen als een 'vliegweide' met vier loodsen, wordt in 2005 uitgebreid met een 5de baan.

Schiphol Airport connects the Netherlands with more than 250 cities in over 100 countries by air. The airport has grown at a spectacular rate over the years to become one of the most important in Europe. This is true not just of passengers, but to an increasing degree of air cargo too. Of the approximately 50,000 people who work at or around Schiphol, 25% are involved in cargo. Schiphol started in 1916 as an air field with four sheds. In 2005 it will expand again when a fifth runway is built.

Schiphol assure les liaisons aériennes avec plus de 250 villes dans plus de 100 pays. L'aéroport a connu une croissance spectaculaire, il est devenu l'un des plus importants d'Europe. Cela concerne non seulement le trafic passagers, mais aussi, à un degré croissant, celui des marchandises. Des 50 000 personnes qui travaillent sur l'aéroport ou à sa périphérie, 25% s'occupent du transport des marchandises. Ayant débuté en 1916 comme un petit terrain d'aviation avec quatre hangars, Schiphol sera agrandi en 2005 avec une cinquième piste.

Schiphol es el punto de comunicación aérea de Holanda con más de 250 ciudades de 100 diferentes paises. El aeropuerto, tras años de espectacular crecimiento, se ha convertido en uno de los mas importantes de Europa. No solamente por la cantidad de viajeros que lo visitan sino que también por la progresión creciente de su tráfico de mercaderías. De las aproximadamente 50.000 personas que trabajan en Schiphol, un 25% se dedica exclusivamente al tráfico de mercaderías. Schiphol, que comenzó siendo en 1.916 un campo de vuelo con 4 almacenes, llegará a tener en el 2.005 su quinta pista de aterrizaje.

Schipol verbindet die Niederlande auf dem Luftweg mit über 250 Städten in mehr als 100 Ländern. Der Flughafen wurde in Jahren des spektakulären Wachstums zu einem der wichtigsten in Europa. Und dies nicht nur im Hinblick auf die Passagierzahlen, sondern auch in zunehmendem Maße für den Frachttransport. Von den ca. 50.000 Personen, die in oder um Schipol tätig sind, arbeiten 25% im Frachtbereich. Schiphol, der 1916 als "Flugplatz mit vier Lotsen" begann, wird im Jahre 2005 um eine fünfte Bahn erweitert.

O aeroporto Schiphol liga pelo ar mais de 250 cidades, em mais de 100 países. O aeroporto desenvolveu-se a um dos mais importantes da Europa, graças ao crescimento espectacular dos últimos anos. Isto não só no que diz respeito aos passageiros, mas também, em medida crescente, à carga transportada. Das cerca de 50.000 pessoas que trabalham no, ou à volta do aeroporto Schiphol, 25% ocupa-se da carga. Schiphol, que começou em 1916 como "um campo de voos" com quatro hangares, será ampliado em 2005 com a 5ª pista de aterragem.

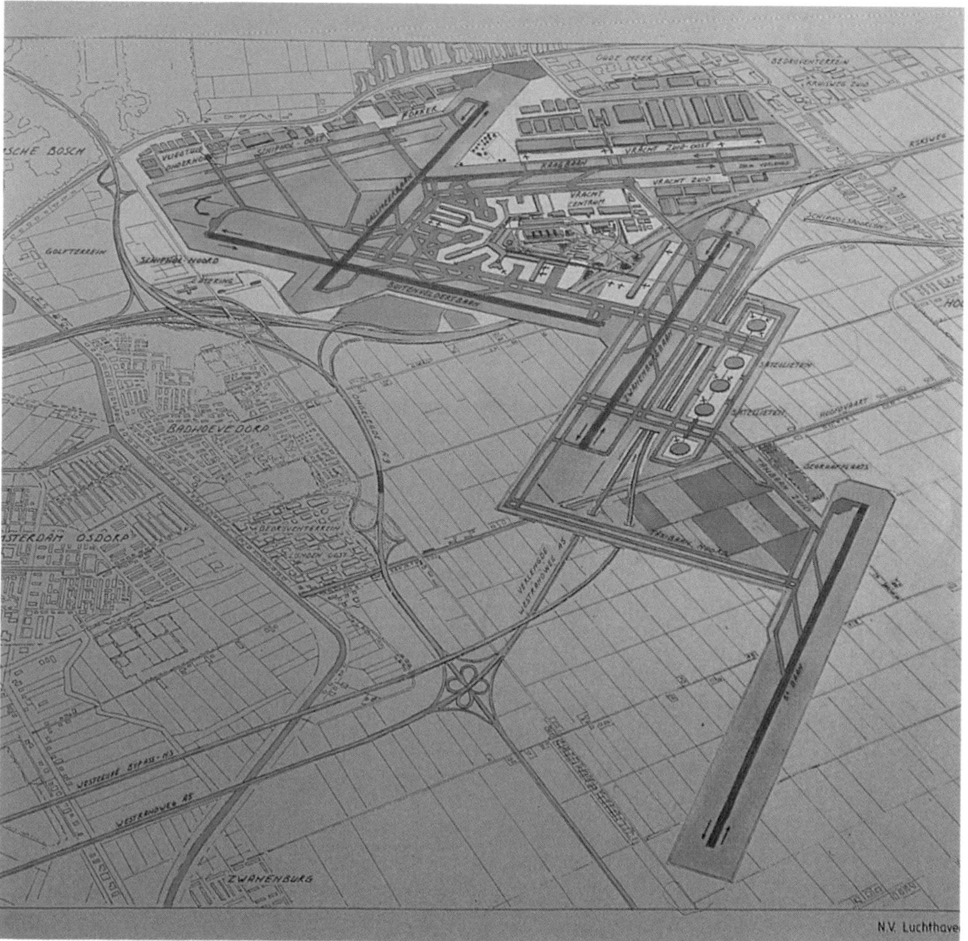

N.V. Luchthave

Wie in Londen, Berlijn of New York bloemen koopt heeft grote kans met Nederlandse bloemen de winkel te verlaten. De Hollanders ontdekten de tulp in de 17de eeuw. De bol was toen zo bijzonder dat men erin speculeerde. Al snel kwam hier de eigen teelt op gang en werd de basis gelegd voor een enorme bedrijfstak. Op de veilingen in Aalsmeer en Poeldijk worden niet alleen bloemen uit Nederland geveild, maar ze worden ook ingevlogen uit Azië en Afrika. Vrijwel de gehele distributie vindt van hieruit plaats.

Someone buying flowers in London, Berlin or New York will more likely than not leave the shop carrying Dutch blooms. The Dutch discovered the tulip in the seventeenth century. The bulb was so special at the time that it was the subject of financial speculation. The Dutch soon started cultivating their own, and the foundations were laid for an enormous industry. The auctions in Aalsmeer and Poeldijk sell flowers flown in from Asia and Africa as well as blooms grown in the Netherlands. Virtually all of the distribution takes place here.

Wer in London, Berlin oder New York Blumen kauft, hat gute Chancen, den Laden mit niederländischen Blumen zu verlassen. Die Holländer entdeckten die Tulpe im 17. Jahrhundert. Die Zwiebel war damals so begehrt, daß sie als Spekulationsobjekt galt. Schon schnell begann man in Holland mit der eigenen Zucht, die die Grundlage für einen immensen Wirtschaftszweig bilden sollte. Auf den Versteigerungen in Aalsmeer und Poeldijk werden nicht nur Blumen aus den Niederlanden versteigert, sie werden auch aus Asien und Afrika eingeflogen. Der gesamte Vertrieb wird allerdings in den Niederlanden koordiniert.

Celui qui achète des fleurs à Londres, Berlin ou New York a une grande chance de quitter le magasin avec des fleurs hollandaises. Les néerlandais découvrirent le bulbe de tulipe au 17e s. A cause de sa rareté, il fut un objet de spéculation. Bientôt, la culture des bulbes démarra aux Pays-Bas même : la base d'une activité économique colossale était créée. Aux marchés de fleurs aux enchères d'Aalsmeer et du Westland, on vend des fleurs hollandaises, mais aussi des fleurs d'Asie et d'Afrique, transportées par voie aérienne. La presque-totalité de la distribution s'effectue depuis ces marchés.

Las personas que compran flores en Londres, Berlín o Nueva York, tienen muchas probabilidades de estar comprando flores holandesas. Los holandeses descubrieron los tulipanes en el siglo XVII. Eran tan especiales en dicha época que se llegó a especular con ellos. Poco despues se empezaron a cultivar en este pais y se formó la base de la gran actividad comercial actual. En las subastas de flores de Alsmeer y el Westland, se subastan no solo flores del pais sino tambien otras procedentes de Asia y Africa. Practicamente toda su posterior distribución se realiza desde aquí.

Quem comprar flores em Londres, Berlim ou Nova Iorque sairá da loja, muito provavelmente, com flores holandesas na mão. Os holandeses descobriram as tulipas no século 17. O bulbo, naquela altura, era tão importante que se começou a especular nele. Brevemente se iniciou uma cultura própria e foi posta a base para um enorme ramo empresarial. Nos leilões de Aalsmeer e Poeldijk são leiloadas não só flores da Holanda, mas também as que vêm da Ásia e da África. Quase toda a distribuição se realiza a partir daqui.

Om de economie aan het begin van de 19de eeuw weer op gang te krijgen werd de Nederlandsche Handelsmaatschappij opgericht. Het markante hoofdkantoor in het centrum van Amsterdam is in 1921 gebouwd door de architect De Bazel. De bank is na een aantal fusies uiteindelijk opgegaan in ABN-AMRO. De AEX komt voort uit de fusie tussen de effectenbeurs en de optiebeurs in 1998. Het beeld van de beurshandelaar op het drukke Amsterdamse Damrak geeft een beeld van de tijd dat de handel plaatsvond zonder computers en beeldschermen. De AEX behoort tot de toonaangevende beurzen van Europa.

The Nederlandsche Handelsmaatschappij was set up at the beginning of the nineteenth century in order to stimulate economic growth. The striking head office in the centre of Amsterdam was built in 1921 by the architect De Bazel. After a number of mergers, the bank has become incorporated in ABN-AMRO. The AEX came about through a merger of the stock exchange and futures exchange in 1998. The statue of the stock exchange dealer in the busy Damrak in Amsterdam gives an impression of the era when bargains were struck without computers and screens. The AEX is one of Europe's leading exchanges.

Zur Wiederbelebung der Wirtschaft zu Beginn des 19. Jahrhunderts wurde die Niederländische Handelsgesellschaft gegründet. Der auffällige Geschäftssitz im Zentrum von Amsterdam wurde 1921 von dem Architekten De Bazel gebaut. Die Bank wurde nach einer Reihe von Fusionen schließlich zur ABN-AMRO. Die AEX entstanden aus dem Zusammenschluß der Effektenbörse und der Optionsbörse im Jahre 1997. Das Standbild des Börsenmaklers auf dem belebten Amsterdamer Damrak zeigt die Zeit, in der der Handel ohne Computer und Bildschirm ablief. Die AEX gehören zu den tonangebenden Börsen Europas.

La Compagnie Commerciale Néerlandaise fut créée au début du 19e s, pour relancer l'économie. Le siège principal est un bâtiment remarquable, situé au centre-ville d'Amsterdam et construit en 1921 par l'architecte De Bazel. La banque a fusionné plusieurs fois, et appartient aujourd'hui au groupe ABN-AMRO. L'AEX est le résultat de la fusion de la bourse des valeurs et du marché à options. L'image du courtier dans l'effervescence du Damrak à Amsterdam donne une idée de l'époque où le commerce s'exerçait sans ordinateurs ni écrans. Aujourd'hui l'AEX se situe parmi les places financières européennes de premier plan.

Para estimular la economía se creó al principio del siglo XIX la compañía Nederlandsche Handelsmaatschappij. Sus oficinas principales fueron construidas en el 1.921 en el centro de Amsterdam por el arquitecto De Bazel. Despues de varias uniones y fusiones, ha recabado finalmente siendo el banco ABN-AMRO. El AEX fué el resultado de la fusión de las bolsas de valores y de opciones que tuvo lugar en 1.998. La imagen de los corredores de bolsa en el concurrido Damrak de Amsterdam nos transporta al tiempo en que dicho comercio se realizaba sin ordenadores y sus correspondientes monitores. La bolsa AEX es una de las más influyentes de Europa.

Para activar a economia no princípio do século 19 foi fundada a Nederlandse Handelsmaatschappij (Companhia Comercial Holandesa). O escritório de características notáveis, no centro de Amsterdão, foi construído em 1921pelo arquitecto De Bazel. O banco, após uma quantidade de fusões, foi finalmente absorvido pelo banco ABN-AMRO. A AEX teve a sua origem na fusão entre a bolsa de valores e a bolsa de opções em 1997. A estátua do negociante da bolsa na movimentada praça Damrak em Amsterdão, dá uma ideia do tempo, em que o negócio se fazia sem computadores e ecrãs. A AEX faz parte das bolsas mais importantes da Europa.

Haringkaken, het schoonmaken van haringen om ze te kunnen bewaren, is een Nederlandse vinding uit de vroege Middeleeuwen. Sindsdien is er veel in de visserij gebeurd. Vooral in de laatste decennia werden de schepen groter en ontstonden er aan de wal grote bedrijven voor de verwerking van vis. De sector speelt hiermee in op de neiging van de consument steeds vaker kanten-klare visproducten te kopen. Belangrijke vissershavens zijn: Lauwersoog, Urk, IJmuiden, Scheveningen en Breskens (links).

The process of gutting herring so that they can be preserved was invented by the Dutch in the early Middle Ages. A lot has changed in the fishing industry since then. Fishing boats have become larger, particularly over the last few decades, and large companies have grown up on shore to process the fish. These facilities reflect consumer trends – people increasingly want to buy ready-to-cook fish products. The most important fishing ports are Lauwersoog, Urk, IJmuiden, Scheveningen and Breskens (left).

Das Kaken, d. h. Ausnehmen von Heringen, um sie haltbar zu machen, ist eine niederländische Erfindung aus dem frühen Mittelalter. Seitdem hat sich in der Fischerei viel getan. Vor allem in den letzten zehn Jahren wurden die Schiffe immer größer, und in Hafennähe entstanden große Fischverarbeitungsbetriebe. Der Sektor reagiert damit auf die steigende Nachfrage der Verbraucher nach tafelfertigen Fischprodukten. Bedeutende Fischereihäfen sind: Lauwersoog, Urk, IJmuiden, Scheveningen und Breskens (links).

Dans le haut moyen âge, afin de pouvoir conserver le hareng, les Néerlandais ont inventé le 'caquage', la préparation du poisson pour le mettre en caque. Depuis, la pêche a beaucoup évolué. Surtout au cours des dernières décennies, la taille des bateaux a augmenté, et une industrie de transformation du poisson s'est développée à terre, répondant ainsi à la demande croissante des consommateurs en produits de la pêche préparés. Lauwersoog, Urk, IJmuiden, Scheveningen et Breskens (à gauche) sont des ports de pêche importants.

La saladura de arenques, para poderlos guardar, es un descubrimiento holandes del principio de la Edad Media. Desde entonces ha cambiado mucho la pesca en sí. Además de hacer los barcos cada vez más grandes, se ha desarrollado en tierra una gran industria para la elaboración del pescado. Este sector mercantil se ha ido acomodando a los deseos del consumidor de comprar cada vez mas unos productos pesqueros ya preparados. Importantes puertos pescadores son: Lauwersoog, Urk, IIJmuiden, Scheveningen y Breskens (izquierda).

"Haringkaken", a limpeza dos arenques, para poderem ser conservados, foi uma invenção holandesa, do princípio da Idade Média. Desde então muito se modificou na indústria da pesca. Em especial durante os últimos decénios os navios tornaram-se maiores e em terra surgiram grandes empresas para elaboração do peixe. O sector aproveita-se da tendência do consumidor de comprar cada vez mais produtos de peixe prontos a consumir. Portos de pesca importantes são: Lauwersoog, Urk, IJmuiden, Scheveningen e Breskens (à esquerda).

De aangevoerde vis wordt dagelijks geveild in de diverse visafslagen. Yerseke in Zeeland (rechtsboven) is het centrum van de oester- en mosselcultuur. De schelpdieren die gedijen in de Oosterschelde en de Grevelingen worden bij de handelaren in grote bakken nagespoeld. De export richt zich voornamelijk op België en Frankrijk.
In Nederland wordt paling overwegend gerookt gegeten. In het IJsselmeer wordt veel paling gevangen. Langs de haven van Volendam (rechtsonder) bevinden zich veel rokerijen.

The catches are auctioned every day in the different fish markets. Ierseke in Zeeland (above right) is the centre of the oyster and mussel industry. The shellfish, which thrive in the Eastern Scheldt and the Grevelingen, are cleaned in large tanks by the dealers. Most exports go to Belgium and France.
In the Netherlands eel is usually eaten smoked. The IJsselmeer is a rich source of eel. There are many fish-smoking companies along the quays in the port of Volendam (below right).

Der angelieferte Fisch wird täglich auf den verschiedenen Fischauktionen versteigert. Ierseke in Zeeland (rechts oben) ist das Zentrum der Austern- und Muschelzucht. Bei den Händlern werden die Schalentiere, die in der Oosterschelde und Grevelingen gezüchtet werden, in großen Becken nachgespült. Exportiert werden sie vor allem nach Belgien und Frankreich. In den Niederlanden wird Aal meist geräuchert gegessen. Im IJsselmeer spielt der Aalfang eine große Rolle. Im Hafen von Volendam (rechts unten) befinden sich viele Räuchereien.

Chaque jour, les arrivages de poisson sont mis aux enchères dans les différentes criées. Yerseke en Zélande (à droite en haut) est le centre de l'ostréiculture et de la mytiliculture. Les coquillages se plaisent dans l'Escaut oriental et dans les Grevelingen. Chez les négociants, ils sont soumis à un deuxième rinçage dans de grands bassins. L'export est principalement orienté vers la Belgique et la France. On pêche beaucoup d'anguilles dans l'IJsselmeer. Les Néerlandais consomment surtout l'anguille fumée. Le long du port de Volendam, on trouve de nombreux fumoirs (à droite en bas).

El pescado es subastado diariamente en los diversos mercados de pescado. Ierseke en Zelandia (arriba derecha) es el centro de venta de ostras y mejillones. Estos moluscos, que se crían en el Oosterschelde y Grevelingen, son limpiados primero en grandes depósitos de agua. Su exportación va dirigida principalmente hacia Belgica y Francia. En Holanda las anguilas se comen principalmente ahumadas. El Ijsselmeer es el lugar por excelencia para la pesca de la anguila. En el puerto de Volendam (derecha abajo) se encuentran muchos ahumaderos.

O peixe vindo do mar é leiloado diariamente, em diversas lotas. Ierseke, na Zelândia (à direita, em cima) é o centro da cultura das ostras e dos mexilhões.
O marisco que cresce no Oosterschelde e Grevelingen são lavados pelos comerciantes em caixas grandes. A exportação é dirigida em especial à Bélgica e à França. Na Holanda comem-se as enguias, em especial, fumadas. O lago IJssel é muito rico em enguias. Ao longo dos cais de Volendam (à direita, em baixo) há muitas empresas de fumagem.

De stad Groningen is door de overheid aangewezen als groeistad. Ook in de gelijknamige provincie wordt de economie enorm gestimuleerd. Ten westen van Delfzijl is de Eemshaven aangelegd. Het havengebied huisvest o.a. chemische industrie en een aluminiumfabriek. Langs het Winschoterdiep liggen van oudsher scheepswerven. In de stad Groningen zijn de meeste werknemers actief in de dienstensector. Groningers staan open voor vernieuwing. Tegenover het station is, als een schip, de futuristische nieuwbouw van het Groninger museum verrezen (links). Het eerste aardgas werd in Slochteren gewonnen. Omdat de activiteiten van de Gasunie zich in het noorden concentreren bevindt zich hier het bijzondere hoofdkantoor (rechts).

The city of Groningen has been designated by the government as a growth city. The economy of the province of Groningen is receiving substantial incentives. The port of Eemshaven was built to the west of Delfzijl. The industrial activities in the port area include chemical plants and an aluminium smelter. The Winschoterdiep is the traditional home of shipyards. Most of the workforce in the city of Groningen is employed in the services sector. The people of Groningen are open to innovation. Across from the station is the ship-like futuristic new building of the Groninger Museum (left). The first Dutch natural gas to be produced came from Slochteren. The activities of the Gasunie are concentrated in the northern part of the country, and it is here that their striking head office is to be found (right).

Die Stadt Groningen wurde von der Regierung zur Wachstumszone erklärt. Auch in der gleichnamigen Provinz wird die Wirtschaft nach Kräften stimuliert. Westlich von Delfzijl wurde der Emshafen angelegt. Im Hafenbereich sind unter anderem chemische Industriebetriebe und eine Aluminiumfabrik angesiedelt. Entlang der Winschoterdiep liegen schon seit jeher Schiffswerften. In der Stadt Groningen arbeiten die meisten Beschäftigten im Dienstleistungssektor. Die Einwohner sind offen für Neues. Gegenüber dem Bahnhof entstand der futuristische Neubau des Groninger Museums in Form eines Schiffs (links). Das erste Erdgas wurde in Slochteren gewonnen. Da sich die Aktivitäten der Gasunion auf den Norden konzentrieren, befindet sich hier die eigene Hauptgeschäftsstelle (rechts).

Groningue a été classée 'ville à vocation de croissance' par le gouvernement. Mais l'économie est également fortement stimulée dans la province du même nom. A l'ouest de Delfzijl, le port d'Eems a été aménagé. Le bassin portuaire comprend entre autres des industries chimiques ainsi qu'une usine d'aluminium. Au bord du Winschoterdiep, se trouvent de tout temps des chantiers navals. A Groningue, la plupart des salariés travaillent dans le secteur tertiaire. La ville est ouverte à l'innovation. En face de la gare, une construction futuriste se dresse, comme un navire, c'est le nouveau Musée de Groningue (à gauche). Les premiers gisements de gaz naturel ont été exploités à Slochteren. Toutes les activités de la Gasunie (l'Union du gaz naturel) se concentrent dans le Nord du pays. Par conséquent, le siège principal, un bâtiment remarquable, se trouve à Groningue (à droite).

El gobierno ha escogido a Groninga como ciudad de crecimiento. En su provincia se ha estimulado tambien la economía enormemente. Al oeste de Delfzijl se ha construido el puerto Eemshaven. En su zona portuaria se encuentra, entre otros, industria química y una fábrica de aluminio. A orillas del Winschoterdiep se encuentran, desde siempre, varios astilleros. En la propia ciudad de Groninga, la ocupación de trabajo mayoritaria se encuentra en el sector de servicios. Sus ciudadanos están abiertos a aceptar innovaciones. En frente de la estación, se ha alzado, como un barco, el futurista edificio que alberga el Museo de Groninga (izquierda). En Slochteren se extrajo el primer gas natural. Dado que las actividades de la empresa de gas natural Gasunie se desarrollan principalmente en esta provincia, se ha edificado aquí su especial oficina central (derecha).

A cidade de Groningen foi indicada pelo governo como cidade de crescimento. Na província com o mesmo nome, a economia é estimulada fortemente. A oeste de Delfzijl foi construído o Eemhaven (o Porto no rio Eem). Esta região portuária abriga, entre outras, uma indústria química e uma fábrica de alumínio. Ao longo do Winschoterdiep existem desde há muito tempo os estaleiros. Na cidade de Groningen a maioria dos habitantes trabalha no sector de serviços. Os habitantes de Groningen aceitam renovações de braços abertos. No lado contrário à estação está, em forma de navio, a nova construção futurística do museu de Groningen (à esquerda). A primeira descoberta de gás natural foi feita em Slochteren. Como as actividades da Companhia do Gás se concentraram no Norte, encontra-se aqui também o seu especial escritório central (à direita).

Friesland wordt in het algemeen beschouwd als een agrarische provincie. Geleidelijk verandert dit aanzien. Steeds meer bedrijven, waaronder ook buitenlandse, zoeken en vinden in Friesland een aangename vestigingsplaats. De hoofdstad Leeuwarden is over de gehele wereld bekend. Hier worden de ingeblikte melkproducten vervaardigd die, met de Friese vlag op het etiket, tot in de verste binnenlanden worden geconsumeerd. Niet voor niets dat in Leeuwarden de koe wordt geëerd met een standbeeld, linksboven, en voorts met de klok mee: de Waag in het stadshart; het Poptaslot te Marssum; de binnenhaven van Harlingen; als er voldoende ijs ligt wordt in Friesland de Elfstedentocht geschaatst; in de jachthaven te Grouw wachten zeilboten om de plas op te gaan.

Friesland is generally considered to be an agricultural province. This is gradually changing. More and more businesses, including foreign companies, are seeking and finding a pleasant spot to locate in Friesland. The provincial capital Leeuwarden is known all over the world. It is here that canned milk products with the Frisian flag on the label are produced and shipped to consumers all over the country. It is with good reason that the cow is honoured in Leeuwarden with a statue, above left. Clockwise: the Waag (Weigh House) in the centre of the city; the Poptaslot in Marssum; the inner harbour of Harlingen; when it is cold enough, Friesland is host to the Elfstedentocht skating race; yachts in the Grouw marina waiting to go sailing on the lake.

Friesland gilt im allgemeinen als landwirtschaftliche Provinz. Doch dies ändert sich allmählich. Immer mehr Betriebe, darunter auch ausländische Unternehmen, suchen und finden in Friesland einen geeigneten Standort. Die Hauptstadt Leeuwarden ist weltweit bekannt. Hier werden die Dosenmilchprodukte hergestellt, die mit der friesischen Flagge auf dem Etikett auch in fernen Ländern verkauft werden. Nicht umsonst wird in Leeuwarden die Kuh mit einem Denkmal geehrt. Von links oben im Uhrzeigersinn: die Stadtwaage im Zentrum; das Popta-Schloß in Marssum; der Binnenhafen von Harlingen; in frostigen Wintern findet auf den zugefrorenen Flüssen und Kanäle Frieslands der "Elfstädtelauf" statt; im Jachthafen von Grouw warten Segelboote darauf, in See zu stechen.

La Frise est en général considérée comme une province agricole. Mais elle change progressivement de visage. De plus en plus d'entreprises, parmi lesquelles des sociétés étrangères, cherchent et trouvent en Frise un lieu d'implantation agréable. La capitale Leeuwarden est mondialement réputée. C'est ici que sont fabriqués les produits laitiers en boîte, à l'étiquette décorée du drapeau de Frise, que l'on consomme dans les contrées les plus éloignées du monde. Ce n'est donc pas pour rien, que l'on a érigé un monument à Leeuwarden, en hommage à la vache (à gauche en haut). Ensuite, dans le sens des aiguilles d'une montre : le Poids public au centre-ville; le château Popta à Marssum; le port intérieur de Harlingen; si l'épaisseur de la glace des canaux le permet, la fameuse course de patinage, le Circuit des Onze Villes (Elfstedentocht) a lieu; dans le port de plaisance de Grouw, les voiliers attendent de cingler vers le lac.

Por lo general se considera a Frisia como una provincia propiamente agraria. Progresivamente se va cambiando esta idea. Cada vez mas empresas, incluidas las extranjeras, buscan y encuentran en Frisia su lugar de asentamiento. Su capital Leeuwarden, tiene fama mundial. Aquí se enlatan los productos lácteos que, con la bandera frisona en sus etiquetas, llegan hasta las partes mas recónditas de muchos paises. Con razón en Leeuwarden se rinde tributo a la vaca por medio de un monumento, izquierda arriba y siguiendo el movimiento del reloj: el Peso público, en el corazón de la ciudad; el Poptaslot en Marssum; el puerto interior de Harlingen; si el hielo natural tiene el suficiente grosor se corre la famosa Elfstedentocht (la carrera de las once ciudades) de unos 200 km.; en el puerto recreativo de Grouw esperan los veleros para hacerse a la mar.

A Frísia é em geral considerada como uma província agrária. A pouco e pouco este aspecto vai-se mudando. Cada vez aparecem mais empresas, entre as quais estrangeiras, que procuram e encontram na Frísia um lugar agradável para se estabelecerem.
A capital Leeuwarden é conhecida em todo o mundo. Aqui são produzidos os produtos de leite enlatados que, com a bandeira da Frísia na etiqueta, são consumidos nos pontos mais afastados do interior dos países. Não é sem razão que em Leeuwarden a vaca é honrada com uma estátua (à esquerda, em cima); em seguida: no sentido dos ponteiros do relógio: "de Waag" (a Balança), no centro da cidade; "het Poptaslot" (o castelo Popta), em Marssum; o porto interior de Harlingen; quando há gelo suficiente realiza-se a corrida em patins na Frísia, a "Elfstedentocht" (a Corrida das Onze Cidades); no porto dos iates em Grouw, os barcos à vela esperam a saída para as águas abertas.

Drenthe is de provincie met de meeste natuur binnen haar grenzen. Talloze recreanten zoeken hier de rust van de bossen en vooral die van de uitgestrekte heidevelden. Assen, de hoofdstad van de provincie, heeft een uitgesproken centrumfunctie. Op de Brink staat een bronzen beeld dat het kuipersambacht in herinnering brengt. In Roderwolde is de opvallende koren- en oliemolen Woldzicht als museum ingericht (midden). De meeste huizen in vrijwel alle Drentse dorpen zijn gegroepeerd om een zogenaamde brink, een ongeplaveid plein met bomen. Op de Brink te Zuidlaren wordt jaarlijks een beroemde paardenmarkt gehouden (rechts). De industrie in de provincie concentreert zich in Emmen en Hoogeveen.

Drenthe is the province with the most extensive nature reserves. Large numbers of people find relaxation and recreation in the peace and quiet of the woods, and above all the vast areas of heath. The provincial capital of Assen is a real centre of activities. On the Brink there is a bronze statue commemorating the cooper's trade. The eye-catching Woldzicht corn and oil windmill in Roderwolde has been turned into a museum (centre). Most houses in virtually every Drenthe village are grouped around a Brink, which is an unpaved square with trees. A famous horse market is held every year in the Brink in Zuidlaren (right). The province's industry is concentrated in Emmen and Hoogeveen.

Drenthe ist die Provinz, in der am meisten Natur zu finden ist. Zahllose Urlauber kommen wegen der Ruhe der Wälder und der ausgedehnten Heide hierher. Assen, die Hauptstadt der Provinz, ist der zentrale Ort Drenthes. Auf dem Brink steht eine Bronzestatue, die an das Böttcherhandwerk erinnert. In Roderwolde wurde die auffällige Korn- und Ölmühle Woldzicht als Museum eingerichtet (Mitte). Die meisten Häuser fast aller Drenther Dörfer sind um einen sogenannten Brink gruppiert, einen ungepflasterten baumbestandenen Dorfplatz. Auf dem Brink in Zuidlaren wird jedes Jahr ein berühmter Pferdemarkt abgehalten (rechts). Die Industrie konzentriert sich in der Provinz Drenthe auf Emmen und Hoogeveen.

La province de Drenthe possède la plus grande superficie d'espaces naturels. De nombreux vacanciers recherchent ici la tranquillité des forêts et surtout des vastes landes. Assen, la capitale de la province, affirme sa fonction de pivot. Sur la place centrale, le Brink, une statue de bronze rappelle la tonnellerie. A Roderwolde, un remarquable moulin à blé et à huile à été aménagé en musée (milieu). Dans les villages, la plupart des maisons sont groupées autour d'une place non-revêtue et bordée d'arbres, le 'Brink'. Une foire aux chevaux importante a lieu chaque année sur celui de Zuidlaren. L'industrie est concentrée à Emmen et à Hoogeveen.

Drenthe es la provincia con la mayor extensión de naturaleza. Numerosos turistas buscan aquí la paz de los bosques y las grandes extensiones de brezales. Assen, la capital de la provincia, tiene un función central de gran importancia. En el Brink se encuentra una estatua de bronce en recuerdo del oficio de tonelería. En Roderwolde se ha adaptado el molino de grano y aceite Woldzicht como museo (en medio). En casi la totalidad de los pueblos de Drenthe, las casas se agrupan alrededor del Brink, una plaza sin asfaltar y rodeada de árboles. En el Brink de Zuidlaren se celebra anualmente un mercado de caballos (derecha). La industria de esta provincia se encuentra concentrada en Emmen y Hoogeveen.

Drenthe é a província com a natureza mais bela, dentro dos seus limites. Muitas pessoas que procuram recreio encontram aqui o sossego dos bosques e, em especial, dos imensos campos de brejos. Assen, a capital da província, tem uma função de centralização bem pronunciada. No Brink está uma estátua de bronze, que faz lembrar o ofício de tanoeiro. Em Roderwolde os moinhos de cereais e de óleos de aspecto notável estão equipados para servir de museu (ao meio). A maioria das casas em quase todas as aldeias de Drenthe agrupam-se à volta do chamado Brink, um largo sem pavimento e com árvores. No Brink de Zuidlaren dá-se todos os anos o famoso mercado dos cavalos (à direita). A indústria na província concentra-se nas cidades Emmen e Hoogeveen.

In 1959 werd in Nederland aardgas aangeboord in het Slochterenveld. Sinds die tijd is er een groot aantal locaties bijgekomen niet alleen op het vasteland maar vooral veel in zee op het continentale plat. Het gas wordt gewonnen door de NAM. De Gasunie zorgt voor transport en distributie. Het bedrijf beheert en controleert een transportnet van ruim 10.000 km. Om tijdens pieken aan een grotere vraag te kunnen voldoen vult de Gasunie diep in de ondergrond buffervoorraden op. Het bedrijf exporteert grote hoeveelheden aardgas naar België, Duitsland, Frankrijk, Zwitserland en Italië.

Natural gas was first found in the Netherlands in 1959, when the Slochteren field was discovered. Since then a large number of locations have been added, both on dry land and offshore on the Continental Shelf. The gas is produced by NAM. The Gasunie is responsible for transport and distribution. The company manages and controls a transport network comprising more than 10,000 kilometres of pipes. The Gasunie fills storage facilities deep underground with natural gas in order to meet high demand during peaks. The company exports large quantities of natural gas to Belgium, Germany, France, Switzerland and Italy.

1959 stieß man in den Niederlanden im Slochterenfeld auf Erdgas. Seit dieser Zeit kamen noch viele weitere Vorkommen hinzu, nicht nur auf dem Festland, sondern vor allem auf dem Kontinentalschelf in der Nordsee. Das Gas wird von der NAM gewonnen. Die Gasunion kümmert sich um Transport und Verkauf. Das Unternehmen betreibt und kontrolliert ein Transportnetz von ungefähr 10.000 km Länge. Um Bedarfsspitzen abfangen zu können, legt die Gasunion tief im Boden unterirdische Lagervorräte an. Das Unternehmen exportiert große Mengen Erdgas nach Belgien, Deutschland, Frankreich, Italien und in die Schweiz.

En 1959, un gisement de gaz naturel a été découvert à Slochteren. Depuis, un grand nombre de puits ont été forés, non seulement sur la terre ferme, mais aussi en mer, sur la partie néerlandaise du plateau continental. La NAM (Société pétrolière néerlandaise) exploite le gaz, et la Gasunie assure son transport et sa distribution. L'entreprise gère et contrôle un réseau de plus de 10 000 km. Afin de pouvoir satisfaire la demande pendant les périodes de pointe, elle en stocke dans des réserves souterraines. L'entreprise exporte de grandes quantités de gaz naturel vers la Belgique, l'Allemagne, la France, la Suisse et l'Italie.

En 1.959 se halló gas natural en Holanda, en los campos de Slochteren. Desde entonces se han encontrado campanas de gas en muchos otros pueblos tanto de tierra firme como de las islas y tambien en el mar del Norte en la plataforma continental. La compañía NAM es la encargada de la extracción del gas. La empresa Gasunie es la responsable de su transporte y distribución. Esta empresa tiene el control y dominio sobre una red de transporte y distribución de mas de 10.000 km. Para poder suplir la demanda en tiempos de necesidad, Gasunie cuenta con diversos depósitos subterráneos de almacenamiento del gas. Tambien se exportan grandes cantidades de gas natural hacia Belgica, Alemania, Francia, Suiza e Italia.

Em 1959 encontrou-se no solo da Holanda gás natural, nos campos de Slochteren. Desde então apareceu uma grande quantidade de locais, não só no continente, mas também no mar no espaço continental, onde o gás é explorado pela companhia NAM. A União do Gás encarrega-se do transporte e da distribuição. A empresa administra e controla uma rede de transporte de mais de 10.000 km. Para que, durante períodos de ponto possa satisfazer à necessidade, a União do Gás pressiona uma grande quantidade de gás, como provisão, na profundidade da terra. A empresa exporta uma grande porção do gás para a Bélgica, a Alemanha, a França, a Suíça e a Itália.

De uitgestrekte akkers in het noorden van Groningen zijn op de zee gewonnen gebieden. De klei is bijzonder vruchtbaar. De voornaamste gewassen zijn graan en suikerbieten. Even buiten de stad Groningen werkt in het najaar de suikerfabriek op volle capaciteit (links). Het grondstation van Station 12 staat in Burum op de grens van Groningen en Friesland. Station 12, een onderdeel van KPN, is de eerste satelliettelefoon- , data- en faxservice ter wereld. Met een mobiele satelliet-telefoon, niet groter dan een laptopcomputer, kan van elke plek op aarde contact worden gemaakt met dit grondstation. Station 12 draagt zorg voor het doorschakelen naar de gewenste abonnee. Vooral de internationale scheepvaart maakt gebruik van deze diensten (rechts).

The huge arable farms in the north of Groningen were reclaimed from the sea. The clay is exceptionally fertile. The main crops are cereals and sugar beet. In the autumn the sugar factory just outside the city of Groningen (left) is at full capacity. The ground station of Station 12 is in Burum, on the border between Groningen and Friesland. Station 12, part of KPN, is the first satellite telephone, data and fax service in the world. Contact can be made with this ground station from anywhere on earth using a mobile satellite telephone no larger than a laptop computer. Station 12 connects the call to the subscriber in question. International shipping is one of the primary users of these services (right).

Die ausgedehnten Felder im Norden von Groningen liegen auf ehemaligem Meeresboden. Das Kleigebiet ist besonders fruchtbar. Hauptanbauprodukte sind Getreide und Zuckerrüben. Gleich am Stadtrand von Groningen arbeitet die Zuckerfabrik im Herbst mit voller Kapazität (links). Die Bodenstation von Station 12 in Burum steht an der Grenze zwischen Groningen und Friesland. Station 12, ein Teil von KPN, ist der erste Satellitendienst der Welt für Telefon, Datenübertragung und Fax. Mit einem mobilen Satellitentelefon, nicht größer als ein Laptop, kann man von jedem Ort der Erde zu dieser Bodenstation Kontakt aufnehmen. Station 12 sorgt für die Verbindung zum gewünschten Teilnehmer. Vor allem die internationale Schiffahrt macht von diesen Diensten Gebrauch (rechts).

Les vastes étendues de terres agricoles dans le Nord de la province de Groningue ont été gagnées sur la mer. Les argiles sont extrêmement fertiles. Les cultures les plus importantes sont les céréales et la betterave sucrière. Située un peu en dehors de la ville de Groningue, la raffinerie de sucre tourne à plein régime en automne (à gauche). 'Station 12' se trouve à Burum, aux limites des provinces de Groningue et de Frise. Cette station à terre fait partie du groupe KPN, le premier service de télécommunications et téléinformatique par satellite dans le monde. A l'aide d'un téléphone mobile pas plus encombrant qu'un micro-ordinateur portable, on peut contacter cette station depuis n'importe quel endroit au monde. Ensuite, elle se charge de la communication avec le correspondant désiré. C'est surtout la navigation internationale qui utilise ces services (à droite).

Los extensos campos al norte de Groninga son terrenos ganados al mar. Su tierra es muy fecunda. Los principales vegetales de cultivo son el grano y la remolacha azucarera. En el otoño, la fábrica de azucar a las afueras de Groninga, funciona por un corto periodo a pleno rendimiento (izquierda). La estación de comunicación con el satélite Station 12 se encuentra en Burum entre las provincias de Frisia y Groninga. Station 12, propiedad de la empresa KPN, es el primer satélite mundial de servicios de teléfono, fax y datos de informática. Con un teléfono móbil, no mayor que un ordenador de bolsillo, se puede tomar contacto con esta estación desde cualquier lugar del mundo. Station 12 se cuida de establecer la conexión con el abonado que se le solicite. Los servicios de esta estación son usados sobretodo por la navegacion maritima internacional (derecha).

Os imensos campos de cultura no Norte de Groningen foram conquistados ao mar. Os terrenos barrentos são muito fecundos. Os produtos que lá se cultivam são principalmente os cereais e a beterraba. Um pouco fora da cidade de Groningen funciona, durante o outono, uma fábrica de açúcar, a toda a capacidade (à esquerda). A estação terrestre da Estação 12 está em Burum na fronteira entre Groningen e Frísia. A Estação 12, que faz parte da KPN (=CTT), é o primeiro serviço no mundo de telefone, dados e fax via do satélite. Com um telefone móvel de satélite, quase do tamanho de um computador 'laptop', pode-se entrar em contacto com esta estação, de qualquer ponto da terra. A Estação 12 encarrega-se da ligação com os clientes desejados. Em especial a navegação internacional serve-se muito destes serviços (à direita).

De jaarlijkse boekenmarkt te Deventer is de grootste van Europa. Langs vrijwel alle straten in de binnenstad staan marktkramen met oude en nieuwe boeken. De duizenden kopers en handelaren komen van heinde en verre.
Deventer en Zwolle hebben beide een geschiedenis die doortrokken is van cultuur. In Zwolle is de Sassenpoort een van de best bewaarde monumenten. De poort is uitgerust met een zogenaamde mezenkooi, een boven de deuren uitgebouwde ruimte om indringers van bovenaf te kunnen bestoken. In de jaren zestig werd in Enschede de Universiteit Twente gesticht. De zesduizend studenten wonen op een moderne campus. De torenspits in de vijver is een grapje van de architect.

Deventer's annual book market is the largest in Europe. There are stalls selling new and second-hand books along virtually every street in the city centre. Thousands of buyers and dealers come from far and wide. Deventer and Zwolle both have histories steeped in culture. The Sassenpoort in Zwolle is one of the best preserved monuments. There is a room built out over the gates from where defenders could bombard attackers from above.
The University of Twente was built in Enschede in the nineteen-sixties. Six thousand students live on the modern campus. The steeple in the middle of the lake is a joke, courtesy of the architect.

Der jährliche Büchermarkt in Deventer ist der größte in ganz Europa. Auf fast allen Straßen des Stadtzentrums werden an Marktständen alte und neue Bücher feilgeboten. Käufer und Händler kommen zu Tausenden aus Nah und Fern. Deventer und Zwolle blicken beide auf eine kulturell reiche Geschichte zurück. In Zwolle ist das Sachsentor eines der besterhaltenen Baudenkmäler. Das Tor ist mit einem sogenannten Meisenkäfig ausgestattet, einem über den Toren ausgebauten Raum, von dem aus Eindringlinge von oben befeuert werden konnten.
In den sechziger Jahren wurde in Enschede die Universität Twente gegründet. Die sechstausend Studierenden wohnen auf einem modernen Campus. Die Turmspitze im Teich ist ein Scherz des Architekten.

La foire annuelle aux livres de Deventer est la plus grande d'Europe. Les rues du centre-ville sont couvertes d'étals où l'on vend des livres anciens et neufs aux milliers d'acheteurs et négociants venus de près et de loin. Deventer et Zwolle ont une histoire imprégnée de culture. A Zwolle, la Sassenpoort est un des vestiges les mieux conservés. La porte est équipée d'une 'mésangette', une sorte de petite pièce surmontant l'entrée, d'où on pouvait riposter aux assaillants. Dans les années soixante, l'université de Twente a été fondée à Enschede. Les six mille étudiants sont logés sur un campus moderne. La tour construite au milieu du bassin est un clin d'oeil humoristique de l'architecte.

En Deventer se celebra el mercado del libro mas grande de Europa. En casi todas las calles hay tenderetes con libros tanto nuevos como antiguos. Los visitantes a este mercado vienen de todas partes del mundo. Tanto Deventer como Zwolle poseen una historia impregnada de cultura. La puerta Sassenpoort de Zwolle es uno de los monumentos mejor conservados. Esta puerta esta provista de un torrejón de defensa situado encima mismo de ella para desde arriba poder defenderla mejor. Durante los años sesenta se fundó en Enschede la universidad de Twente. Los seis mil estudiantes son cobijados en un moderno campus universitario. La puntiaguda torre en el estanque fué una broma del arquitecto.

O mercado anual do livro em Deventer é o maior da Europa. Por quase todas as ruas no centro da cidade se encontram os lugares de venda de livros velhos e novos. Os milhares de compradores e negociantes vêm de toda a parte. Deventer e Zwolle têm ambas uma história rica de cultura. Em Zwolle o portal 'de Sassenpoort' é um dos monumentos mais bem conservados. O portal tem em cima uma chamada 'gaiola de pássaros', que era usada para se defenderem dos estranhos indesejáveis. Nos anos sessenta foi fundada em Enschede a Universidade de Twente. Os seis mil estudantes moram na moderna 'cidade universitária'. A ponta da torre, que está na água, foi uma brincadeira do arquitecto.

De witte watermolen behoort bij het Park Sonsbeek te Arnhem. In dit park worden sinds de jaren vijftig een internationale exposities van moderne beeldhouwkunst georganiseerd.In de provincie Gelderland ligt ook Bronkhorst, het kleinste stadje van Nederland. Het bezit officiële stadsrechten vanaf het begin van de Middeleeuwen. Een deel van het natuurgebied de Veluwe ten noorden van Arnhem is het Nationaal Park de Hoge Veluwe. Het park is mede bekend vanwege het Jachtslot Hubertus en het Rijksmuseum Kröller-Müller.

The white water mill is in Park Sonsbeek in Arnhem. International exhibitions of modern sculpture have been held in the park since the beginning of the nineteen-fifties. Elsewhere in the province is Bronkhorst, the smallest town in the Netherlands. It has had official town status since the early Middle Ages. The National Park the Hoge Veluwe is part of the Veluwe nature reserve to the north of Arnhem. The park's well-known attractions include the Hubertus hunting lodge and the Kröller-Muller Museum.

Die weiße Wassermühle gehört zum Sonsbeek Park in Arnheim. In diesem Park werden seit den fünfziger Jahren internationale Ausstellungen moderner Bildhauerei organisiert. In derselben Provinz liegt auch Bronkhorst, die kleinste Stadt der Niederlande. Seit Beginn des Mittelalters besitzt sie offiziell die Stadtrechte. Ein Teil des Naturgebiets Veluwe nördlich von Arnheim ist der Nationalpark De Hoge Veluwe. Der Park ist unter anderem bekannt durch das Jagdschloß St. Hubertus und das Reichsmuseum Kröller-Müller.

Le 'moulin blanc', un moulin à eau, se dresse dans le Parc de Sonsbeek aux environs d'Arnhem. Depuis les années cinquante, des expositions internationales de sculpture moderne sont organisées ici. Dans la même province se trouve la plus petite ville des Pays-Bas, Bronkhorst. Elle possède les droits de cité depuis le début du moyen âge. Une partie de l'espace naturel au nord d'Arnhem est occupé par le parc national de la Haute Veluwe, qui abrite le célèbre musée Kröller-Müller et le pavillon de chasse St-Hubert.

Los blancos molinos de agua se encuentran en el parque Sonsbeek de Arnhem. Desde los años cinquenta se organiza en este parque una exposición internacional del arte escultórico moderno. En esta misma provincia se encuentra Bronkhorst, la ciudad mas pequeña de Holanda. Sus derechos de ciudadanía le fueron concedidos ya al principio de la edad media. Una parte de la zona natural llamada Veluwe, la situada al norte de la ciudad de Arnhem, compone el Parque Nacional Hoge Veluwe. Ademas de por sus campos y bosques, en este parque encontramos el museo Rijksmuseum Kröller-Muller y el castillo Jachtslot Hubertus.

O moinho de água branco faz parte do Parque de Sonsbeek, em Arnhem. Neste parque organizam-se desde os anos cinquenta exposições internacionais de arquitectura moderna. Na mesma província encontra-se também Bronkhorst, a cidade mais pequena da Holanda. Ela possui, oficialmente, os direitos de cidade já desde os princípios da Idade Média. Uma parte da região natural 'de Veluwe', ao norte de Arnhem é o Parque Nacional 'de Hoge Veluwe'. O parque é também muito conhecido graças ao Castelo da Caça Hubertus e o Museu Nacional Kröler-Muller.

In Nederland zijn 9000 tuinbouw-bedrijven verenigd in één coöperatie, The Greenery. Het aanbod van de kwekers is zeer uitgebreid, want in Nederland wordt sinds tientallen jaren een groot aantal subtropische producten onder glas geteeld. Vele kassen worden verwarmd met de restwarmte van de industrie. Zo worden het hele jaar door tomaten, paprika's, courgettes en allerlei soorten sla vers naar de veiling aangevoerd. Naast de traditionele verkoop via de veilingklok houdt The Greenery zich bezig met marketing, consumentenonderzoek en onderhoudt ze de langlopende contacten met buitenlandse afnemers.

Nine thousand horticulture firms in the Netherlands belong to one cooperative, The Greenery. The range of products from the growers is very broad, because for decades a large number of subtropical plants have been cultivated in the Netherlands under glass. Many of the greenhouses are heated with waste heat from industry. The auctions are therefore supplied with tomatoes, peppers, courgettes and all sorts of salad vegetables all year round. In addition to selling through the auctions, The Greenery is also active in marketing and consumer surveys, and it maintains long-term contacts with foreign customers.

In den Niederlanden haben sich 9000 Gartenbaubetriebe zu einer Genossenschaft, The Greenery, zusammengeschlossen. Das Angebot der Züchter ist sehr breit gefächert, denn in den Niederlanden werden schon seit Jahrzehnten unzählige subtropische Produkte unter Glas gezüchtet. Viele der Treibhäuser werden mit der Abwärme von Industriebetrieben geheizt. So werden das ganze Jahr frische Tomaten, Paprika, Zucchini und allerlei Salatsorten zu den Auktionshallen gebracht. Neben dem traditionellen Verkauf per Versteigerungsuhr befaßt sich The Greenery mit Marketing oder Verbraucherstudien und pflegt langjährige Kontakte zu ausländischen Abnehmern.

Aux Pays-Bas, 9000 exploitations horticoles sont réunies en une seule coopérative. Les néerlandais ont une longue tradition de culture en serres, ce qui explique la grande diversité des produits. De nombreuses serres sont chauffées avec l'énergie restante des industries. Ainsi, le marché est alimenté toute l'année en tomates, courgettes et diverses laitues. 'The Greenery', le service marketing-vente de la coopérative, s'occupe de la traditionnelle vente aux enchères, effectue des études de marché auprès des consommateurs et entretient les contacts avec les clients étrangers.

En Holanda hay 9.000 empresas de horticultura agrupados en una sola asociación: The Greenery. La oferta de los horticultores es muy variada dado que desde hace ya bastantes años se cultivan productos tropicales en invernaderos. Muchos de estos invernaderos proveen su calefacción del calor sobrante de empresas industriales. De esta manera se abastecen las subastas durante todo el año de verduras frescas como tomates, pimientos, pepinos y varios tipos de ensaladas. La asociación The Greenery, ademas de dirigir la venta tradicional de estos productos por medio de subastas, se encarga de realizar estudios de venta y de mercado asi como de mantener las largas relaciones con sus clientes extranjeros.

Na Holanda existem 9000 empresas de horticultura ligadas numa Cooperativa, 'The Greenery'. Os produtos postos à disposição pelos horticultores são imensos, porque na Holanda são produzidos, há dezenas de anos, muitíssimos produtos subtrópicos cultivados em estufas de vidro. Muitas destas estufas são aquecidas com o calor desperdiçado pela indústria. Desta maneira durante todo o ano são apresentados no leilão tomates, pimentos, 'courgetes' e uma grande variedade de alfaces, sempre frescos. Paralelamente à venda tradicional, por meio do 'relógio do leilão', The Greenery pratica também o 'marketing', os estudos do consumo e mantém os contactos a longo prazo com os compradores estrangeiros.

Vroeger werd er alleen kaas gemaakt in de weidegebieden van Noord-Holland en Zuid-Holland. Dat was de tijd dat alleen de kazen uit Edam en Gouda in het buitenland bekend waren. Nog steeds is de export van Goudse en Edammer het grootst, maar genieten ook de kazen uit andere streken van Nederland grotere bekendheid. De afbeeldingen tonen het kaasmaken op de boerderij. De melk wordt op temperatuur gebracht en er wordt stremsel toegevoegd om de melk te verdikken. De wrongel, de verdikte melk wordt in een kaasvorm uitgeperst. Hierna gaan de kazen in een pekelbad en moeten zij rijpen.

In past times cheese was only made in the pasture regions of North Holland and South Holland. In those days the only cheeses known outside the country were from Edam and Gouda. The export of Gouda and Edam cheeses still represents the biggest slice, but cheeses from other parts of the Netherlands are now becoming better known. The illustrations show cheese being made on the farm. The milk is heated up and then rennet is added to thicken it. The curd or thickened milk is pressed into a cheese mould. The cheeses go into a brine bath and then they are left to mature.

Früher wurde nur in den Weidegebieten von Nordholland und Südholland Käse hergestellt. Damals kannte man im Ausland nur Käse aus Edam und Gouda. Zwar wird noch immer am meisten Gouda und Edamer exportiert, doch sind inzwischen auch Käse aus anderen Gegenden der Niederlande bekannt. Die Abbildungen zeigen die Käseherstellung auf dem Bauernhof. Die Milch wird auf die richtige Temperatur gebracht, und es wird Lab hinzugefügt, damit die Milch gerinnt. Der Käsebruch, d. h. die eingedickte Milch, wird in einer Käseform gepreßt. Danach werden die Käselaibe in Salzlake eingelegt, und anschließend beginnt der Reifungsprozeß.

A l'époque, on ne fabriquait du fromage que dans les terres de pâturage de la Hollande-Septentrionale et Méridionale. Seuls étaient connus à l'étranger les fromages d'Edam et de Gouda. Bien qu'ils représentent toujours la plus grande part des exportations, les fromages d'autres régions se font également un nom. Les images montrent la fabrication du fromage à la ferme. Le lait est rechauffé, on y ajoute de la présure pour le faire cailler, puis la caillebotte est pressée dans une forme à fromage. Après avoir été salés, les fromages sont mis en affinage.

Antiguamente se hacia queso solo en las regiones de tierras de pasto de la Holanda septentrional y meridional. Era el tiempo en que en el extranjero solo se conocían los quesos de Edam y Gouda. Hoy en día continúan siendo estos quesos los de mayor exportación pero hay tambien quesos de otras regiones que empiezan a gozar de merecida fama. La ilustracion nos muestra la forma de realizar el queso en la granja. La leche se calienta a la temperatura ideal y se le añade cuajo para espesarla. La cuajada resultante se coloca en un molde para ser exprimida. Seguidamente se le da un baño de salmuera y se la deja madurar.

Antigamente só se fazia queijo nas regiões de pastagem de Noord-Holland e Zuid-Holland. Era nesse tempo, que no estrangeiro só se conhecia o queijo de Edam e Gouda. Ainda agora os Queijos de Edam e de Gouda são os mais exportados, mas também os queijos de outras regiões da Holanda gozam de grande fama. As imagens mostram a feitura do queijo numa granja. O leite é levado à temperatura e adiciona-se-lhe coalheira para engrossar o leite. O requeijão adquirido é, em seguida, prensado numa forma do queijo. Depois disso os queijos são metidos em salmoura e têm que 'amadurecer'.

KERK
61

De Nederlandse Spoorwegen werken samen met de overheid aan twee grote projecten om de infrastructuur te verbeteren. In 2005 wordt het laatste deel voltooid van de HSL-verbindingen in zuidelijke richting. De reistijden per trein naar Parijs en naar Londen worden dan dermate verkort dat de trein een aantrekkelijk alternatief voor het vliegtuig moet worden. Voorts wordt tussen de Rotterdamse haven en de Duitse grens de Betuwelijn aangelegd. Het wordt een min of meer geautomatiseerde goederenspoorlijn van 160 kilometer. Het vervoer van containers zal hierdoor drastisch worden ontlast.
De uitvoering van dergelijke projecten grijpen diep in in een dichtbevolkt land als Nederland.

NS Netherlands Railways are working with the government on two major projects to improve the infrastructure. The last section of the southbound HSL links will be completed in 2005. Journey times by rail to Paris and London will be cut to such an extent that the train will become an attractive alternative to flying. The Betuwe Line is also being built between the port of Rotterdam and the German border. This will be an almost totally automated goods line 160 kilometres long, which will significantly relieve the pressure on container transport. Projects like these have a major impact in a densely populated country like the Netherlands.

Die niederländische Eisenbahngesellschaft arbeitet mit der Regierung an zwei Großprojekten zur Verbesserung der Infrastruktur zusammen. 2005 wird der letzte Abschnitt der Hochgeschwindigkeitstrasse nach Süden fertiggestellt. Die Reisezeiten per Zug nach Paris und London reduzieren sich dadurch so stark, daß die Bahn zur echten Alternative zum Flugzeug wird. Ferner wird zwischen dem Rotterdamer Hafen und der deutschen Grenze die Betuwe-Strecke gebaut. Dabei handelt es sich um eine mehr oder weniger automatisierte Güterbahnlinie mit einer Länge von 160 Kilometern. Der Container-Transport soll dadurch beträchtlich entlastet werden.
Derartige Projekte stellen in einem so dicht besiedelten Land wie den Niederlanden einen tiefgreifenden Einschnitt dar.

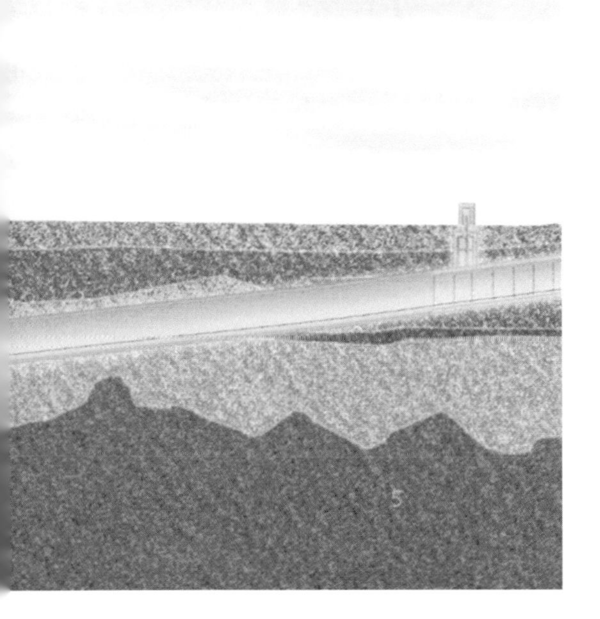

En association avec le gouvernement, les chemins de fer néerlandais (Nederlandse Spoorwegen) travaillent sur deux projets importants visant à l'amélioration de l'infrastructure. En 2005, le dernier tracé du réseau TGV en direction du sud sera achevé. La durée des voyages en train vers Paris et Londres sera raccourcie à tel point, que le train peut devenir une solution attrayante remplaçant l'avion. Le deuxième projet concerne la construction de la ligne du Betuwe, un tracé de 160 km semi-automatisé pour le transport de marchandises entre le port de Rotterdam et la frontière allemande. Cette ligne décongestionnera considérablement le transport par conteneurs. La réalisation de tels projets a un impact énorme sur un pays à population aussi dense que les Pays-Bas.

Los ferrocarriles holandeses cooperan con el gobierno en dos proyectos importantes de mejora de la infraestructura del pais. En el 2.005 se terminará el último trayecto en dirección meridional del tren HSL de gran velocidad. El tiempo de viaje a Paris y Londres se habrá acortado tanto que el tren será una buena alternativa para competir con el viaje aéreo. Al mismo tiempo se está construyendo una línea de ferrocarril entre el puerto de Rotterdam y la frontera alemana, la llamada Betuwelijn. Esta trayecto de 160 km. se convertirá en una línea de transporte de mercancías mas o menos automática que descongestionará en gran medida el actual transporte de contenedores. La realización de estos proyectos es de gran importancia en un pais tan densamente poblado como es Holanda.

Os Caminhos de Ferro holandeses colaboram com as autoridades nacionais em dois projectos grandes para melhorar a infraestrutura. Em 2005 será acabada a última parte de uma ligação para o Sul do CGV. Os tempos de viagem por comboio para Paris e para Londres serão de tal maneira reduzidos que o comboio deverá passar a ser uma alternativa vantajosa, par o avião. Além disso será construída a Linha da Betuwe, entre o porto de Roterdão e a fronteira da Alemanha. Será uma linha de mercadorias automatizada de 160 km. O transporte de contentores passará, assim, a ser bastante descongestionado. A realização de projectos deste calibre têm muita influência num país populoso como a Holanda.

Bewoners uit andere delen van Nederland gaan graag met vakantie naar Limburg. Het landschap is er heuvelachtig en de mensen zijn er vriendelijk, gastvrij en zijn liefhebbers van lekker eten. Jaarlijks wordt op Het Vrijthof in Maastricht een groot culinair feest gehouden, het Preuvenement, maar ook op andere mooie dagen zijn de terrassen hier overvol.
Na het sluiten van der kolenmijnen heeft de overheid maatregelen genomen om de werkgelegenheid te stimuleren. De oude staatsmijnen zijn omgevormd tot het chemie-concern DSM; het vliegveld bij Beek is uitgebouwd tot Maastricht-Aachen Airport en in Born is een automobielfabriek gebouwd waar Volvo's en Mitsubishi's gezamenlijk van de band rollen.

People who live in other parts of the Netherlands love holidaying in Limburg. The landscape is hilly, and the people are friendly, hospitable and enjoy good food. A huge culinary festival – the Preuvenement – is held annually in a square in Maastricht, but the pavement cafés are full here on any fine day.
When the pits were closed, the government took steps to stimulate employment opportunities in the region. The old state-owned coal mines were transformed into the chemical company DSM, the airfield at Beek was expanded to become Maastricht-Aachen Airport and a car factory producing Volvos and Mitsubishis was built in Born.

Bewohner anderer Teile der Niederlande verbringen ihren Urlaub gerne in der Provinz Limburg. Die hügelige Landschaft hat es ihnen ebenso angetan wie die netten, gastfreundlichen Menschen dort, die zudem als kulinarische Genießer gelten. Jedes Jahr findet auf einem Platz in Maastricht ein großes kulinarisches Fest statt, das Preuvenement, aber auch an anderen schönen Tagen sind die Terrassen hier gut besucht.
Nach der Schließung der Kohlebergwerke wurden staatliche Förderprogramme zur Schaffung von Arbeitsplätzen eingerichtet. Die ehemaligen Staatsminen wurden zum Chemie-Konzern DSM; der Flughafen bei Beek wurde zum Maastricht-Aachen-Airport ausgebaut, und in Born entstand eine Automobilfabrik, in der Volvo und Mitsubishi gemeinsam vom Band rollen.

Les habitants des autres régions néerlandaises aiment partir en vacances au Limbourg. Le paysage est vallonné, les gens sont sympathiques, ils ont le sens de l'hospitalité et sont des amateurs de gastronomie. Tous les ans, une grande fête culinaire se tient sur une place à Maastricht, le 'Preuvenement'. Mais, les terrasses sont également très fréquentées à chaque rayon de soleil. Après la fermeture des mines de charbon, le gouvernement a pris des mesures pour stimuler l'emploi. Les anciennes mines se sont transformées en industrie chimique, le groupe DSM; l'aéroport de Beek, agrandi, est devenu le Maastricht-Aachen Airport, et à Born a été construite une usine d'automobiles. De ses chaines sortent des véhicules Volvo et Mitsubishi.

La región de Limburgo es muy apreciada por los habitantes de las otras partes de Holanda como lugar de vacaciones. El paisaje es ligeramente montañoso, sus gentes son muy amables y hospitalarias y aficionados al buen comer. En Maastricht se celebra anualmente una popular fiesta culinaria, la llamada Preuvenement. En los buenos dias del resto del año las terrazas de la ciudad son tambien animadamente concurridas. Despues del cierre de las minas de carbón, el gobierno tomó medidas para estimular la creación de puestos de trabajo en esta región. Las viejas minas estatales han dado paso a la actual industria química DSM; el aeropuerto de Beek ha crecido para ser ahora el aeropuerto Maastricht-Aachen (Aquisgran) y en Born se ha construido una moderna fábrica de automóbiles en la que se fabrican al mismo tiempo coches de la marca Volvo y Mitsubishi.

Habitantes de outras partes da Holanda gostam de ir de férias a Limburg. A paisagem é montanhosa e as pessoas lá são simpáticas, hospitaleiras e gostam muito de boas comidas. Todos os anos se realiza, numa praça em Maastricht, uma grande festa culinária, o 'Preuvenement', mas também em outros dias as esplanadas estão cheias de gente. Depois do encerramento das minas de carvão as autoridades tomaram medidas de precaução para criar pontos de trabalho. As velhas minas do Estado foram transformadas numa companhia química a DSM; o campo de aviação de Beek foi ampliado e passou a ser o Maastricht-Aachen Airport e em Born foi construída uma fábrica de automóveis, onde os Volvos e os Mitsubishis saiem da faixa lado a lado.

De bewoners van Noord-Brabant hebben ook een ietwat Bourgondische levensstijl. Net als de Limburgers vieren zij uitbundig carnaval. Deze van oudsher agrarische provincie is de bakermat van het elektronica-concern Philips, maar ook buitenlandse bedrijven als General Electric en Fuji hebben hier hun vestigingen.
In Zeeland beperkt de industrie zich tot de steden Vlissingen (links) en Terneuzen. Eerst door de aanleg van de dammen in het kader van de Deltawerken zijn de Zeeuwse eilanden ontsloten. Vooral het toerisme profiteert hiervan.

The people of North Brabant also have a good feel for the fine things in life. Like the people of Limburg, they celebrate the carnival (Mardi Gras) in a big way. This province, which traditionally was heavily reliant on agriculture, was the cradle of the electronics giant Philips, and now foreign firms like General Electric and Fuji have located here. Industry in Zeeland is limited to the cities of Vlissingen (left) and Terneuzen. Access to the Zeeland islands was provided by the construction of dams which were part of the Delta project. Tourism has benefitted greatly from this.

Die Einwohner von Nord-Brabant pflegen ebenfalls einen lebensfrohen und ausgelassenen Lebensstil. Ebenso wie die Limburger feiern sie ausgiebig Karneval. Diese von jeher landwirtschaftlich geprägte Provinz war die Wiege des Elektronikkonzern Philips, aber auch ausländische Firmen wie General Electric und Fuji haben hier ihre Niederlassungen. In Zeeland beschränkt sich die Industrie auf die Städte Vlissingen (links) und Terneuzen. Erst durch den Bau der Dämme im Rahmen der Deltawerke wurden die zeeländischen Inseln erschlossen. Davon profitiert vor allem der Fremdenverkehr.

On reconnaît les habitants du Brabant-Septentrional à leur style de vie quelque peu bourguignon. Comme les Limbourgeois, ils fêtent le carnaval avec exubérance. La province, à l'origine agricole, était le berceau du groupe électronique Philips, mais des sociétés étrangères, comme General Electric et Fuji, ont ici aussi leurs établissements. En Zélande, l'industrie se limite aux villes de Vlissingen (à g.) et Terneuzen. Le désenclavement des îles zélandaises a commencé seulement après la construction des barrages dans le cadre du plan Delta. C'est le tourisme qui en tire le plus grand profit.

Los habitantes del Brabante septentrional tienen también una forma de vida algo borgoñesa. Al igual que los limburgueses celebran de forma extraordinaria el carnaval. En esta provincia típicamente agraria, nació la gran empresa electrónica Philips y se han establecido aquí tambien grandes empresas internacionales como General Electric y Fuji. En Zelandia la situación de la industria se localiza en las ciudades de Vlissingen y Terneuzen. Las islas zeelandesas se cerraron con la construcción de los diques necesarios para el plan del Deltawerken. Los turistas son los mas beneficiados de ello.

Os habitantes de Noord-Brabant têm também de certo modo o estilo de vida borgonhês. Assim como os limburgueses eles festejam o Carnaval com grande entusiasmo. Esta província desde há muito tempo com um carácter agrário, foi o berço da companhia electrónica Philips, mas também empresas estrangeiras como a General Electric e a Fuji têm aqui as suas sucursais. Na Zelândia a indústria limita-se às cidades Vlissingen (à esquerda) e Terneuzen. Só depois da construção de diques, no âmbito das Obras do Delta, as ilhas da Zelândia perderam o seu isolamento. Especialmente o turismo ganhou muito com isso.

Reeds eeuwen worden hier koopvaardijschepen en marineschepen gebouwd. Op de werven van de Koninklijke Schelde Groep te Vlissingen lopen beide categorieën van stapel. Sinds de Tweede Wereldoorlog is Nederland sterk in het ontwerpen en bouwen van geavanceerde marineschepen. De ontwerpers werken nauw samen met de Koninklijke Marine. Vooral de fregatten worden geleverd naar alle werelddelen. Links: koningin Beatrix bij de doop van een veerboot; midden: een fregat op volle zee en rechts: de marinehaven in Den Helder tijdens open dagen.

Merchant vessels and fighting ships have been built here for centuries. Both categories are still being launched from the yards of the Royal Schelde Group in Vlissingen. The Netherlands has had a strong position since the Second World War in the design and building of advanced naval ships. The designers work closely with the Royal Netherlands Navy. Ships, particularly frigates, are sold in all parts of the world. Left: Queen Beatrix at the launch of a ferry; centre: a frigate on the high seas and right: the naval base at Den Helder during an open day.

Bereits seit Jahrhunderten werden hier Handels- und Marineschiffe gebaut. Auf den Werften der Koninklijke Schelde Groep in Vlissingen laufen beide Schiffsarten vom Stapel. Seit dem Zweiten Weltkrieg sind die Niederlande groß im Entwerfen und Bauen fortschrittlicher Marineschiffe. Die Schiffsbauer arbeiten eng mit der Königlichen Marine zusammen. Vor allem die Fregatten werden in alle Welt geliefert. Links: Königin Beatrix bei der Taufe eines Fährschiffs; Mitte: Fregatte auf hoher See und rechts: Tag der offenen Tür im Marinehafen von Den Helder.

Depuis de longs siècles, on construit ici des navires marchands et de marine de guerre. Les deux catégories sont lancées au chantier naval du Groupe Koninklijke Schelde à Vlissingen. Depuis la Deuxième Guerre Mondiale, les Pays-Bas se sont fortement développés en matière de conception et de construction de bateaux de marine. Les constructeurs collaborent étroitement avec la Marine Royale. On exporte notamment des frégates sur tous les continents. A gauche : La Reine Béatrix lors du baptême d'un ferry; au milieu : une frégate en pleine mer, et à droite : la base navale à Den Helder, pendant une journée portes ouvertes.

Desde siglos se construyen aquí barcos tanto mercantes como de la marina. De los astilleros de la empresa Koninklijke Schelde Groep de Vlissingen se botan continuamente ambos tipos de barcos. A partir de la Segunda Guerra Mundial Holanda se ha especializado en el diseño y construcción de barcos para la marina. Sus diseñadores trabajan en estrecha cooperación con la Marina Real. En especial sus fragatas son exportadas a paises de todo el mundo. Izquierda: la reina Beatriz en la ceremonia bautismal de un transbordador; en medio: una fragata en alta mar y derecha: el puerto naval de Den Helder durante su dia de visita.

Jà há séculos se construíam aqui barcos das marinhas mercante e de guerra. Nos estaleiros do Grupo Real Schelde, em Vlissingen são lançados ambos os tipos de navios. Desde a Segunda Guerra Mundial a Holanda é um país predominante no desenho e na construção de barcos de guerra, de qualidade superior. Os desenhadores colaboram intimamente com a Marinha Real da Holanda. Nomeadamente as fragatas são fornecidas para todas as partes do mundo. À esquerda: a Rainha Beatriz na inauguração de um barco de travessia; ao meio: uma fragata em pleno mar e à direita: o porto da Marinha em Den Helder, durante um dia de visitas.

Na de aanleg van de Nieuwe Waterweg ontwikkelde Rotterdam zich in hoog tempo tot een van de belangrijkste havens van Europa. Havensteden hebben vaak schilderachtige plekken. De stoomsleepboot 'Furie' dateert nog uit de beginperiode van de grote zeesleep- en bergingsbedrijven. De Oude Haven is in gebruik als Museum voor de Binnenvaart. Het water wordt omzoomd door tientallen terrassen. De zeilschepen maken van de Parkkade een oase van rust in een overigens hectische stad. In het voormalige hoofdkantoor van de Holland Amerika Lijn is nu hotel New York gevestigd. In de periode tussen de twee wereldoorlogen vertrokken van hieruit duizenden emigranten naar Amerika.3

After the construction of the New Waterway, Rotterdam grew fast to become one of the most important ports in Europe. Ports often have picturesque corners. The steam tug Furie dates back to the initial period of the major tug and salvage companies. The Oude Haven is used as a museum of inland shipping. The water is surrounded by dozens of pavement cafés. Sailing craft make the Parkkade an oasis of peace in an otherwise hectic city. The former head office of the Holland America Line is now the New York Hotel. It was from here that hundreds of thousands of emigrants set sail to America between the two world wars.

Nach dem Bau des Nieuwe Waterweg entwickelte sich Rotterdam schnell zu einem der wichtigsten Häfen Europas. In Hafenstädten findet man oft malerische Fleckchen. Das Dampfschleppschiff Furie stammt noch aus der Anfangszeit der großen Hochseeschlepp- und Bergungsbetriebe. Der Alte Hafen dient als Museum für die Binnenschiffahrt. Das Wasser ist von unzähligen Terassen umsäumt. Die Segelschiffe machen die Parkkade zu einer Oase der Ruhe inmitten der sonst so hektischen Stadt. Im ehemaligen Hauptsitz der Holland Amerika Lijn befindet sich jetzt das Hotel New York. Zwischen den beiden Weltkriegen legten von hier Tausende Auswanderer nach Amerika ab.

Après le creusement de la voie d'eau, la Nieuwe Waterweg, Rotterdam devint très vite l'un des ports les plus important d'Europe. Les villes portuaires possèdent souvent des coins pittoresques. La Furie, un remorqueur à vapeur, la Furie, date du début de l'ère des grandes entreprises de renflouement et de remorquage en haute mer. L'Ancien Port, bordé sur son pourtour de terrasses, n'accueille que des barges désaffectés appartenant au musée de la navigation fluviale. Les voiliers transforment le Parkkade en une oasis de tranquillité au milieu de cette ville agitée. Dans l'ancien siège principal de la Ligne Hollande-Amérique s'est établi aujourd'hui l'hôtel New York. Entre les deux guerres mondiales, des milliers d'émigrants ont embarqué d'ici pour l'Amérique.

Despues de la construccion de salida al mar Nieuwe Waterweg, Rotterdam se convirtió en poco tiempo en uno de los puertos mas importantes de Europa. Las ciudades portuarias tienen a menudo rincones pintorescos. El remolcador de vapor Furie fué construido al principio de la formación de las grandes compañías de remolcadores y de salvamento. El puerto viejo es usado actualmente como museo de la navegación interior. Alrededor del agua se han establecido numerosas terrazas. Los barcos veleros hacen del Parkkade un oasis de paz dentro del bullício de la ciudad. En lo que fueran las oficinas centrales de la compañia naviera Holland-America, se encuentra actualmente el hotel New York. En los años de entre las dos guerras mundiales salieron de aquí miles de emigrantes hacia America.

Depois da construção da Nieuwe Waterweg (Nova Via Fluvial), Roterdão desenvolveu-se rapidamente a um dos portos mais importantes da Europa. Cidades portuárias têm muitas vezes locais pitorescos. O barco a vapor Furie data ainda do período inicial das grandes empresas de rebocagem e salvação. O Antigo Cais é usado presentemente com Museu da Navegação Fluvial. A água está rodeada por dezenas de esplanadas. Os barcos à vela formam no Cais do Parque um oásis de sossego numa cidade, de resto, turbulenta. No antigo escritório central da Holland Amerika Lijn está agora "alojado' o hotel New York. No período entre as duas guerras mundiais partiram daqui milhares de emigrantes para a América.

Door de overslag van olie, erts en containers is Rotterdam de grootste haven van de wereld geworden. Bij de terminal van ECT zijn alle activiteiten computergestuurd. Weinigen weten dat in de haven meer dan een miljoen ton fruit per jaar wordt gelost. De citrusveiling is de enige in Europa.

The handling of oil, ore and containers made Rotterdam the biggest port in the world. All the activities at the ECT terminal are computer controlled. Not many people know that more than a million tonnes of fruit a year are unloaded in the port. The citrus auction is the only one in Europe.

Durch den Umschlag von Erdöl, Erz und Containern wurde Rotterdam zum größten Hafen der Welt. Am ECT-Terminal werden alle Abläufe computergesteuert. Nur wenige wissen, daß im Hafen mehr als eine Million Tonnen Obst gelöscht wird. Die Zitrusfrüchteauktion ist europaweit die einzige.

Le transbordement du pétrole, des minerais et des conteneurs a fait de Rotterdam le premier port du monde. Au terminal du groupe ECT, toutes les activités sont pilotées par ordinateur. Peu de gens savent que plus qu'un million de tonnes de fruits sont déchargés dans le port. Le marché aux agrumes est le seul en Europe

Como consecuencia del transbordo de petróleos, minerales y contenedores, Rotterdam se ha convertido en el puerto mayor del mundo. Un ordenador regula todas las actividades de la terminal de ECT. Poco conocido es el hecho de que en Rotterdam se descarga un millon de toneladas de fruta. Su subasta de frutos cítricos es la única en Europa.

Graças ao transbordo de nafta, minérios e contentores Roterdão passou a ser o maior porto do mundo. No terminal da ECT as actividades são dirigidas por meio de computadores. Pouca gente sabe que no porto são descarregadas mais de um milhão de toneladas de fruta. O leilão de frutos citrinos é o único na Europa.

ect
26
NELCON
SEA-LAND QUALITY
544
525

EVERGREEN
EVERGREEN

Rond de datum 5 december kloppen de harten van veel kinderen sneller. De verjaardag van Sint Nicolaas wordt op deze dag gevierd. In elke stad en in elk dorp wordt de goedheiligman ingehaald en toegezongen door de schooljeugd. Meestal rijdt Sinterklaas op een schimmel, maar in het dorp Zegveld wordt hij rond gereden in een open koets. Het feest wordt hier gevierd sinds de 16de eeuw.
De verjaardag van de Koningin wordt gevierd op 30 april. In Amsterdam en in vele andere steden is een vrijmarkt onderdeel vande festiviteiten. De vrijmarkt in Amsterdam is oorspronkelijk bedoeld voor kinderen. Jaarlijks trekken rond een miljoen bezoekers naar dit festijn.

The hearts of Dutch children start to beat a little faster around 5 December. That's the day when the birthday of Sint Nicolaas, or Santa Claus, is celebrated in the Netherlands. The holy man is welcomed in every town and village and sung to by school children. The Sint usually rides a white horse, but in the village of Zegveld he rides in an open coach. His arrival has been celebrated here since the sixteenth century.
The Queen's birthday is celebrated on 30 April. A market where members of the public can sell items is part of the festivities in Amsterdam and many other towns and cities. The market in Amsterdam was originally intended for children. It attracts around a million visitors every year.

Um den 5. Dezember schlagen viele Kinderherzen höher. An diesem Tag wird der Geburtstag des Heiligen Nikolaus gefeiert. In jeder Stadt und jedem Dorf wird der Heilige ins Haus geholt und von den Schulkindern besungen. Meist reitet der Nikolaus auf einem Schimmel, aber im Dorf Zegveld wird er in einer offenen Kutsche gefahren. Das Fest wird hier seit dem 16. Jahrhundert gefeiert.
Der Geburtstag der Königin wird am 30. April gefeiert. In Amsterdam und vielen anderen Städten gehört zum Fest auch ein Jahrmarkt. Der Amsterdamer Jahrmarkt war ursprünglich für Kinder bestimmt. Jedes Jahr zieht dieses Ereignis rund eine Million Besucher an.

Autour du 5 décembre, beaucoup d'enfants ont le coeur qui bat plus fort. Ce soir-là, on fête Saint Nicolas. Dans chaque ville et dans chaque village, le Saint fait son entrée, et la jeunesse l'accueille avec des chants. Le plus souvent, le Saint monte sur un cheval blanc, mais dans le village de Zegveld il est promené en calèche. Cette tradition remonte au 16e s.
Le 30 avril, tout le pays célèbre l'anniversaire de la reine. Amsterdam et beaucoup d'autres villes se transforment en un vaste marché libre de taxes. A l'origine, ce marché fut organisé par les enfants. Chaque année, l'événement attire un million de visiteurs.

Acercándose la fecha del 5 de diciembre, los corazones de todos los niños empiezan a latir mas aceleradamente. Ese dia se celebra el cumpleaños de San Nicolas. Todas las ciudades y pueblos del pais acogen festivamente la llegada del santo al que cantan los niños de todas las escuelas. Normalmente San Nicolas cabalga sobre un caballo blanco menos en el pueblo de Zegveld que lo hace en una carroza abierta. Esta fiesta se celebra en Holanda desde el siglo XVI.
La fiesta de cumpleaños de la reina se celebra el 30 de abril. En Amsterdam y otras muchas ciudades el mercado libre de baratillo forma parte de esta celebración. Originalmente se trataba de un mercadillo para niños que con el tiempo ha tomado dimensiones extraordinarias. Cada año cerca de un millon de visitantes se acercan a esta celebración en Amsterdam.

Por volta da data de 5 de dezembro os corações de muitas crianças batem com maior força. O aniversário do São Nicolau é festejado nesse dia. Em todas as cidades e aldeias é recebido o santo homem, ao qual as crianças cantam cantigas especiais. Na maioria dos casos o São Nicolau anda no seu cavalo branco, mas na aldeia Zegveld foi transportado de coche aberto. O acontecimento é aqui festejado desde o século 16.
O aniversário da Rainha festeja-se no dia 30 de Abril. Em Amsterdão e em muitas outras cidades, um mercado livre faz parte das festividades. Originalmente o mercado livre em Amsterdão era para as crianças. Todos os anos visitam este festim um milhão de pessoas.

Gedurende de zomermaanden worden er op veel plaatsen antiekmarkten in de openlucht gehouden. Op mooie dagen trekken deze veel belangstelling. Twee markten zijn zeer bekend vanwege de prachtige plekken waar zij worden gehouden: in Den Haag onder de bomen van het Voorhout en, zoals hierboven, in Amsterdam op de Nieuwmarkt bij het vroegere Waaggebouw.
Slechts een gering aantal Nederlanders loopt op klompen. Op het platteland worden klompen het meest gedragen. In deze ouderwetse 'veiligheidsschoenen' blijven de voeten heerlijk warm.

During the summer months there are open air antique markets to be found in many places. They can get very crowded in good weather. Two markets are very well known because of their beautiful surroundings. These are in The Hague under the trees of the Voorhout and, see above, in Amsterdam's Nieuwmarkt near the old Weigh House.
Very few Dutch people still regularly wear clogs. Most clogs are worn on farms. Your feet stay lovely and warm inside these old-fashioned 'safety shoes'.

In den Sommermonaten werden vielerorts Antiquitätenmärkte im Freien veranstaltet. An schönen Tagen ziehen sie viele Interessenten an. Zwei Märkte sind besonders bekannt wegen der schönen Plätze, an denen sie stattfinden: in Den Haag unter den Bäumen des Voorhout und – wie hier oben – in Amsterdam auf dem Nieuwmarkt an der alten Stadtwaage.
Nur sehr wenige Niederländer tragen tatsächlich Holzschuhe. Am häufigsten sieht man sie noch auf dem Land. In diesen altmodischen "Sicherheitsschuhen" bleiben die Füße wohlig warm.

L'été, des marchés d'antiquités en plein air se tiennent dans de nombreux endroits et suscitent une forte affluence, quand il fait beau. Deux marchés sont particulièrement courus : celui de La Haye, installé sous les arbres de l'élégante Voorhout et, ci-dessus, celui du Nieuwmarkt à Amsterdam, à côté de l'ancien Poids public.
Très peu de Néerlandais portent des sabots. C'est surtout à la campagne que l'on se chausse de ces 'chaussures de sécurité' d'autrefois, qui tiennent les pieds bien au chaud.

En los meses de verano se celebran numerosos mercados de antiguedades al aire libre. Si el tiempo es bueno atraen a gran numero de curiosos. Dos de estos mercados son conocidos debido a los lugares en donde se celebran: en La Haya bajo los árboles del Voorhout, como se puede apreciar arriba, y en Amsterdam en el mercado Nieuwmarkt junto al antiguo edificio del peso publico Waag.
No quedan ya muchos holandeses que usen zuecos. La mayoría de gente que los usa vive en el campo. Dentro de estos antiguos zapatos de seguridad se tienen los pies siempre calientes.

Durante os meses do verão organizam-se em muitos lugares mercados de antiguidades ao ar livre. Em dias bonitos estes acontecimentos atraem muita gente. Dois mercados são muito conhecidos devido aos locais lindos em que eles se realizam: em Haia sob as árvores do Voorhout e, como aqui em cima, em Amsterdão no Nieuwemarkt, junto do antigo Waaggebouw (Edifício da Balança).
Poucos holandeses andam ainda de tamancos. Os tamancos são usados, em geral, nos campos. Nestes "sapatos de segurança" antigos, os pés ficam muito quentinhos.

Nederland in feiten

The Netherlands in facts

Fakten zu Holland

Les Pays-Bas dans les faits

Holanda en hechos

Os factos da Holanda

De chemische industrie

De chemische industrie is met meer dan 80.000 werknemers een van de grootste industrieën in Nederland. Drie grote multinationals hebben er hun hoofdkantoor.

Bovendien heeft een groot aantal buitenlandse chemische concerns grote belangen in Nederland. En tenslotte is er een aantal kleinere, meestal gespecialiseerde, Nederlandse bedrijven die ook op dit terrein werkzaam zijn.
Nederland heeft een van de laagste energieprijzen voor grote industrieën in Europa. En die energieprijzen vormen ruwweg 60% van de kostprijs van de meeste chemicaliën. Bovendien heeft Nederland ruime voorraden aan aardgas en zout, sleutelcomponenten in tal van chemische producten.
Het uitgebreide raffinaderijcomplex van Rotterdam zorgt voor een groot aantal grondstoffen voor de productie van chemicaliën. Tal van chemische bedrijven zijn gevestigd in de haven, waar zij probleemloos de grondstoffen binnen kunnen krijgen en de eindproducten kunnen verschepen. De chemicaliën worden niet alleen over zee en via de Rijn getransporteerd maar ook via een uitgebreid Europees netwerk van pijplijnen die aan de nationale netwerken elders in Europa zijn gekoppeld. Speciale pijplijnen voor chemicaliën verbinden Rotterdam met het Ruhr-gebied en er komt een nieuwe pijplijn tussen Rotterdam en Antwerpen, het grootste centrum voor chemische industrie in België. Rotterdam heeft ook een groot tankopslagcomplex waar verschillende bedrijven zijn gespecialiseerd in de tijdelijke opslag van speciale soorten chemicaliën.

Na de oorlog herrees Rotterdam uit haar as om Europa's grootste petrochemisch centrum te worden....
De Nederlandse chemiesector produceert het gehele scala aan chemicaliën voor markten over de gehele wereld. Er zijn speciale opleidingscentra voor de chemische industrie, alsook door de overheid opgerichte R&D-centra. Veel bedrijven hebben hun eigen R&D-faciliteiten in Nederland.
De komende jaren zijn aanzienlijke investeringen voorzien in nieuwe fabrieken, opslag- en transportfaciliteiten.
De Nederlandse regering stimuleert actief investeringen in deze sector. Er zijn strikte voorschriften die ervoor moeten zorgen dat de chemische industrie geen grote vervuiler wordt.

Een kant-en-klaar deel van een romp wordt uit de constructieloods gereden

De Nederlandse scheepswerven

Scheepsbouw is een van de oudste industrieën in Nederland. Gegeven de haat-liefderelatie met water, de geografische ligging met de grote Noord-Europese rivieren die uitmonden in de Noordzee en de handelstraditie, waren en zijn schepen essentieel voor de economie.

Al in de Middeleeuwen waren er overal scheepswerven: zelfs in de kleinste nederzettingen waren er altijd wel een paar mensen die een schip konden bouwen. Toen men begon te handelen met de Baltische staten pendelden kleine houten zeilschepen tussen de grote nederzettingen in Holland en in Noord-Europa. Er werden grotere schepen gebouwd toen de handelsroutes werden uitgebreid naar Zuid-Europa en later naar Oost- en West-Indië.
Holland was eeuwenlang een belangrijke zeenatie; de Hollandse oorlogsschepen beschermden de vitale handelsroutes en kusten, voornamelijk tegen de Engelsen. De Nederlandse handelsvloot blijft er een om rekening mee te houden hoewel de vloot nu kleiner is geworden door de grotere tonnage van de schepen. De Nederlandse scheepsbouw is in de afgelopen jaren gemoderniseerd en behoort thans tot de efficiëntste en meest concurrerende ter wereld.
In de jaren zestig bouwden Nederlandse scheepswerven elk type schip, variërend van supertankers tot onderzeeboten. Op dit moment concentreert de afgeslankte industrie zich op datgene waar zij het best in is: middelgrote koopvaardijschepen. Hiertoe behoren containerschepen, koelschepen, veerboten, sleepboten en offshore-bevoorradingsschepen. De grootste scheepsbouwgroep laat zelfs schepen van de assemblagelijnen aflopen. In grote, moderne industriehallen worden modules vervaardigd volgens de exacte maten van de klant. De Nederlandse werven hebben de hoogste productiviteit per werknemer ter wereld.
De jachtbouw is ook een specialiteit. Nederlandse jachten staan bekend om hun kwaliteit, luxe en zeewaardigheid. De international jet set bestelt in Nederland haar grote motorjachten. Zeiljachten worden veel gevraagd door oceaanzeilers die meedoen aan races en door levensgenieters die graag comfortabel en in stijl over de oceanen zeilen. Net als de handelsschepen van de Nederlandse werven worden de jachten beschouwd als de besten ter wereld.

De bierexport

Het Hollandse brakke water werd in de Middeleeuwen ongeschikt geacht voor menselijke consumptie. Als gevolg hiervan werd er een zwakke vorm van bier gedronken door iedereen, mannen, vrouwen en kinderen.

De bierbrouwtechniek kwam uit Duitsland, maar de Hollanders begonnen al snel hun eigen bier te produceren en verfijnden daarbij het proces. In de 16e eeuw waren er in elke stad brouwerijen. De meeste wijken in de grote steden hadden hun eigen brouwerij: bier werd dagelijks gebrouwen en was niet houdbaar.
Aan het eind van de 18e eeuw waren er alleen al in de provincie Limburg 512 brouwerijen, één voor elke 290 inwoners. In 1900 waren er nog 132 over, een niet gering aantal gezien de in totaal 500 brouwerijen in het hele land.
Met de komst van de koeling begonnen de brouwerijen hun productie te concentreren. Ze hoefden de verkoop van hun producten nu niet meer te beperken tot de onmiddellijke omgeving van de brouwerij. Toen de markten zich uitbreidden, kwam de productie steeds meer in handen van een klein aantal brouwers en daalde het aantal brouwerijen drastisch. Op dit moment wordt 95% van het binnenlandse bier gebrouwen door enkele grote brouwers. De kleinere brouwers hebben zich een plaatsje bevochten in niche-markten; ze doen het over het algemeen goed.
Net zoals met zo veel andere producten beschouwde men de Nederlandse binnenlandse markt als te klein voor grootschalige productie. Nederlandse brouwers hebben grote overzeese markten en staan in praktisch elk land bovenaan bij de verkoop van geïmporteerd bier.
De Nederlandse bierconsumptie staat op ongeveer 85 liter per persoon per jaar, ongeveer evenveel als in de Verenigde Staten. De Nederlandse consumptie blijft echter achter bij die in Duitsland en Polen waar de bewoners 125 liter per jaar drinken. De Nederlandse brouwers hebben hun blik nu gericht op de export naar groeimarkten in Zuid-Europa, Azië, Afrika en Latijns-Amerika. De grotere brouwers produceren hun bier overal ter wereld onder hun eigen supervisie. De kwaliteit van Nederlands exportbier is een belangrijke positieve factor bij de verkoop in het buitenland.

De schone kunsten

Nederland is synoniem voor schone kunsten. Er is heel veel lucht bij de Hollandse landschapsschilders te bewonderen, net als in het landschap zelf overigens.

De kunstzinnige traditie stamt uit de 17e eeuw, de Gouden Eeuw van Amsterdam, de bloeiperiode van schilders als Rembrandt, Vermeer en Hals. Soms stichtten deze kunstenaars scholen om samen met de leerlingen hun eigen werken af te kunnen maken, maar ook om jonge kunstenaars op te leiden.
Hun werken zijn te zien in de vele belangrijke musea, waaronder het Rijksmuseum in Amsterdam. Er zijn musea die zijn gewijd aan de meer hedendaagse kunst, zoals Boymans-Van Beuningen in Rotterdam en het Stedelijk in Amsterdam. Het Kröller-Müller Museum in de buurt van Arnhem heeft een uitgebreide en gevarieerde collectie en een belangwekkende beeldentuin.
Het Van Gogh Museum in Amsterdam is een van de weinige dat geheel aan één enkele kunstenaar is gewijd.
Overal in het land staan gebouwen op de monumentenlijst - in Amsterdam alleen al meer dan 7000. Hierdoor worden de historische, meest 17e-eeuwse stadscentra bewaard als een soort openluchtmuseum.
Ballet, concerten en opera's zijn ook zeer populair in Nederland. Het Nederlands Dans Theater is een beroemd balletgezelschap dat regelmatig op tournee gaat over de hele wereld. Het Concertgebouworkest is internationaal gezien een van de beste orkesten ter wereld en het Concertgebouw met zijn perfecte akoestiek maakt ook internationaal furore. Amsterdam huisvest ook Nederlandse Opera, die vooral bekend staat om zijn avantgardistische producties. In Rotterdam wordt jaarlijks een filmfestival gehouden en in Maastricht is jaarlijks een antiekbeurs.
Heel veel Nederlandse kunst wordt geveild bij veilinghuizen in Amsterdam en Den Haag. Deze worden geleid door internationale kunstveilingshuizen maar ook door Nederlandse deskundigen. Er zijn in de grote huizen regelmatig veilingen van schilderijen, tekeningen, zilver, meubilair en objets d'art.
Kunst- en muziekopleidingen zijn zeer populair, zowel bij jong als bij oud. Er zijn verschillende officieel erkende instellingen zoals de Rietveld Academie, die zich richt op schilder- en beeldhouwkunst en architectuur.

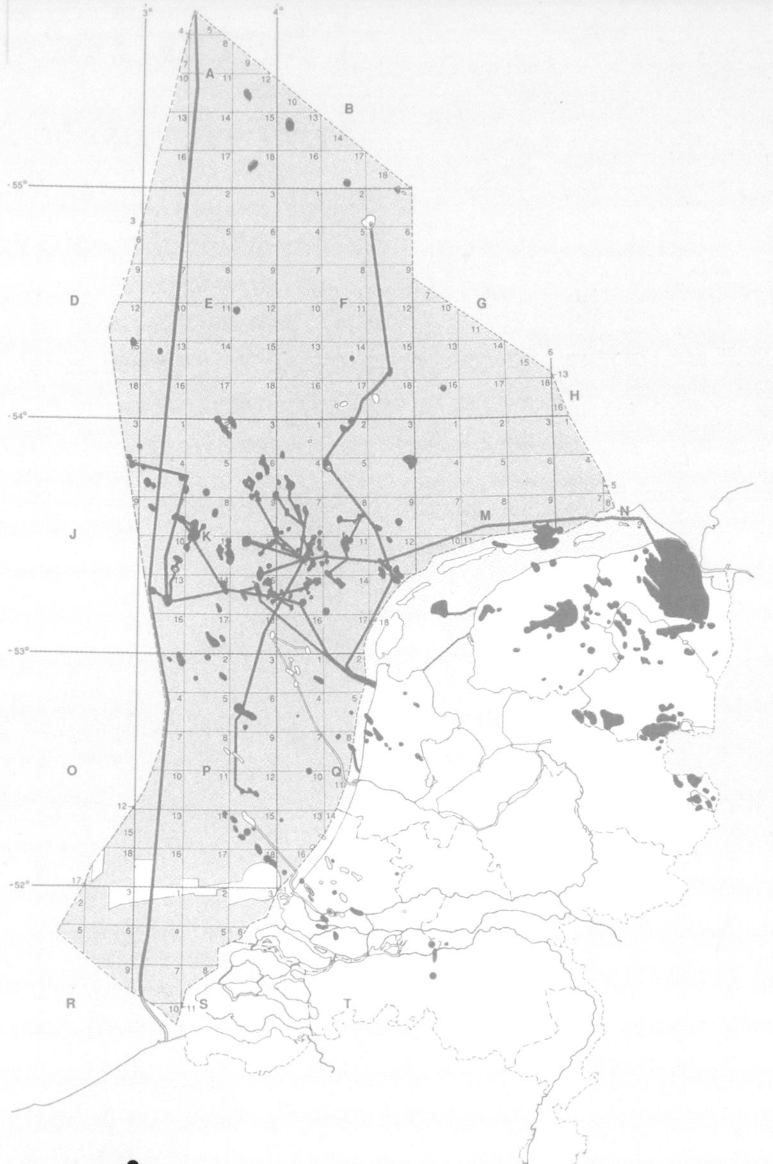

Energie

Nederland heeft de grootste aardgasreserves in West-Europa. Tot de jaren zestig was Nederland een groot producent van steenkool. Maar door de dalende voorraden en de grote hoeveelheden goedkope steenkool uit het buitenland besloot de overheid de kolenmijnen in Limburg te sluiten.

Ongeveer tezelfdertijd werd het Groningse aardgasveld ontdekt. Latere ontdekkingen van nog meer aardgas- en olievelden, zowel op het land als offshore, legden de basis voor de forse economische groei in de daaropvolgende decennia. Er werd besloten om deze gasreserves te ontzien door het beleid voor de komende 50 jaar te richten op het gebruik van verschillende energiebronnen. Ondertussen werden nieuwe technieken ontwikkeld om gas uit kleinere velden te halen.
Op dit moment exporteert Nederland per jaar ongeveer even veel aardgas als het zelf verbruikt. De reserves zijn voldoende om dit nog verschillende decennia vol te houden. Er zijn contracten om aardgas te importeren, bijvoorbeeld uit Rusland dat de grootste reserves ter wereld heeft en ook uit Engeland. Weer andere contracten regelen de aardgasexport.
De verwachting is dat Nederland in de nabije toekomst de voornaamste leverancier van aardgas zal worden in West-Europa. Daartoe zijn complete netwerken van pijplijnen aangelegd. Uitgangspunt is dat de eigen gasvoorraden van Nederland, gedeeltelijk opgeslagen in recentelijk aangelegde ondergrondse opslagdepots, kunnen worden aangewend om de exportleveranties te kunnen garanderen in het geval dat de gasimport onverhoopt stil komt te liggen. De continuïteit is daarmee gewaarborgd. En daar zijn zowel importeurs als exporteurs bij gebaat.

Financieel centrum

Amsterdam is een van Europa's belangrijkste financiële centra en speelt een steeds belangrijker rol in de zich uitbreidende Europese Unie.

Amsterdam heeft een historisch verankerde bank- en verzekeringssector, actieve aandelen- en goederenbeurzen, innovatieve beleggingsmaatschappijen en een zich uitbreidende sector van financiële dienstverlening; hiermee neemt de stad een plaats in net achter de belangrijkste Europese financiële centra Londen, Frankfurt en Parijs.
De wortels zijn diep verankerd: financiering was altijd al nodig ter ondersteuning van de handel, eeuwenlang een steunpilaar van de Nederlandse economie. In 1602 werd in Amsterdam de eerste aandelenvennootschap opgericht om fondsen te werven voor de Verenigde Oostindische Compagnie (VOC). De VOC bracht specerijen vanuit Indië naar Europa en breidde de handel later uit naar andere goederen in andere delen van de wereld.
De banken werden aan het begin van de 19e eeuw begunstigd door Koning Willem I, na de nederlaag van Napoleon bij Waterloo en de daaropvolgende terugtrekking van de Fransen uit Nederland.
In 1997 werden de aandelen-, optie-, goederen- en termijnbeurzen samengevoegd tot de Amsterdam Exchanges, beter bekend als de AEX. Dit werd gedaan om overlappende dienstverlening tegen te gaan en om deze beursactiviteiten prominenter te profileren. De AEX handelt in een groot aantal Amerikaanse en andere buitenlandse aandelen, en is een belangrijke schakel in de 24-uurs effectenhandel. De AEX staat open voor buitenlandse banken en makelaars. Op de AEX vinden regelmatig nieuwe beursgangen plaats; de AEX wordt beschouwd als een uitstekende omgeving voor kleine beginnende bedrijven.
Nederlandse banken en verzekeringsbedrijven behoren tot de grootste ter wereld en zijn actief in alle delen van de wereld. Veel van deze banken zijn al langer dan 100 jaar aanwezig in Noord- en Zuid-Amerika en Azië. Latere uitbreidingen werden gestimuleerd door de intrede van Nederlandse industriële bedrijven op nieuwe markten. De banken en verzekeringsbedrijven spelen een sleutelrol bij de introductie van nieuwe financiële producten over de hele wereld.

De infrastructuur

De transportinfrastructuur in Nederland is modern en efficiënt. De weg- en spoorverbindingen zijn verbonden met de rest van Europa, terwijl via de rivieren en binnenwateren een groot deel van het binnenlandse en internationaal vrachtverkeer wordt afgehandeld.

Het wegen- en spoornet wordt momenteel verder uitgebreid met het oog op een nog betere toegankelijkheid van de steden en de internationale routes.
Schiphol Airport, nabij Amsterdam, is de snelst groeiende luchthaven in Europa; en het single terminal systeem staat garant voor een hoge graad van efficiency. Schiphol is de op drie na grootste luchthaven van Europa als het gaat om passagiers en op twee na wat betreft luchtvracht. Meer dan 80 luchtvaartmaatschappijen vliegen dagelijks op 200 bestemmingen. De luchthaven en de ondersteunende bedrijfstakken zijn een van de grootste werkgevers in dit gebied.
Rotterdam is 's werelds grootste zeehaven en gezamenlijk handelen de Nederlandse zeehavens ruwweg 50% van alle internationale vracht af van de Noordzeehavens tussen Hamburg en Le Havre. De Rotterdamse haven heeft een ideale ligging aan de monding van de Rijn en de Maas die respectievelijk Duitsland, Zwitserland en midden Europa, en België en Noord-Frankrijk als achterland hebben.
Er zijn plannen voor forse uitbreidingen van de infrastructuur. Zo wil men Amsterdam/Rotterdam via de hogesnelheidstrein verbinden met Brussel en Parijs in het zuiden, en met Keulen en andere locaties in Duitsland in het oosten. Passagierstreinen worden gezien als een levensvatbaar en efficiënt alternatief voor het luchtverkeer waarmee de druk van de Europese luchthavens kan worden weggehaald, terwijl het tegelijkertijd een plezierige manier van reizen is tussen stadscentra.
In Nederland wordt een spoorlijn gebouwd die uitsluitend bestemd is voor vrachtvervoer tussen de haven van Rotterdam en het Ruhr-gebied in Duitsland. Een groot deel van de Duitse export en grondstoffenimport loopt al via Rotterdam en de spoorverbinding zorgt voor een alternatief voor het transport over de weg of de binnenwateren.
Schiphol heeft zijn maximale capaciteit nog lang niet bereikt, maar er zijn toch al plannen om de luchthaven uit te breiden met een satelliet-luchthaven op een kunstmatig eiland in de Noordzee. De bouw van zo'n luchthaven zou kunnen worden uitgevoerd door Nederlandse bagger- en bouwmaatschappijen die de specifieke expertise hebben ontwikkeld bij soortgelijke projecten in het buitenland.

Distributie

Nederland staat bekend als de Poort naar Europa en is het voornaamste distributiecentrum voor het continent.

De ligging aan de monding van de Rijn en Maas en aan de Noordzee, 's werelds drukst bevaren zeeroute, heeft van Nederland de natuurlijke toegang gemaakt voor goederen uit Noord- en Zuid-Amerika, Azië, Afrika en het Midden-Oosten. Tegelijkertijd worden Europese goederen via Hollandse havens naar buitenlandse bestemmingen verscheept.
De Nederlandse transportmaatschappijen zijn experts in alle vormen van distributie en veel bedrijven uit deze sector treden als partner op voor buitenlandse bedrijven die toegang willen krijgen tot de Europese markt. Europa wordt dan misschien wel beschouwd als één enkele markt, maar er zijn natuurlijk taal- en cultuurverschillen. Vaak is daarbij deskundige hulp nodig en die is in Nederland bij uitstek voorhanden. Er wonen ongeveer 300 miljoen mensen binnen een straal van 500 kilometer van Rotterdam en Amsterdam. Dat is een lucratieve markt van consumenten met een grote koopkracht. Er zijn uitstekende verbindingen naar de rest van Europa, over de weg, via het spoor, door de lucht, over zee en via de binnenvaart.
De Value Added Logistics, of VAL, is het meest recente distributiemiddel dat door de Nederlanders is ontwikkeld. Via de VAL worden goederen in bulk naar een magazijn vervoerd waar zij worden geüpgraded (er worden bijvoorbeeld anderstalige toetsenborden toegevoegd aan computers), verpakt, gelabeld en soms geassembleerd. Een uniek systeem van gekoppelde magazijnen door het hele land zorgt ervoor dat er geen invoerbelastingen hoeven te worden betaald aangezien de goederen nog steeds in transit zijn. Er wordt uitstekend samengewerkt met de douaneautoriteiten.
Europese Distributiecentra worden steeds populairder. Daarbij centraliseert een buitenlandse producent zijn Europese distributieactiviteiten op één plek. De voordelen zijn evident: de exportladingen kunnen voor elke klant apart op maat toegesneden worden. Bovendien is er een meertalige staf aanwezig die kan helpen met de back office dienstverlening. Deze medewerkers zijn opgeleid om met cliënten door heel Europa de problemen in hun eigen taal te bespreken.

Landbouw

Nederlanders behoren nog altijd tot de meest efficiënte landbouwers ter wereld. In de 16e eeuw werden al grote hoeveelheden haver verbouwd ten behoeve van de veeteelt, en ook wintervoedsel en weidegras door klaver en knollen te zaaien op de dunne grond.

Nederland is geen natuurlijk landbouwgebied met zijn dorre en droge grond. Maar de Nederlanders hebben er wat van gemaakt, met wisselende gewassen om aan hun voedingsstoffen te komen.
De moderne Nederlandse schuur van staal en gegalvaniseerd ijzer kan overal ter wereld bezichtigd worden aangezien Nederlandse boeren verhuisden naar groenere weiden.
In 1890 was een derde van de werkende bevolking werkzaam in de landbouw en veeteelt. Op dit moment is dit nog geen 10%, maar de opbrengst is indrukwekkend. Nederland is de op één na grootste exporteur van agrarische producten ter wereld, na de Verenigde Staten.
De vee- en varkensteelt is wijdverspreid in Nederland; grootschalige boerderijen zijn een alledaags verschijnsel. Nederlandse koeien hebben de hoogste melkopbrengst ter wereld. Er vindt ruime export plaats van vee en varkens(vlees). Pootaardappelen zijn ook een belangrijk exportartikel.
De Hollanders hebben ook altijd voorop gelopen in de voedselverwerkende industrie. Een zekere Willem Breukels uit Zeeland valt de eer te beurt om in de 14e eeuw als eerste haring “gekaakt” te hebben. Margarine werd zo’n 100 jaar geleden voor het eerst geproduceerd in Nederland.
Veel van de melkopbrengst wordt gebruikt voor boter, kaas, en gecondenseerde en poedermelk, vaak door coöperaties van boeren. Kaas is een belangrijk exportartikel; de Goudse en Edammer zijn over de hele wereld te krijgen.
Fruit en groenten zijn een ander exportproduct; Nederlandse tomaten, wortels, kool en paprika’s zijn overal ter wereld in winkels te koop, vers en vaak goedkoper dan de lokale producten. Gespecialiseerde transportbedrijven zorgen ervoor dat het fruit en de groenten vers worden verscheept.

Een van de laboratoria van de Universiteit Twente

Research & Development

Nederland kent een lange wetenschappelijke traditie. De Hollandse, in Rotterdam geboren humanist Diderius Erasmus spande zich in het begin van de 16e eeuw als geen ander in voor het verwerven van kennis.

De vroegste Hollandse wetenschappelijke ontdekkingen lagen vooral op het gebied van de navigatie; de Hollandse kooplieden lieten namelijk geen kans onbenut om hun greep op de handelsroutes te verstevigen.
Dat de Hollandse cartografie op zeer hoog peil stond, hoeft dan ook geen verbazing te wekken.
De Hollanders ontwikkelden ook verschillende baanbrekende chirurgische technieken.
Vandaag is Nederland een belangrijk research- en developmentcentrum. De overheid financiert verschillende R&D-instituten die op hun beurt nauw samenwerken met de particuliere sector. De grootste Nederlandse universiteiten hebben allemaal gespecialiseerde R&D-centra: landbouw in Wageningen, medicijnen in Utrecht, biotechnologie in Amsterdam enz. Onderzoek op het gebied van de humaniora wordt uitgevoerd door verschillende academische en door de overheid gefinancierde instellingen.
Ook de particuliere sector beschikt overal in het land over R&D-centra. Nederland heeft zich in dat opzicht een zekere populariteit verworven vanwege het grote aantal meertalige academici dat elk jaar van de universiteiten komt. Er vindt een uitgebreide kennisoverdracht plaats tussen de verschillende R&D-centra.
Overal bevinden zich wetenschapscentra. Deze worden door de Nederlandse overheid gestimuleerd om nieuwe producten en nieuwe dienstverlening te ontwikkelen. Deze zogenaamde denktanks hebben behoorlijk wat buitenlandse interesse getrokken.
In de wetenschapscentra kunnen individuele bedrijven samenwerken en gebruikmaken van producten en ideeën die ter plekke zijn ontwikkeld. Het concept omhelst universitaire researchcentra om bedrijven en wetenschap met elkaar in contact te brengen, maar ook technologiecentra voor de commerciële exploitatie van high technology.
De overheid heeft verschillende ‘centres of excellence’ als zodanig erkend, bijvoorbeeld op het gebied van landbouw en scheikunde. Het idee achter deze centra is de stimulering van verder onderzoek en de ontwikkeling van nieuwe producten.

Het nieuwe gebouw van de veiling te Poeldijk

The chemical industry

The chemical industry is one of the largest in the Netherlands, employing more than 80,000. Three large groups, all of which operate around the world, are headquartered in the country.

In addition, a number of foreign chemical concerns have large operations in the Netherlands. On top of that, there are a number of smaller, usually very specialised, Dutch companies which operate in the field.
The Netherlands has one of the lowest energy costs for large industries in Europe. Energy costs account for roughly 60% of the cost price of most chemicals. Also, the country has ample supplies of natural gas and salt, key components in many chemical products.

Rotterdam's vast refinery complex provides a large number of feedstocks for the production of chemicals. Many chemical operations are located in the port where they can easily receive raw materials and ship out the end products. In addition to ocean and Rhine shipping, chemicals are moved throughout Europe by a vast pipeline network which connects up to national grids elsewhere in continental Europe. Special chemicals pipelines connect Rotterdam with Germany's Ruhr industrial complex, and a new pipeline will link Rotterdam and Antwerp, the chief Belgian chemical industry centre.
Rotterdam also has a large tank farm complex, with several companies specialising in the temporary storage of special types of chemicals. In fact, Rotterdam rose from the ashes of the war t become Europe's largest petro-chemical centre.

Chemical producers in the Netherlands manufacture both bulk and fine chemicals, with markets all over the world. There are a number of specialised educational institutes which turn out graduates to work in the chemical industry. There are also government operated research and development centres. Many companies have their own R&D facilities in the Netherlands. Considerable investment in new plants, storage and transport facilities are planned for the coming years.

The Dutch government actively encourages investment in the sector. Strict norms see to it that the chemical industry is not a major polluter.

The Dutch shipyards

Shipbuilding is one of the oldest industries in the Netherlands. Given the country's love/hate relationship with water, its geographical position where northern Europe's major rivers meet the North Sea and its traditions of trade, ships were and remain vital to the economy.

A ready-made module is leaving the construction hall before being assembled

In the Middle Ages, there were shipyards everywhere: there were always a few people skilled in building boats in even the tiniest settlements.
When the early Dutch first began trading with the Baltic states, small wooden sailing ships plied between the larger settlements and their counterparts in the Nordic countries. Larger vessels were built when the trading routes extended to southern Europe and later the East and West Indies.

The Netherlands was a major sailing power for many centuries, its men-of-war protecting the vital trading routes and it shores, largely from the British. The Dutch merchant fleet remains a major force, although it is now slimmed down as ships' sizes' increase. The Dutch shipbuilding industry has been rationalised in recent years and is now among the most efficient and most competitive in the world. In the 1960s, Dutch shipyards built practically every type of vessel, ranging from Very Large Crude Carriers to submarines.

Today, the slimmed-down industry concentrates at what it does best: medium-sized merchant vessels. These include container ships, reefer vessels, passenger ferries, tugs and offshore supply vessels. The largest shipbuilding group produces ships which are virtually built on an assembly line. Modules are assembled in large, modern covered halls to the exacting requirements of buyers. Dutch yards have the highest productivity per worker in the world.
Yachts are another speciality. Dutch-built yachts are known for the quality, luxury and seaworthiness. Large motor vessels are ordered by potentates and tycoons from all over the world. Sailing yachts are in demand from ocean racers as well as discerning individuals who enjoy sailing the world's oceans in comfort and style. Like the merchant vessels produced in Dutch shipyards, the yachts are considered top-of-the-line and good value for money.

The exportation of beer

The brackish water prevailing in the Netherlands during the Middle Ages was considered unfit for human consumption. As a result, a weak form of beer was used by all, men women and children.

The brewing techniques came from Germany, but the Dutch soon began to produce beer on their own, refining the process along the way. By the 16th century there were breweries in every town. Most neigbourhoods in the cites had their own breweries: beer was produced daily and would not keep.
At the end of the 18thcentury there were 512 breweries in the Province of Limburg alone, one for every 290 inhabitants. By 1900, 132 remained, a high number considering there were just over 500 in the entire country.
With the advent of refrigeration, the breweries began to consolidate. It was now possible to sell their production further away than the immediate few hundred metres around the brewery. As markets expanded, individual brewers became bigger and the total number of brewing companies fell drastically. Today there are several large brewers which produce 95% of the domestic beer produced in the country. The score of so of smaller brewers have carved out niche markets which increase their sales.
As with so many other products, the Dutch domestic market is considered to be too small for large scale production. Dutch brewers have huge overseas markets, leading the sales of imported beers in practically every country in the world. Dutch beer consumption is about 85 litres per capita a year, about the same level as in the United States. However, Dutch consumption trail Germany and Poland where per capita consumption tops 125 litres a year. Dutch brewers, however, are looking to the growth markets in southern Europe, Asia, Africa and Latin America to increase their export sales. The larger brewers produce beer under their own supervision worldwide. The quality of Dutch export beer helps promote sales abroad.

The Arts

The Netherlands is synonymous with the arts. There is a lot of sky in Dutch landscapes just as there is all over the country.

The tradition of the arts dates back to the 17th century, Amsterdam's Golden Age, when painters like Rembrandt, Vermeer and Hals thrived. Some of these artists set up schools to help finish their own works and to provide training for younger artists. Their works are seen in the country's many grand museums which include the Rijksmuseum in Amsterdam. There are museums dedicated to more contemporary art, such as the Boymans-Van Beuningen in Rotterdam and Amsterdam's Stedelijke. The Kroller-Muller Museum near Arnhem has a vast and wide-ranging collection as well as an important sculpture garden. The Van Gogh Museum in Amsterdam is one of the few in the world devoted entirely to a single major artist.
Many buildings throughout the country are listed monuments - there are more than 7,000 in Amsterdam alone. This preserves the historic, mostly 17th century, city centres which form a sorting of living museum as a result.
Dance, concerts and opera are also popular in the Netherlands. The Nederlands Dans Theatre is a well-known ballet company which tours the world on a regular basis. Amsterdam's Concertgebouworkest is constantly rated one of the best internationally as is its home the acoustically near-perfect Concertgebouw. The Netherlands Opera is also based in Amsterdam and is known best for its avant-garde productions.
Music and the arts are encouraged everywhere. Rotterdam hosts an annual film festival , Maastricht has its fine arts fair.
A lot of Dutch art is auctioned in auction houses in Amsterdam and The Hague. These are operated by the international art auction houses as well as by Dutch specialists. There are regular sales of paintings, drawings, silverware, furniture and objects d'art at the main houses.
Art and music classes are very popular, among the young and old alike. There are several accredited institutions, such as the Rietveld Academy which specialises in painting, architecture and sculpture.

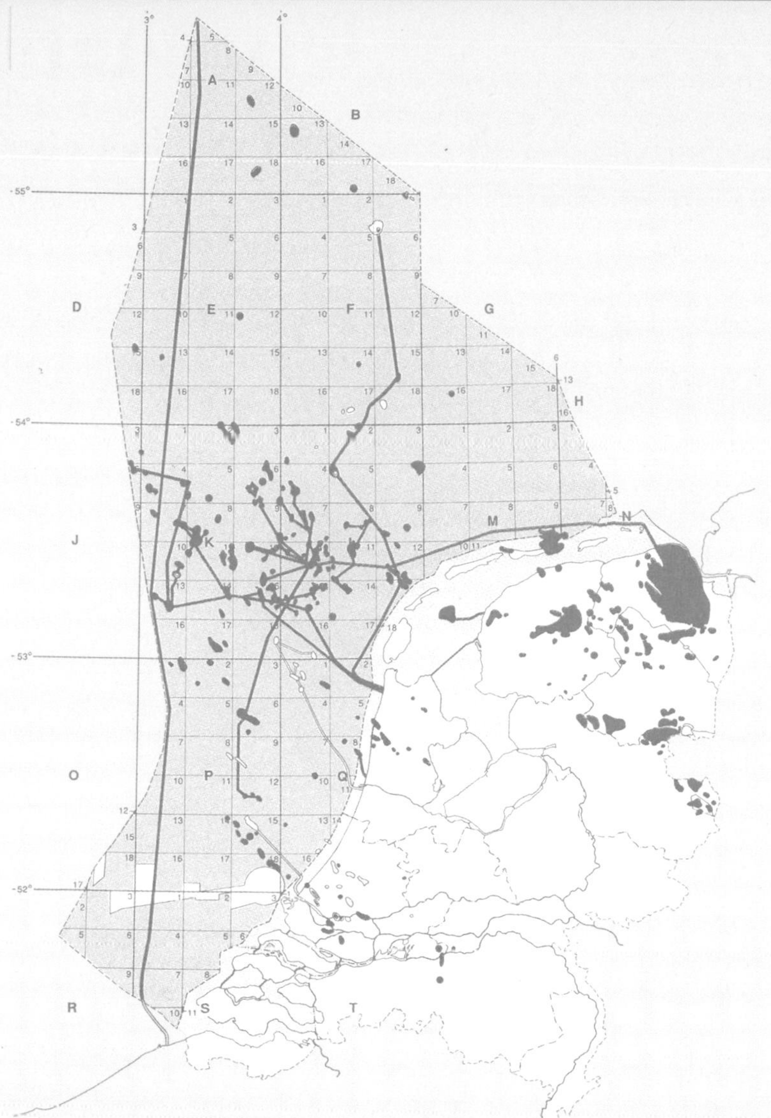

Exploitation of natural gas

The Netherlands has the largest reserves of natural gas in western Europe. The country was a producer of coal until the 1960s when dwindling supplies and heavy supplies of cheap coal from abroad led the government to the conclusion that the coal mines in the southern Province of Limburg should be closed.

It was at about the same time that the Groningen field was discovered in the northern province of the same name. Later discoveries of additional fields of natural gas and oil both onshore and offshore laid the basis for the country's robust economic growth in the ensuing decades. It was decided to conserve these gas reserves by adopting a policy of using several sources of energy for the coming 50 years. In the meantime, new techniques for extracting gas from smaller, marginal fields were developed.
Today, the Netherlands exports about the same amount of natural gas as it consumes each year. Reserves are sufficient to continue this supply for several decades. There are contracts to import natural gas from Russia which has the world's biggest reserves, as well as from other producers including England. Other contracts have been made to supply additional export markets in the future.
The Netherlands is expected to emerge as the main gas supplier in western Europe in the near future. There are pipeline grids connecting to import and export markets. The most important point is that the Netherlands' own gas supplies, partly held in recently developed underground storage depots, can be used to ensure export supplies in the event that gas imports are interrupted. This guarantees a steady supply of gas to foreign buyers, and will serve to avoid economic problems to importers and exporters alike.

Financial centre

Amsterdam is one of Europe's leading financial centres which is playing an increasingly important role in the expanded European Union.

With a strong banking and insurance sector, active stock and commodities exchanges, innovative asset management teams and a rising financial services sector, Amsterdam is ranked just behind London, Frankfurt and Paris as the leading European financial centre. The roots go deep: financing was always needed to support trade, a mainstay of the Dutch economy for centuries. In 1602, the world's first joint stock company was formed in Amsterdam to raise funds for the United East Indies company, known as the VOC. The VOC was started to bring back to Europe spices from the Indonesian archipelago, and later branched out into the trade of other commodities in other parts of the world.
The country's banks were given a boost by King Willem I in the early 19th century after Napoleon's defeat at Waterloo and the subsequent withdrawal of the French from the Netherlands.
In 1997, Amsterdam's stocks, options, commodities and futures exchanges were merged to form Amsterdam Exchanges , better known as the AEX. The move was made to eliminate overlapping services and to bring a stronger presence to these exchange activities.
The AEX handles a significant number of American and other foreign shares, and is a major link in the 24-hour trading of many issues. The options exchange was the first in Europe to handle international issues. The AEX is open to foreign banks and brokers. Initial public offerings are common on the AEX which is widely regarded as an excellent place for small, start-up companies.
Dutch banks and insurance companies are among the largest in the world, and are active in all parts of the world. Many of these banks have been present in the Americas and Asia for more than 100 years. Later expansion was fueled by the moves of Dutch industrial companies into new markets. The banks and insurance companies are key innovators of new financial products worldwide.

ENGLISH

The infrastructure

The transport infrastructure in the Netherlands is modern and efficient. Road and rail links connect to the rest of Europe, while the rivers and inland waterways handle a large share of domestic and international cargo traffic.

The road and rail network is being extended to provide easier access to cities and international routes.
Schiphol Airport, near Amsterdam, is the fastest-growing airport in Europe and its sophisticated single terminal operation ensures efficiency. Schiphol is Europe's fourth-largest in terms of passengers and third in air freight. More than 80 airlines serve over 200 destinations on a daily basis. The airport and its supporting industries are one of the area's largest employers.
Rotterdam is the world's largest seaport, and together the Dutch seaports handle roughly 50% of all the international cargo handled in the Hamburg-Le Havre range of northern continental North Sea ports. The port has a superb location at the mouth of the Rhine and Maas Rivers leading to Germany, Switzerland and central Europe and Belgium and northern France respectively.
There are plans for major extensions to the infrastructure. High-speed rail lines are planned to link Amsterdam/Rotterdam with Brussels and Paris to the south and with Cologne and further points in Germany to the east. Passenger trains are thought to be a viable and efficient alternative to air travel and is expected to relieve pressure on European airports as well as to provide a pleasant means of transport between city centres.

The Netherlands is going ahead with an all-freight rail line between the Port of Rotterdam and Germany's Ruhr industrial area. Much of German exports and its supplies of raw materials already move through Rotterdam and the rail connection will provide an alternative to transport of these goods by road or inland waterway.
Schiphol Airport is far from reaching its capacity, but already there are proposals to extend the airport by building a satellite airport on an artificial island in the North Sea. Construction of such an airport could be undertaken by Dutch dredging and building companies which have developed the expertise at similar projects abroad.

Distribution

Known as the Gateway to Europe, the Netherlands is the continent's primary distribution centre.

Its location on the delta of the Rhine and Maas rivers and the North Sea, the world's busiest shipping region, has made the country the natural point-of-entry for goods from North and South America, Asia, Africa and the Middle East.
At the same time, European goods are moved to destinations abroad through Dutch ports.

Dutch transporters are adept at all forms of distribution and many companies in the sector are able to serve as partners to foreign firms wanting access to the European market. Europe may seem to be a single market, but there are language differences and varying needs and tastes among the Europeans. Expert help is often needed and is readily available in the Netherlands.
About 300 million people live within a 500-kilometre radius of Rotterdam and Amsterdam. It is a lucrative market, where consumers have high spending powers.
There are excellent connections to the rest of Europe by road, rail, air, sea and inland waterway. Dutch truckers move nearly 30% of the cross-border road cargo in Europe.

Value Added Logistics, or VAL, is the latest distribution tool to be developed by the Dutch. Under Val, goods are shipped in bulk to a warehouse where they are upgraded (foreign language keyboards are added to computers, for instance), packaged, labeled and under certain circumstances, assembled. A unique system of bonded warehouses throughout the country means that import duty need not be paid because the goods are still in transit. There is excellent cooperation from the customs authorities.
European Distribution Centres are becoming increasing popular. Under this system a foreign producer of goods centralises their European distribution activities in one spot. The advantages are obvious as export shipments can be customised for each customer. In addition, multilingual staff are available to help with back office service operations. They are trained to discuss problems with users throughout Europe in their own language.

Agriculture

The Dutch remain among the most efficient farmers in the world. In the 16th century, the region was already producing magnificent crops of oats for their cattle and providing winter feed and good pastures by sowing clover and turnips on the thin soils.

The Netherlands is not a natural agricultural area with its barren and sandy soil. But the Dutch have made something of it, alternating crops to build up the nutrients. The modern steel and galvanised iron Dutch barn is seen all over the world as Dutch farmers moved to greener pastures. In 1890, agriculture and farming employed one-third of the working population. Today, the figure is less than 10%, but the output is impressive. The Netherlands is the world's second-largest exporter of agricultural products, after the United States. Cattle and pig farming is widespread in the Netherlands, with large-scale farms quite common. Dutch cows give the highest milk yields in the world. Exports of live cattle and pigs as well as meat are high. Seed potatoes are also a major export.
The Dutch have always been one of the leaders in food processing. A certain Willem Breukels of the Province of Zeeland is credited with being the first to salt herring for preservation in the 14th century. Margarine was first extensively produced in the Netherlands 100 years ago.
Much of the milk yield is processed into butter, cheese and condensed and powdered milk, often by cooperatives which are owned by the farmers. Cheese is a major export, Gouda and Edam cheeses are available worldwide.
Fruit and vegetables are another export product, with Dutch tomatoes, carrots, cabbages and peppers sold in stores around the world, fresh and often cheaper than local produce. Specialist transporters see to it that the fruit and vegetables are ripened and shipped in prime condition.

One of the laboratories of the University Twente.

Research & Development

There is a long tradition of science in the Netherlands. Born in Rotterdam, the Dutch humanist Diderius Erasmus did more than anyone else in the early 16th century to advance learning.

Many of the early Dutch scientific discoveries were related to navigation as Dutch merchants sought to strengthen their grip on their trading routes. The art of map-making was a subsequent development. Several pioneering surgical methods were developed by the Dutch as well.
Today, the Netherlands is the centre of a vast research and development complex. The government funds several R&D institutes which, in turn, work closely with the private sector. The leading Dutch universities all have R&D centres geared to their specialities: agriculture in Wageningen, medicine in Utrecht, biotechnology in Amsterdam, and so on. Research in the humanities is undertaken by several academic and government-funded institutions.
The private sector has many R&D centres throughout the country. The Netherlands is often selected for such activities because of the large number of multi-lingual academics turned out by the universities every year. There is wide interchange of knowledge between the various RD centres.
Science parks are located everywhere. The Dutch government pursues a policy of encouraging their development to stimulate new developments in manufacturing and services. These so-called brain parks have attracted a lot of foreign interest. These parks allow individual businesses to cooperate and make use of products and ideas developed on the site. The concept includes research parks established at universities to promote academic and business links in science, as well as technology parks designed for the commercial exploitation of high technology.
The government has recognised several 'centres of excellence' in a number of fields including agriculture and chemistry. The idea behind these centres is to encourage further research in these areas, and to stimulate the development of new products.

The new building of the auction at Poeldijk.

Die chemische Industrie

Mit über 80.000 Beschäftigten ist die chemische Industrie eine der größten in den Niederlanden. Drei Großkonzerne haben ihren Hauptsitz im Land. Zudem agiert eine Vielzahl ausländischer Chemieunternehmen in den Niederlanden.

Und schließlich existiert noch eine ganze Reihe kleinerer, meist spezialisierter niederländischer Betriebe, die ebenfalls im Chemiesektor tätig sind.
Die Niederlande haben mit die niedrigsten Energiepreise für Großindustrien in ganz Europa. Und diese Energiepreise machen rund 60% des Herstellungspreises der meisten Chemikalien aus. Außerdem verfügen die Niederlande über umfassende Erdgas- und Salzvorkommen, wichtigen Ausgangsstoffen vieler chemischer Produkte.
Der riesige Raffineriekomplex Rotterdams liefert unzählige Grundstoffe für die Herstellung von Chemikalien. Zahlreiche Chemieunternehmen haben ihren Sitz im Hafen, wo sie leicht an die Rohstoffe herankommen und ihre Endprodukte verschiffen können. Die Chemikalien werden nicht nur über das Meer und auf dem Rhein transportiert, sondern auch über ein weitverzweigtes europäisches Pipeline-Netz, das an die Netze der einzelnen europäischen Länder angeschlossen ist. Spezielle Chemikalien-Pipelines verlaufen vom Rotterdamer Hafen ins Ruhrgebiet, und eine neue Pipeline soll zwischen Rotterdam und Antwerpen, dem größten Zentrum der belgischen Chemieindustrie, entstehen. Rotterdam verfügt auch über ein riesiges Gelände von Tanklagern mit zahlreichen Betrieben, die sich auf die Zwischenlagerung verschiedener Chemikalien spezialisiert haben.
So entwickelte sich Rotterdam, das im Krieg völlig zerstört wurde, zum größten Zentrum der Petrochemie in Europa. Niederländische Chemieunternehmen produzieren die gesamte Bandbreite an Chemikalien für alle internationalen Absatzmärkte. Es gibt eine Reihe spezieller Bildungseinrichtungen für die Chemieindustrie sowie staatlich geführte R&D-Zentren. Viele Betriebe haben ihre eigene Forschungs- und Entwicklungsabteilung in den Niederlanden.
Für die kommenden Jahre sind beträchtliche Investitionen in neue Werke, Lager- und Transportmöglichkeiten geplant. Solche Investitionen werden von der niederländischen Regierung aktiv gefördert. Strikte Vorschriften sorgen dafür, daß die Chemieindustrie nicht zum großen Umweltverschmutzer wird.

Die niederländischen Schiffswerften

Der Schiffbau ist eine der ältesten Industrien in den Niederlanden. Aufgrund des von Haßliebe geprägten Verhältnisses der Niederländer zum Wasser, der geographischen Lage des Landes, in dem die wichtigsten nordeuropäischen Flüsse in die Nordsee münden, und der langen Handelstradition spielten und spielen Schiffe für die Wirtschaft eine ungeheuer wichtige Rolle.

Ein Fertigteil eines Schiffsrumpfs wird aus der Konstruktionshalle gefahren.

Bereits im Mittelalter fanden sich überall Schiffswerften: Selbst in den kleinsten Siedlungen gab es immer ein paar Menschen, die ein Schiff bauen konnten. Als der Handel mit den Ländern an der Ostsee in Gang kam, pendelten kleine hölzerne Segelschiffe zwischen den wichtigsten Ansiedlungen in Holland und Nordeuropa. Im Zuge des Ausbaus der Handelswege nach Südeuropa und später auch nach Ost- und Westindien baute man dann größere Schiffe.
Holland war jahrhundertelang eine wichtige Schiffahrtsnation, seine Kriegsschiffe schützten die wichtigsten Handelsrouten und Küsten, hauptsächlich gegen die Engländer. Die niederländische Handelsflotte ist immer noch bedeutend, obwohl sie durch die größere Tonnage der Schiffe stark reduziert wurde. Der niederländische Schiffbau wurde in den vergangenen Jahren rationalisiert und gilt derzeit weltweit als besonders effizient und wettbewerbsfähig.
In den sechziger Jahren baute man in den niederländischen Werften jeden Schiffstyp, vom Supertanker bis zum U-Boot. Heute konzentriert sich die abgespeckte Industrie auf das, was sie am besten kann: mittelgroße Handelsschiffe. Darunter fallen Containerschiffe, Kühlschiffe, Fähren, Schleppschiffe und Versorgungsschiffe für Bohrinseln. Beim größten Schiffbaukonzern laufen ganze Schiffe vom Montageband. In riesigen modernen Industriehallen werden Module ganz nach Kundenwunsch angefertigt. Die niederländischen Werften weisen weltweit die höchste Produktivität pro Beschäftigtem auf.
Auch im Jachtbau sind die Niederlande tonangebend. Die hier hergestellten Jachten sind bekannt für ihre Qualität, luxuriöse Ausstattung und Seetauglichkeit. Der internationale Jet-set bestellt seine großen Motorjachten in den Niederlanden. Segeljachten sind gleichermaßen gefragt bei Segelsportlern, die an Hochseeregatten teilnehmen, und Lebenskünstlern, die gerne stilvoll und mit allem Komfort über die Weltmeere segeln. Wie die Handelsschiffe der niederländischen Werften werden auch die Jachten zur Weltspitze gerechnet.

Bierexport

Im Mittelalter galt das brackige Wasser in Holland als ungenießbar. Deshalb tranken alle, Männer, Frauen und Kinder, eine schwache Art von Bier.

Die Bierbrautechnik kam aus Deutschland, aber schon sehr bald stellten die Niederländer ihr eigenes Bier her und verfeinerten dabei das Herstellungsverfahren. Im 16. Jahrhundert gab es in jeder Stadt Brauereien. Die meisten Viertel größerer Städte hatten ihre eigene Brauerei; Bier wurde täglich gebraut und war nicht haltbar.
Ende des 18. Jahrhunderts zählte allein die Provinz Limburg 512 Brauereien, eine für jeweils 290 Einwohner. 1900 waren es immer noch 132, eine stolze Zahl angesichts der Tatsache, daß im ganzen Land nur gut 500 Brauereien bestanden.
Mit dem Aufkommen der Kühltechnik erfolgte eine Konzentration der Bierproduktion. Die Brauereien waren beim Verkauf ihrer Erzeugnisse nun nicht mehr auf die unmittelbare Umgebung ihres Standorts beschränkt. Mit der Entwicklung der Märkte ging die Bierherstellung immer mehr in die Hände einer kleinen Zahl von Brauern über, und die Zahl der Brauereien nahm drastisch ab. Heute werden 95% des heimischen Biers von wenigen Großbrauereien produziert. Die kleineren Brauereien haben sich Marktnischen geschaffen, in denen sie ganz gut leben können.
Wie bei vielen anderen Produkten galt der heimische Markt in den Niederlanden für eine Produktion im großen Stil als zu klein. Die niederländischen Brauer haben große Absatzmärkte in Übersse und sind praktisch in jedem Land beim Verkauf von Importbier die Nummer 1.
Der niederländische Bierkonsum liegt bei etwa 85 Litern pro Kopf im Jahr und entspricht damit in etwa dem der USA. Hinter dem deutschen und polnischen Bierkonsum von 125 Litern pro Jahr bleiben die Niederländer allerdings weit zurück.
Jetzt haben die niederländischen Brauereien den Export in die Wachstumsmärkte Südeuropas, Asiens, Afrikas und Lateinamerikas ins Auge gefaßt. Die Großbrauereien stellen ihr Bier überall auf der Welt unter eigener Leitung her. Die Qualität des niederländischen Exportbiers hat im Ausland einen starken positiven Einfluß auf die Verkaufszahlen.

Kunst

Die Niederlande stehen synonym für Kunst. Auf den Bildern der holländischen Landschaftsmaler ist viel Himmel zu bewundern, wie übrigens auch in der Landschaft selbst.

Die Tradition der schönen Künste geht ins 17. Jahrhundert zurück, Amsterdams Goldenen Zeitalter, die Blütezeit von Malern wie Rembrandt, Vermeer und Hals. Einige dieser Künstler richteten Schulen ein, um ihre eigenen Werke gemeinsam mit den Schülern zu vollenden, aber auch zur Ausbildung junger Künstler. Ihre Werke sind in den vielen bekannten Museen des Landes ausgestellt, darunter das Rijksmuseum in Amsterdam. Andere Museen sind der zeitgenössischen Kunst gewidmet wie das Boymans-Van Beunigen in Rotterdam und das Stedelijke Museum in Amsterdam. Das Kröller-Müller-Museum in der Nähe von Arnheim umfaßt eine große und abwechslungsreiche Sammlung sowie einen interessanten Skulpturenpark. Das Van Gogh-Museum in Amsterdam ist eines der wenigen, das ganz einem einzigen Künstler gewidmet ist. Überall im Land stößt man auf Gebäude, die unter Denkmalschutz stehen - mehr als 7000 allein in Amsterdam.
Ballett, Konzerte und Opern sind in den Niederlanden ebenfalls sehr beliebt. Das Nederlands Dans Theater ist ein berühmtes Tanzensemble, das regelmäßig auf Welttournee geht. Das Amsterdamer Concertgebouworkest gilt international als eines der besten Orchester der Welt, und das Concertgebouw, in dem es zuhause ist, macht mit seiner ausgezeichneten Akustik ebenfalls weltweit Furore. In Amsterdam steht auch die niederländische Staatsoper, die vor allem für ihre avantgardistischen Produktionen bekannt ist. Kunst und Kultur werden überall gefördert. In Rotterdam wird jedes Jahr ein Filmfestival organisiert, in Maastricht findet eine alljährliche Antiquitätenmesse statt.
Viele niederländische Kunstobjekte kommen in den Auktionshäusern in Amsterdam und Den Haag unter den Hammer. Diese Häuser werden von internationalen Kunstauktionatoren, aber auch von niederländischen Fachleuten geführt.
Künstlerische und musikalische Kurse sind in den Niederlanden sehr beliebt, und zwar bei Jung und Alt. Angeboten werden sie von verschiedenen offiziell anerkannten Einrichtungen wie beispielsweise der Rietveld Academie, die sich auf Malerei, Architektur und Bildhauerei spezialisiert hat.

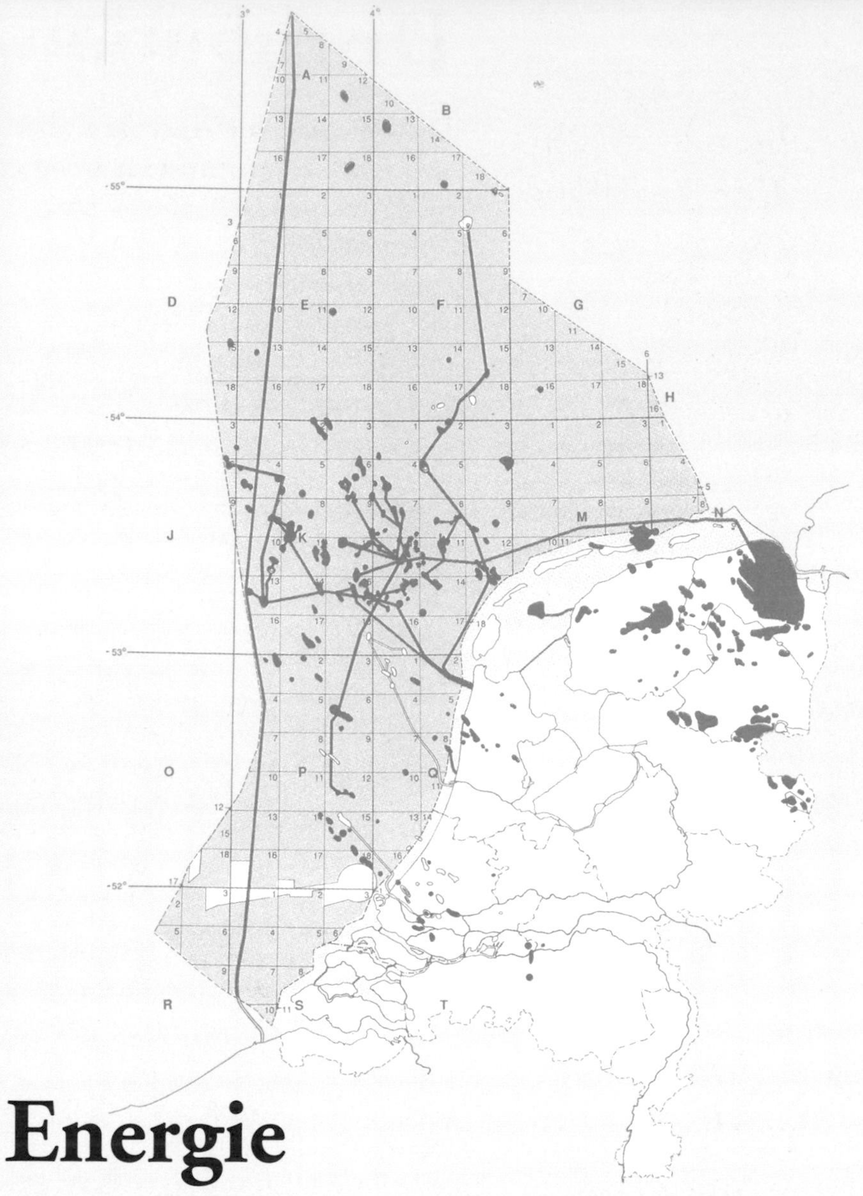

Energie

Die Niederlande besitzen die größten Erdgasreserven in Westeuropa. Bis zu den sechziger Jahren war das Land ein wichtiger Steinkohleproduzent.

Doch dann gingen die Vorräte zur Neige, und billige Steinkohle aus dem Ausland kamen in großen Mengen ins Land. So beschloß die Regierung, die Kohlebergwerke in der südlichen Provinz Limburg zu schließen. Ungefähr zur selben Zeit wurde das Erdgasfeld von Groningen entdeckt. Spätere Entdeckungen weiterer Erdgas- und Erdölfelder an Land und im Meer bildeten den Grundstein für das starke Wirtschaftswachstum in den nächsten Jahrzehnten.
Man beschloß, diese Erdgasreserven zu erhalten, indem man die Politik in den kommenden 50 Jahren auf die Nutzung unterschiedlicher Energiequellen ausrichtete. Inzwischen wurden neue Techniken entwickelt, mit denen auch Erdgas aus kleineren Feldern gewonnen werden kann.
Derzeit exportieren die Niederlande jährlich ungefähr genauso viel Erdgas wie sie selbst verbrauchen. Die Reserven reichen dafür noch etliche Jahrzehnte aus. Es wurden Verträge für den Import von Erdgas beispielsweise aus Rußland, das die größten Vorkommen der Welt besitzt, aber auch aus anderen Ländern wie England abgeschlossen. Auch über den zukünftigen Export von Erdgas in neue Märkte bestehen vertragliche Vereinbarungen.
Man geht davon aus, daß sich die Niederlande in nächster Zukunft zum wichtigsten Erdgaslieferanten Westeuropas entwickeln. Pipeline-Netze zur Verbindung der Import- und Exportmärkte existieren bereits. Der wichtigste Faktor für den Export ist, daß die heimischen Erdgasvorräte, die teilweise in kürzlich angelegten unterirdischen Depots gelagert werden, zur Sicherung der Exportlieferungen verwendet werden können, falls der Erdgasimport plötzlich stagniert. Dies garantiert Kontinuität, was sowohl Importeuren als auch Exporteuren zupaß kommt.

Finanzzentrum

Amsterdam ist eines der wichtigsten Finanzzentren in Europa und spielt in der größer werdenden Europäischen Union eine immer wichtigere Rolle.

Die Stadt hat einen historisch begründeten Bank- und Versicherungssektor, aktive Aktien- und Warenbörsen, innovative Anlagegesellschaften und einen stetig wachsenden Sektor der Finanzdienstleistungen; damit sichert sich Amsterdam seinen Platz direkt hinter den wichtigsten europäischen Finanzzentren London, Frankfurt und Paris.
Die Finanzgeschichte hat eine lange Tradition: Schon immer brauchte man zur Unterstützung des Handels auch die entsprechende Finanzierung, und der Handel war jahrhundertelang einer der Stützpfeiler der niederländischen Wirtschaft. 1602 wurde in Amsterdam die erste Aktiengesellschaft gegründet, um Mittel für die Vereinigte Ostindische Compagnie (VOC) zu beschaffen. Die VOC brachte Gewürze aus Indien und dehnte den Handel später auf andere Waren und andere Regionen der Welt aus.
Die Banken wurden zu Beginn des 19. Jahrhunderts nach der Niederlage Napoleons bei Waterloo und dem anschließenden Rückzug der Franzosen aus den Niederlanden von König Wilhelm I. gefördert.
1997 wurden die Aktien-, Options-, Waren- und Terminbörse zu den Amsterdam Exchanges, besser bekannt unter der Abkürzung AEX, zusammengelegt. Durch diesen Zusammenschluß sollte die Überschneidung der Leistungsangebote beendet und die Präsenz dieser Börsenaktivitäten gefördert werden. An den AEX werden viele amerikanische und andere ausländische Aktien gehandelt. Zudem sind sie ein wichtiges Glied im 24-Stunden-Effektenhandel. Die AEX stehen ausländischen Banken und Maklern offen. An den AEX finden regelmäßig neue Börsengänge statt, da sie als ausgezeichnetes Umfeld für junge Kleinunternehmen betrachtet werden.
Die niederländischen Banken und Versicherungsgesellschaften gehören zu den größten weltweit und sind in allen Teilen der Welt aktiv. Viele dieser Banken sind bereits seit über 100 Jahren in Nord- und Südamerika sowie Asien präsent. Spätere Erweiterungen wurden von der Eroberung neuer Märkte durch niederländische Industriebetriebe begünstigt. Die Banken und Versicherungen spielen eine Schlüsselrolle bei der Einführung neuer Finanzprodukte auf der gesamten Welt.

Infrastruktur

Die Niederlande verfügen über eine moderne und effiziente Transportinfrastruktur. Straßen- und Schienennetz sind mit dem übrigen Europa verbunden, während ein Großteil des inländischen und internationalen Frachtverkehrs über die Flüsse und Wasserstraßen abgewickelt wird.

Derzeit wird das Straßen- und Schienensystem noch weiter ausgebaut, um für eine bessere Erreichbarkeit der Städte und internationalen Routen zu sorgen.
Schiphol Airport in der Nähe von Amsterdam ist der am schnellsten wachsende Flughafen Europas, und das ausgeklügelte single terminal-System garantiert eine effiziente Abwicklung. Schiphol ist der viertgrößte Passagierflughafen und drittgrößte Frachtflughafen in Europa. Mehr als 80 Fluggesellschaften starten täglich von hier aus zu 200 verschiedenen Zielorten. Der Flughafen und seine Zulieferfirmen sind einer der größten Arbeitgeber der Region.
Rotterdam hat den größten Seehafen der Welt, und an allen niederländischen Seehäfen werden insgesamt rund 50% aller internationalen Fracht der Nordseehäfen zwischen Hamburg und Le Havre verschifft.
Der Rotterdamer Hafen ist ideal an der Mündung von Rhein und Maas gelegen, die weiter nach Deutschland, die Schweiz und Mitteleuropa bzw. nach Belgien und Nordfrankreich führen.
Weitere Ausbauten der Infrastruktur sind geplant. So soll Amsterdam/Rotterdam per Hochgeschwindigkeitszug in südlicher Richtung mit Brüssel und Paris und im Osten mit Köln und anderen deutschen Städten verbunden werden. Personenzüge werden als realistische und effiziente Alternative zum Luftverkehr gesehen, was die Überlastung der europäischen Flughäfen reduzieren kann; zugleich sind Bahnreisen eine angenehme Art, von Stadtzentrum zu Stadtzentrum zu gelangen.
In den Niederlanden wird eine reine Güterzugstrecke für Transporte zwischen dem Hafen von Rotterdam und dem Ruhrgebiet gebaut. Ein Großteil des deutschen Exports und Rohstoffimports läuft ohnehin bereits über Rotterdam, und die Schienenverbindung wird daher eine echte Alternative zum Straßen- oder Schiffstransport darstellen.
Zwar ist Schiphol noch lange nicht ausgelastet, aber es gibt schon Pläne für eine Erweiterung des Flughafens um einen Satellitenflughafen auf einer künstlichen Insel in der Nordsee. Der Bau eines solchen Flughafens könnte von niederländischen Bagger- und Bauunternehmen ausgeführt werden, die bei ähnlichen Projekten im Ausland bereits die nötige Erfahrung erworben haben.

Distribution

Die Niederlande sind als Tor zu Europa bekannt und stellen das wichtigste Distributionszentrum für den europäischen Kontinent dar.

Ihre Lage an der Mündung von Rhein und Maas sowie an der Nordsee, der weltweit dichtbefahrendsten Schiffahrtsstraße, machte die Niederlande zu einem Zugangstor für Waren aus Nord- und Südamerika, Asien, Afrika und dem Mittleren Osten. Gleichzeitig werden europäische Waren über holländische Häfen in die ganze Welt verschifft.
Die niederländischen Transportgesellschaften sind Experten für alle Formen der Distribution, und viele Firmen aus diesem Sektor treten als Partner für ausländische Betriebe auf, die auf dem europäischen Markt Fuß fassen wollen. Europa wird in solchen Fällen vielleicht als ein homogener Markt betrachtet, aber es gibt natürlich sprachliche und kulturelle Unterschiede. Häufig wird deshalb kompetente Hilfe benötigt, und die ist in den Niederlanden in Hülle und Fülle vorhanden. Ca. 300 Millionen Menschen wohnen in einem Umkreis von 500 km um Rotterdam und Amsterdam - ein lukrativer Verbrauchermarkt mit großer Kaufkraft. Die Verbindungen in andere europäische Länder sind per Straße, Zug oder Flugzeug sowie über das Meer und die Binnenschiffahrt ausgezeichnet. Value Added Logistics, oder kurz VAL, ist das jüngste Distributionsmittel, das von den Niederländern entwickelt wurde. Mit VAL werden Waren lose in ein Depot verschickt, wo sie ein Upgrade durchlaufen (beispielsweise Hinzufügen anderssprachiger Tastaturen für Computer), verpackt, etikettiert und zum Teil zusammengebaut werden. Ein einzigartiges System miteinander verbundener Depots im ganzen Land gewährleistet, daß keine Importzölle gezahlt werden müssen, da die Waren sich immer noch auf der Durchreise befinden. Die Zusammenarbeit mit den Zollbehörden ist ausgezeichnet.
Europäische Distributionszentren werden immer populärer. Dabei zentriert ein ausländischer Hersteller seine Distributionsaktivitäten in Europa auf einen einzigen Ort. Die Vorteile liegen auf der Hand: Die Exportladungen können für jeden Kunden gesondert und maßgeschneidert zusammengestellt werden. Zudem steht ein mehrsprachiges Team zur Verfügung. Diese Mitarbeiter sind speziell dafür ausgebildet, mit Kunden aus ganz Europa deren Probleme in ihrer eigenen Sprache zu besprechen.

Landwirtschaft

Die Niederländer gehören immer noch zu den produktivsten Landwirten der Welt. Bereits im 16. Jahrhundert baute man große Mengen Hafer für die Viehzucht an, aber durch das Aussäen von Klee und Rüben wurden dem kargen Boden auch Winterfutter und Grünfutter abgerungen.

Die Niederlande mit ihrem dürren und trockenen Boden sind kein natürliches Landwirtschaftsgebiet. Aber seine Bewohner haben es zu einem gemacht, indem sie durch Fruchtwechsel den Nährstoffreichtum erhöhten.
Die modernen niederländischen Scheunen aus Stahl und galvanisiertem Eisen sind überall auf der Welt zu sehen, da die niederländischen Bauern auf grünere Weiden umsiedelten. 1890 arbeitete ein Drittel der Erwerbsbevölkerung in der Land- und Viehwirtschaft. Derzeit sind es weniger als 10%, aber das Resultat ist beeindruckend. Die Niederlande sind - nach den Vereinigten Staaten - der zweitgrößte Exporteur von Agrarprodukten.
Die Rinder- und Schweinezucht ist in den Niederlanden weit verbreitet, wobei landwirtschaftliche Großbetriebe durchaus üblich sind. Niederländische Kühe liefern den höchsten Milchertrag der Welt. Die Exportzahlen für lebende Rinder und Schweine sowie ihr Fleisch liegen sehr hoch. Auch Saatkartoffeln sind ein wichtiger Exportartikel. Die Holländer hatten bei der Erzeugung von Nahrungsmitteln schon immer die Nase vorn. Ein gewisser Willem Breukels aus Zeeland gilt als der erste, der im 14. Jahrhundert Heringe gesalzen hat, um sie haltbar zu machen. Margarine wurde vor gut 100 Jahren zum ersten Mal in den Niederlanden hergestellt.
Ein Großteil der Milcherzeugung fließt in die Herstellung von Butter, Käse, Kondensmilch und Milchpulver, oft auch durch Bauerngenossenschaften. Käse ist ein Exportschlager, Gouda und Edamer werden in der ganzen Welt verkauft.
Obst und Gemüse sind weitere Exportprodukte; niederländische Tomaten, Karotten, Kohl und Paprika sind in allen Geschäften der Welt zu finden, frisch und oft billiger als die einheimischen Produkte. Spezialtransportunternehmen sorgen dafür, daß das Obst und Gemüse frisch verschifft wird.

Ein Labor der Universität Twente

Forschung & Entwicklung

Wissenschaft hat in den Niederlanden eine lange Tradition. Der in Rotterdam geborene holländische Humanist Diderius Erasmus engagierte sich zu Beginn des 16. Jahrhunderts wie kein anderer für den Wissenserwerb.

Viele der frühesten wissenschaftlichen Entdeckungen in Holland fielen in den Bereich Navigation; die holländischen Kaufleute ließen nämlich keine Chance ungenutzt, ihre Position auf den Handelsrouten zu stärken. Daß die holländische Kartographie sehr weit entwickelt war, dürfte deshalb auch kaum jemanden erstaunen. Die Holländer entwickelten auch verschiedene bahnbrechende Techniken in der Chirurgie. Heutzutage sind die Niederlande ein wichtiges Forschungs- und Entwicklungszentrum. Der Staat finanziert unterschiedliche R&D-Institute, die ihrerseits eng mit der Privatwirtschaft zusammenarbeiten. Die größten niederländischen Universitäten haben alle spezielle R&D-Zentren: Landwirtschaft in Wageningen, Medizin in Utrecht, Biotechnologie in Amsterdam usw. Humanistische Forschung wird von verschiedenen akademischen und öffentlich finanzierten Einrichtungen durchgeführt.

Das neue Auktionsgebäude in Poeldijk

Auch im privaten Sektor existieren zahlreiche, über das Land verstreute R&D-Zentren. Die Niederlande haben in dieser Hinsicht aufgrund der großen Zahl mehrsprachiger Akademiker, die Jahr für Jahr von den Universitäten kommen, eine gewisse Popularität errungen. Die einzelnen R&D-Zentren pflegen einen permanenten Kontakt zum Austausch von Erfahrungen und Forschungsergebnissen.
Überall existieren Wissenschaftszentren. Sie werden von der niederländischen Regierung gefördert, um neue Produkte und Dienstleistungen zu entwickeln. Diese sogenannten "Denkfabriken" werden im Ausland mit großem Interesse verfolgt. In den Wissenschaftszentren können einzelne Betriebe zusammenarbeiten und vor Ort entwickelte Produkte und Ideen nutzen. Das Konzept umfaßt auch universitäre Forschungszentren, um den Kontakt zwischen Wirtschaft und Wissenschaft zu fördern, sowie Technologiezentren für die Vermarktung von Spitzentechnologie.
Verschiedene "Centres of Excellence" sind staatlich anerkannt, beispielsweise im Bereich Landwirtschaft oder Chemie. Dahinter steckt der Gedanke, daß so die weitere Forschung in diesen Bereichen und die Entwicklung neuer Produkte gefördert wird.

L'industrie chimique

Avec plus de 80.000 employés, l'industrie chimique est une des industries les plus importantes aux Pays-Bas. Trois multinationales importantes y ont leur siège social.

En outre, plusieurs trusts de chimie étrangers ont des intérêts importants en Hollande. De plus, il existe un bon nombre de petites entreprises néerlandaises, souvent fort spécialisées, opérant dans ce domaine.
Aux Pays-Bas, le prix de l'énergie pour les grandes industries est un des plus bas en Europe. Le co˚t de l'énergie représente plus ou moins 60% du prix de revient de la plupart des produits chimiques. En outre, le pays a d'immenses réserves de gaz naturel et de sel, des éléments indispensables à de nombreux produits chimiques.
Le grand complexe de raffineries de Rotterdam procure énormément de matières premières nécessaires à la production de produits chimiques. Bon nombre d'entreprises chimiques sont situées dans le port où elles peuvent recevoir facilement les matières premières et expédier les produits finis. Outre la mer et le Rhin, les produits chimiques sont également transportés dans toute l'Europe grâce à un énorme réseau de pipelines relié aux réseaux nationaux des autres pays d'Europe. Des pipelines spéciaux relient Rotterdam à la région industrielle de la Ruhr, en Allemagne, et un nouveau pipeline reliera Rotterdam à Anvers, le plus important centre d'industrie chimique en Belgique.
Rotterdam dispose aussi d'un immense complexe de réservoirs et plusieurs compagnies sont spécialisées dans l'entreposage temporaire de certains produits chimiques spéciaux. Après la guerre, Rotterdam s'est relevée de ses cendres pour devenir le centre européen de pétrochimie le plus important.

Une partie de la coque prête pour l'assemblage sort de la halle de montage

Aux Pays-Bas, l'industrie chimique produit toute une série de produits chimiques destinés aux marchés dans le monde entier. Il y a également des centres de formation professionnelle spécialisés pour l'industrie chimique ainsi que des centres de recherche et de développement fondés par le gouvernement. De nombreuses entreprises aux Pays-Bas ont leur propre centre de R&D.
D'importants investissements dans de nouvelles fabriques, entrepôts et dans le domaine des transports sont prévus pour les prochaines années. Le gouvernement hollandais stimule les investissements dans ce secteur. Des normes sévères garantissent que l'industrie chimique ne deviendra pas un pollueur important.

Les chantiers navals néerlandais

La construction navale est une des plus vieilles industries des Pays-Bas. Etant donné les rapports haine-amour que ce pays entretient avec l'eau, son emplacement géographique où les rivières les plus importantes de l'Europe septentrionale se jettent dans la mer du Nord et ses traditions commerciales, les bateaux occupaient et occupent toujours une place essentielle au sein de l'économie du pays.

Déjà au moyen âge, il y avait des chantiers navals partout, et même dans les endroits les plus dépeuplés, il y avait toujours des gens capables de construire un bateau.
Quand les premiers hollandais ont commencé à faire du commerce avec les pays Baltes, de petits bateaux à voile en bois naviguaient entre les grandes villes des Pays-Bas et d'Europe septentrionale. Des bateaux plus grands ont été construits lorsque les routes commerciales ont commencé à se développer vers l'Europe méridionale et, plus tard, vers les Indes orientales et occidentales.
Pendant bien des siècles, les Pays-Bas ont eu une force navale importante, les bâtiments de guerre hollandais protégeaient les routes commerciales principales et les côtes, en particulier contre les Anglais. Bien que le nombre de ses bateaux soit réduit et que ceux-ci soient maintenant plus grands, la flotte marchande hollandaise est encore puissante. En Hollande, la construction navale a été modernisée ces dernières années et fait maintenant partie des plus performantes et des plus compétitives au monde. Durant les années 60, les chantiers navals hollandais ont construit tous les bateaux possibles, allant des pétroliers géants aux sous-marins.
De nos jours, cette industrie amincie se concentre sur ce qu'elle fait de mieux : des bateaux de taille moyenne pour la marine marchande, ceci comprenant les porte-conteneurs, les navires frigorifiques, les ferry-boats, les remorqueurs et les avitailleurs offshore. Le groupe de construction navale le plus important livre même des bateaux qui sont pour ainsi dire fabriqués à la chaÓne. Les modules sont confectionnés dans de grands hangars modernes, d'après les dimensions exactes du client. Les chantiers navals hollandais ont la productivité la plus élevée au monde par employé.
Les yachts sont une autre spécialisation. Les yachts construits en Hollande sont réputés pour leur qualité, leur luxe et leur navigabilité. Le jet set international commande ses yachts en Hollande. Les voiliers sont fort appréciés tant par les amateurs de voile en haute mer que par les personnes de go˚t qui aiment à naviguer sur les océans dans le confort et la classe. Tout comme les navires marchands construits dans les chantiers navals hollandais, les yachts sont considérés comme les meilleurs au monde.

Exportation de la bière

Au moyen âge, aux Pays-Bas, l'eau saumâtre n'était pas potable. C'est pourquoi la plupart des gens, hommes, femmes et enfants buvaient une sorte de bière à faible degré d'alcool.

Les techniques de brassage provenaient d'Allemagne, mais les hollandais ont produit rapidement leur propre bière en améliorant le processus. Au 16e siècle, chaque ville avaient ses propres brasseries et dans les grandes villes, la plupart des quartiers avaient aussi leur propre brasserie : la bière était faite chaque jour et ne pouvait pas être conservée.
A la fin du 18e siècle, la province du Limbourg, à elle seule, comptait 512 brasseries, une par 290 habitants. En 1990, il n'en restait plus que 132, un chiffre cependant élevé quand on pense qu'il y en avait à peine plus de 500 dans tout le pays.
L'arrivée de la réfrigération a permis aux brasseries de consolider leur position. Elles ne devaient plus limiter la vente de leurs produits aux environs directs de la brasserie. Avec l'expansion du marché, la production s'est de plus en plus retrouvée entre les mains d'un petit nombre de brasseurs et le nombre total des brasseries a baissé de manière drastique. De nos jours, quelques brasseries importantes produisent 95% des bières nationales. Environ 80 petits brasseurs se sont fait une petite place dans le marché et leurs affaires marchent bien.
Comme c'est le cas de nombreux autres produits, le marché néerlandais est trop petit pour une production à grande échelle. Les brasseurs hollandais disposent d'importants marchés étrangers, et dans pratiquement tous les pays, la bière hollandaise tient la première place parmi les bières importées. Le hollandais consomme environ 85 litres de bière par an, à peu près autant qu'aux Etats-Unis. La Hollande est cependant derrière l'Allemagne et la Pologne où l'on consomme 125 litres de bière par habitant par an. Les brasseurs hollandais visent cependant les marchés en expansion d'Europe méridionale, d'Asie, d'Afrique et d'Amérique latine. Les brasseurs les plus importants produisent leur bière partout dans le monde sous leur propre supervision. La qualité de la bière d'exportation hollandaise est un facteur important lors des ventes à l'étranger.

Les beaux-arts

La Hollande est synonyme de beaux-arts. Il y a autant de cieux dans les paysages des peintres hollandais qu'il y en a dans le pays.

Cette tradition artistique remonte au 17e siècle, l'âge d'or d'Amsterdam, une époque où prospéraient des peintres tels que Rembrandt, Vermeer et Hals. Certains de ces artistes ont fondé des écoles pour finir leurs propres travaux avec leurs élèves et pour former de jeunes artistes. Leurs oeuvres peuvent être admirées dans les nombreux musées importants que compte le pays, dont le Rijksmuseum à Amsterdam. Certains musées sont dédiés à l'art contemporain, tels que le Boymans-Van Beuningen à Rotterdam et le Stedelijk à Amsterdam. Le musée Kröller-Müller, situé près de Arnhem, a une collection très étendue et très variée ainsi qu'un jardin de sculptures digne d'intérêt. Le musée Van Gogh à Amsterdam est un des rares au monde à n'être dédié qu'à un seul artiste.
Partout dans le pays, de nombreux bâtiments sont classés, la ville d'Amsterdam à elle seule en compte plus de 7000.
La danse, les concerts et l'opéra connaissent également une grande popularité en Hollande. Le Nederlands Dans Theatre a une troupe de danse célèbre qui fait des tournées régulières dans le monde entier. L'Orchestre du Concertgebouw d'Amsterdam est constamment classé parmi les meilleurs au niveau international, et le Concertgebouw, avec son acoustique parfaite, fait fureur dans le monde entier. L'Opéra Néerlandais est également situé à Amsterdam et est surtout connu pour ses productions d'avant-garde. La vie culturelle est encouragée dans tout le pays. Un festival du cinéma a lieu chaque année à Rotterdam et Maastricht a sa foire aux antiquités.
Une grande partie de l'art hollandais est vendu aux enchères à Amsterdam et à La Haye. Ces ventes sont effectuées par des maisons de vente aux enchères internationales mais aussi par des experts hollandais. Dans les grandes maisons, il y a des ventes régulières de peintures, de dessins, d'argenterie, de meubles et d'objets d'art.
Les formations artistiques et musicales jouissent d'une grande popularité et ce, tant parmi les jeunes que les personnes âgées. Il existe plusieurs établissements reconnus, tels que l'Académie Rietveld qui se spécialise dans la peinture, l'architecture et la sculpture.

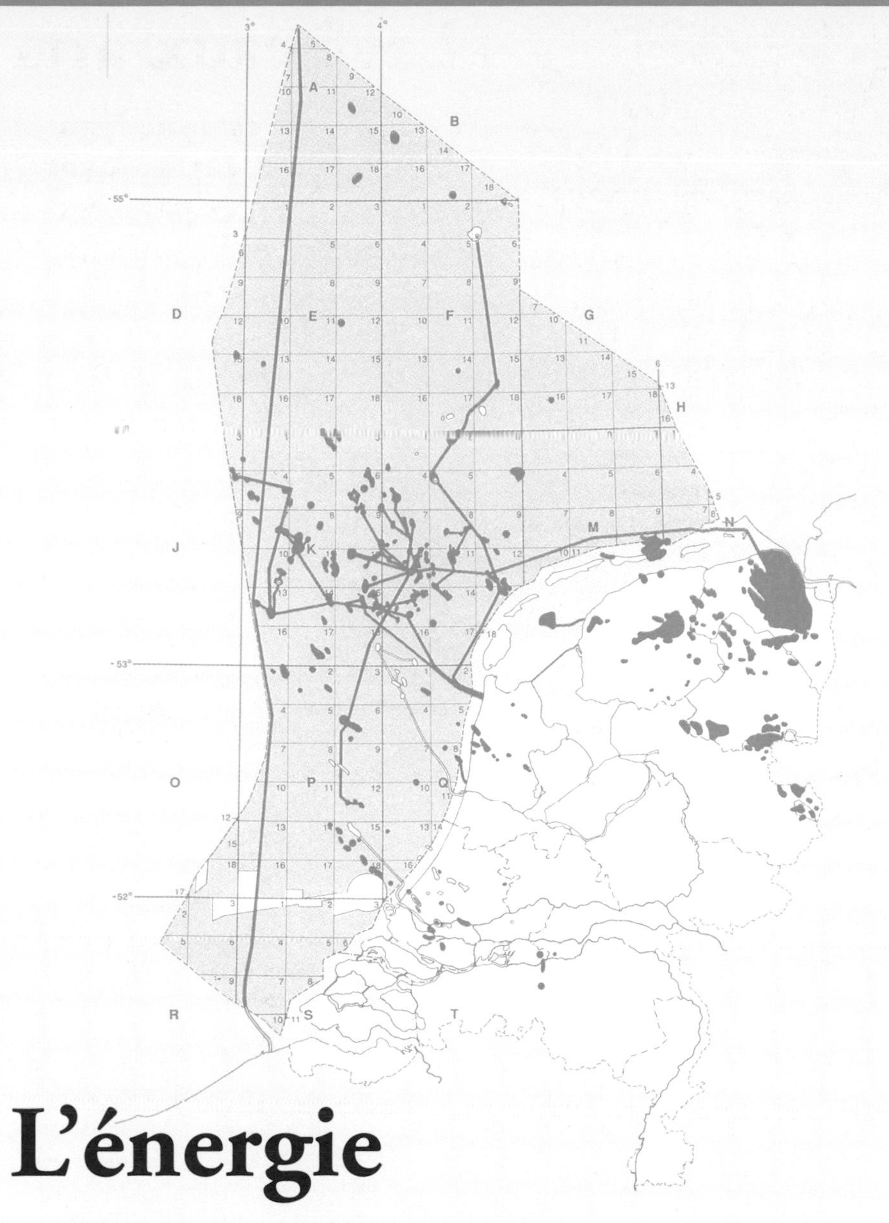

L'énergie

Les Pays-Bas ont les réserves de gaz naturel les plus importantes d'Europe occidentale. Ce pays était un important producteur de charbon jusque dans les années 60.

Mais le gouvernement a décidé de fermer les mines de charbon de la province méridionale du Limbourg quand la production a commencé à diminuer et que du charbon bon marché a commencé à venir de l'étranger. C'est environ au même moment que la poche de gaz naturel de Groningue (de la province qui porte le même nom) fut découverte. La découverte d'autres poches de gaz naturel et de nappes de pétrole en mer et sur terre ont été à l'origine de la croissance économique dans le pays dans les décennies qui ont suivi. On a décidé de préserver ces réserves de gaz pendant les 50 années à venir en utilisant différentes sources d'énergie. Entre-temps, de nouvelles techniques d'extraction de gaz ont été développées pour les poches moins importantes.

De nos jours, les Pays-Bas exportent annuellement environ une quantité de gaz naturel égale à celle qu'ils consomment. Les réserves sont suffisantes pour répondre à la demande durant plusieurs décennies. Il existe des contrats d'importation de gaz naturel avec la Russie qui a les plus grandes réserves au monde, ainsi qu'avec l'Angleterre. D'autres contrats règlent à leur tour l'exportation de gaz naturel.

On s'attend à ce que, dans un avenir proche, les Pays-Bas deviennent le fournisseur de gaz naturel le plus important d'Europe occidentale. Il existe des réseaux de pipelines qui relient les marchés d'importation et d'exportation.

Le point le plus important est que les réserves de gaz naturel néerlandais, stockées en partie dans des entrepôts souterrains récents, peuvent être utilisées pour assurer l'exportation au cas où, contre toute attente, l'importation du gaz naturel était paralysée. Ceci garantit la continuité, ce qui profite aussi bien aux importateurs qu'aux exportateurs.

Le centre financier

Amsterdam est un des centres financiers européens les plus importants et joue un rôle de plus en plus prépondérant dans une Union Européenne grandissante.

Avec un puissant secteur de banques et d'assurances, une bourse des valeurs et une bourse de commerce actives, des sociétés d'investissement novatrices et un secteur de services financiers en pleine expansion, Amsterdam se trouve juste après Londres, Francfort et Paris, les centres financiers les plus importants en Europe. Les racines sont profondes : le financement a de tout temps été nécessaire pour assister le commerce, qui est depuis des siècles un des piliers de l'économie néerlandaise. En 1602, la première société par actions a été fondée à Amsterdam dans le but de se procurer des fonds pour la Compagnie des Indes orientales, connue sous le nom de VOC. La VOC avait été fondée pour ramener des épices de l'archipel indonésien et a étendu plus tard ses activités en important des marchandises venant d'autres continents. Au début du 19e siècle, les banques ont pris de l'essor sous le règne de Guillaume 1er, après la défaite de Napoléon à Waterloo et la retraite des troupes françaises.

En 1997, la bourse des valeurs, le marché à options, la bourse de commerce et le marché à terme d'Amsterdam ont fusionné pour former la Bourse d'Amsterdam, plus connue sous le nom d'AEX. La décision avait été prise afin d'éliminer les services qui faisaient double emploi et de permettre aux activités boursières de jouer un rôle de premier plan. L'AEX traite un nombre élevé d'actions américaines et étrangères et joue un rôle de premier plan dans le commerce continu des valeurs. Le marché à options a été le premier en Europe à traiter des affaires internationales. L'AEX est ouverte aux banques et aux courtiers étrangers. Il est courant de voir de nouvelles entreprises cotées en bourse, l'AEX est considérée comme un endroit idéal pour les petites entreprises et celles qui débutent. Les banques et les compagnies d'assurance néerlandaises font partie des plus importantes au monde, et elles sont actives dans le monde entier. Une grande partie de ces banques sont installées aux Amériques et en Asie depuis plus de 100 ans. L'expansion ultérieure a été stimulée par l'établissement d'entreprises industrielles néerlandaises dans ces nouveaux marchés. Les banques et les compagnies d'assurance jouent un rôle-clé lors de l'introduction de nouveaux produits financiers dans le monde entier.

FRANÇAIS

L'infrastructure

En Hollande, l'infrastructure des transports est moderne et efficace. Les routes et les chemins de fer relient le pays au reste de l'Europe, tandis qu'une grande partie du transport de marchandises national et international passe par les rivières et les eaux intérieures.

Le réseau routier et ferroviaire est en train de se développer afin d'offrir un meilleur accès aux villes et aux routes internationales. Schiphol Airport, près d'Amsterdam, est l'aéroport qui croÓt le plus rapidement en Europe et le système sophistiqué de single terminal garantit une grande efficacité. En se basant sur le nombre de passagers, Schiphol est le quatrième aéroport européen et le troisième en ce qui concerne le fret aérien. Plus de 80 compagnies aériennes partent chaque jour pour plus de 200 destinations. L'aéroport et le secteur industriel qui le soutient représentent un des employeurs les plus importants de la région.
Rotterdam est le port maritime le plus important au monde et l'ensemble des ports maritimes hollandais traitent environ 50% de la totalité des chargements internationaux traités dans les ports de la mer du Nord entre Hambourg et Le Havre. Le port de Rotterdam a un emplacement idéal à l'embouchure du Rhin et de la Meuse, et dessert l'Allemagne, la Suisse, l'Europe centrale, la Belgique et le nord de la France.
Il existe des plans d'expansion de l'infrastructure. Des lignes de TGV doivent relier Amsterdam/Rotterdam à Bruxelles et Paris au sud et à Cologne ainsi qu'à d'autres villes allemandes à l'est. Les trains de voyageurs sont considérés comme une solution de remplacement viable et efficace pour le trafic aérien, ils réduiront l'affluence dans les aéroports européens tout en offrant un moyen de transport agréable entre les différentes villes.
Les Pays-Bas ont décidé de construire une ligne de chemin de fer pour le transport de marchandises entre le port de Rotterdam et le bassin de la Ruhr, en Allemagne. Une grande partie des exportations allemandes et l'importation des matières premières passent déjà par Rotterdam et la liaison ferroviaire offre une solution de remplacement pour les transports routiers et la navigation intérieure.
Schiphol est loin d'avoir atteint son point de saturation, mais des propositions ont cependant déjà été faites afin d'agrandir l'aéroport en construisant un aéroport satellite sur une Óle artificielle dans la mer du Nord. La construction d'un tel aéroport pourrait être faite par des entreprises néerlandaises de dragage et de construction qui sont passées maÓtre en la matière en effectuant ce genre de travail à l'étranger.

La distribution

Connus sous le nom de porte de l'Europe, les Pays-Bas sont le principal centre de distribution du continent.

Leur emplacement dans le delta du Rhin et de la Meuse et au bord de la mer du Nord, la route maritime la plus utilisée au monde, a fait de ce pays une entrée naturelle pour les marchandises en provenance d'Amérique du Nord, d'Amérique du Sud, d'Asie, d'Afrique et du Moyen-Orient.
Au même moment, des marchandises européennes passent par les ports néerlandais afin d'être expédiées par bateau vers des destinations étrangères.
Les entreprises de transports hollandaises sont experts dans toutes les formes de distribution et de nombreuses entreprises dans ce secteur agissent en tant que partenaires pour les firmes étrangères qui désirent accéder au marché européen. L'Europe pourrait sembler être un marché unique, mais elle connaÓt différentes langues et civilisations. Une aide spécialisée est souvent nécessaire et elle est heureusement facilement disponible en Hollande. 300 millions de personnes environ vivent dans un rayon de 500 km de Rotterdam et d'Amsterdam. C'est un marché lucratif où le pouvoir d'achat des consommateurs est important. L'accès au reste de l'Europe est facile et cela grâce aux routes, aux voies ferrées, aux voies aériennes, à la mer et à la navigation intérieure.
Le Value Added Logistics (ou VAL) est le dernier moyen de distribution développé par les néerlandais. Avec VAL, les marchandises sont transportées en vrac dans un entrepôt où elles sont mises à jour (des claviers pour langues étrangères sont par exemple ajoutés aux ordinateurs), emballées, étiquetées et, dans certains cas, assemblées. Un système unique d'entrepôts interconnectés dans tout le pays permet de ne pas avoir à payer de droits d'entrée étant donné que les marchandises sont toujours en transit. Les autorités douanières coopèrent sans le moindre problème.
Les Centres de Distribution Européens deviennent de plus en plus populaires. Grâce à ce système, un producteur étranger est en mesure de centraliser sa distribution européenne en un seul endroit. Les avantages en sont évidents vu que les transports pour l'étranger peuvent être 'ajustés' pour chaque client. De plus, un personnel polyglotte est disponible pour assister en ce qui concerne les opérations de service. Ce personnel est formé pour discuter dans toute l'Europe avec les clients qui ont des problèmes et ce, dans leur propre langue.

L'agriculture

Le fermier hollandais est un des plus performants au monde. Au 16e siècle, l'on produisait déjà de grandes quantités d'avoine pour le bétail ainsi que du fourrage d'hiver et de l'herbage en semant du trèfle et des navets dans les terres peu abondantes.

En fait, avec leur sol aride et sablonneux , les Pays-Bas ne sont pas une région agricole naturelle. Mais les hollandais en ont fait quelque chose, alternant les récoltes pour augmenter les substances nutritives. La grange hollandaise moderne en acier et en fer galvanisé a fait son apparition dans le monde entier étant donné que les fermiers hollandais étaient partis à la recherche de nouveaux horizons.
En 1890, l'agriculture et l'élevage procuraient du travail à un tiers de la population ouvrière. De nos jours, ce chiffre n'atteint même plus les 10%, mais la production est impressionnante. La Hollande est le deuxième pays exportateur de produits agricoles, après les Etats-Unis. L'élevage de bétail et de porcs est très répandu aux Pays-Bas et les fermes de grande envergure sont une chose assez courante. Les vaches hollandaises ont le plus grand rendement en lait au monde. Les exportations de bétail et de (viande de) porcs sont importantes. Les plants de pommes de terre représentent également un produit d'exportation important.
Les hollandais ont toujours été les leaders dans le domaine du traitement des aliments. Au 14e siècle, un certain Willem Breukels, originaire de la province de Zélande, semble être le premier à avoir salé des harengs pour les conserver. Il y a environ cent ans, la margarine a été produite pour la première fois aux Pays-Bas.
Une grande partie du lait est utilisée pour la production du beurre, du fromage, du lait en poudre et du lait condensé, la plupart du temps par les coopératives qui appartiennent aux fermiers. Le fromage est un produit d'exportation important, le Gouda et l'Edam sont connus dans le monde entier.
Des autres produits d'exportation sont les fruits et les légumes. Les tomates, les carottes, les choux et les poivrons de Hollande se vendent dans le monde entier, ils sont frais et souvent moins chers que les produits locaux. Des entreprises de transport spécialisées font en sorte que les fruits et les légumes soient transportés frais.

Un des laboratories de l'Université de Twente

Recherche & Developpement

Les Pays-Bas jouissent d'une longue tradition en ce qui concerne les sciences. Né à Rotterdam, Didier Erasme, l'humaniste hollandais, a fait plus que n'importe qui d'autre pour faire avancer les connaissances au début du 16e siècle.

Au départ, un grand nombre des découvertes scientifiques aux Pays-Bas avaient à voir avec la navigation ; en effet, les marchands hollandais visaient à renforcer leur prise sur les routes commerciales. Il n'est donc pas étonnant que les Hollandais soient passés maîtres dans l'art de la cartographie.
Certaines techniques novatrices en chirurgie ont aussi été développées par des Hollandais. De nos jours, les Pays-Bas sont un centre important de recherche et de développement. Le gouvernement finance plusieurs institutions de R&D qui, de leur côté, travaillent en étroite collaboration avec le secteur privé. Les plus importantes universités hollandaises disposent toutes d'un centre de R&D spécialisé : l'agriculture à Wageningen, la médecine à Utrecht, la biotechnologie à Amsterdam, et ainsi de suite. Les recherches dans les sciences humaines sont effectuées par plusieurs institutions académiques financées par le gouvernement. Le secteur privé dispose de nombreux centres de R&D à travers le pays. Les Pays-Bas ont acquis une grande popularité grâce au nombre important d'universitaires polyglottes qui terminent leurs études chaque année. Il existe un échange important des connaissances entre les différents centres de R&D.
On trouve des centres scientifiques un peu partout dans le pays. Le gouvernement hollandais pratique une politique d'encouragement en stimulant les nouveaux développements dans le domaine de l'industrie et des services. Ces ëgroupes d'experts' ont soulevé un intérêt important à l'étranger. Ces centres permettent aux entreprises individuelles de coopérer et de faire usage des produits et des idées développés sur place. Ce concept comprend des centres de recherche établis dans les universités afin de promouvoir les contacts entre les entreprises et la science ainsi que les centres de technologie destinés à l'exploitation commerciale de la haute technologie.
Le gouvernement a reconnu plusieurs ëcentres of excellence', par exemple dans le domaine de l'agriculture et de la chimie. Le but de ces centres est d'encourager les recherches dans ces domaines et de stimuler le développement de nouveaux produits.

Le nouveau bâtiment du marché de gros à Poeldijk

La industria química

La industria química, con un índice de empleo superior a 80.000 personas, es una de las industrias más importantes de Holanda. En el país tienen su sede tres grandes multinacionales y otros muchos consorcios extranjeros realizan amplias operaciones.

El país cuenta con otras empresas menores generalmente muy especializadas que operan también en este terreno.
En los Países Bajos los costes de energía para las grandes industrias son de los más bajos de Europa y suponen grosso modo un 60% del precio de coste de la mayoría de los productos químicos. El país posee grandes reservas de gas natural y sal, elementos clave de muchos productos químicos.
El vasto complejo de refinería de Rotterdam proporciona gran número de materias primas para la producción de productos químicos. Muchas empresas químicas se encuentran localizadas en el puerto desde donde pueden recibir las materias primas y expedir los productos acabados con gran facilidad. Los productos químicos no sólo se transportan por vía marítima y fluvial, por el Rin, sino también a través de una red de tuberías que conecta con las conducciones nacionales en otras partes de Europa. Unas tuberías de productos químicos especiales conectan a Rotterdam con el complejo industrial alemán de la cuenca del Ruhr, estando proyectada una nueva conducción entre Rotterdam y Amberes, el principal centro de industria química de Bélgica.

Rotterdam cuenta también con un amplio parque de depósitos y diversas compañías especializadas en el almacenaje temporal de tipos especiales de productos químicos. De hecho, Rotterdam, resucitando de las cenizas de la guerra, se ha convertido en el centro petroquímico más importante de Europa.
El sector químico holandés manufactura tanto productos en bruto como productos refinados para todos los mercados del mundo. Numerosas instituciones especializadas de enseñanza forman graduados que luego trabajarán en la industria química. También existen centros de investigación y desarrollo dependientes del Estado. Muchas empresas poseen en Holanda sus propias instalaciones de I+D.
Para los años próximos se están planeando inversiones en nuevas plantas e instalaciones de almacenaje y transporte. El gobierno holandés estimula activamente las inversiones en el sector y, por medio de unas normas muy estrictas trata de evitar que la industria química se convierta en un elemento polucionador.

Una parte acabada del casco es sacada de los muelles de construcción

Los astilleros holandeses

La construcción de barcos es una de las industrias más antiguas de los Países Bajos. Dada la relación de amor y odio que tiene el país con el agua, su situación geográfica, en el punto de confluencia de los grandes ríos septentrionales con el mar del Norte, y sus tradiciones mercantiles, los barcos eran y siguen siendo imprescindibles para la economía.

En la Edad Media surgían astilleros en todas partes; en cualquier aldea, por pequeña que fuese, había alguien que sabía el oficio de construir barcos. Cuando los holandeses empezaron a comerciar con los estados bálticos, pequeños veleros de madera hacían el viaje entre los grandes asentamientos holandeses y sus contrapartidas en los países nórdicos. Los barcos aumentaron de tamaño cuando las rutas comerciales se extendieron al sur de Europa y más tarde a las Indias Orientales y Occidentales.
Los Países Bajos fueron una potencia marítima importante durante varios siglos, sus barcos de guerra protegían, sobre todo de ingleses, sus vitales rutas de comercio y sus costas. La flota mercante holandesa sigue siendo muy fuerte aunque en la actualidad se va reduciendo a medida que va aumentando el tonelaje de los barcos. La industria naviera holandesa ha sido racionalizada recientemente y en la actualidad se cuenta entre las más eficientes y competitivas del mundo. En los años sesenta los astilleros holandeses construyeron prácticamente todos los tipos de barcos existentes, desde grandes petroleros hasta submarinos.

Hoy en día, la recortada industria se concentra en lo que mejor sabe hacer: barcos mercantes de tamaño medio entre los que se incluyen buques de contenedores, navíos refrigeradores, transbordadores de pasajeros, remolcadores y barcos de abastecimiento de plataformas marinas. El mayor grupo de construcción de navíos produce barcos virtualmente construidos en la línea de montaje. Los módulos se montan en grandes y modernas naves cubiertas según las instrucciones exactas de los compradores. Los astilleros holandeses poseen la productividad por trabajador más alta del mundo.
Otra especialidad de los holandeses son los yates, que son famosos por su calidad, lujo y navegabilidad. Magnates del mundo entero encargan en Holanda sus grandes yates de motor. Los barcos de vela los encargan participantes en regatas oceánicas así como particulares que disfrutan navegando a vela cómoda y lujosamente por los cuatro océanos. Al igual que los buques mercantes, los yates producidos en los astilleros holandeses están considerados como lo mejor y en buena relación calidad/precio.

La exportación de cerveza

El agua salobre que había en Holanda durante la Edad Media se consideraba como impropia para el consumo humano. El resultado fue la elaboración de una cerveza ligera que consumía todo el mundo, hombres, mujeres y niños.

Las técnicas de elaboración procedían de Alemania, pero los holandeses empezaron enseguida a producir su propia cerveza, refinando el proceso poco a poco. En el siglo XVI había cervecerías en todos los pueblos. En las ciudades, había cervecerías en todos los barrios: la cerveza se producía cada día y no podía conservarse.
A fines del siglo XVIII, solamente en la provincia de Limburgo había 512 cervecerías, una por cada 290 habitantes. En 1900, quedaban 132, un número bastante elevado, si se tiene en cuenta que en todo el país no quedaban más que 500.
Con el advenimiento de la refrigeración, las cervecerías empezaron a fusionarse. Ahora podían vender su producción más lejos y no sólo en el inmediato entorno de la cervecería. Al ampliarse los mercados, las cervecerías se hicieron mayores y el número total de empresas bajó drásticamente. Hoy en día, el 95% de la cerveza doméstica producida en el país es elaborada por unas cuantas fábricas grandes. Una veintena de pequeños cerveceros han hecho unos nichos en el mercado y están incrementando sus ventas.
Como ocurre con tantos otros productos, el mercado doméstico holandés se considera demasiado pequeño para la producción a gran escala. Los cerveceros holandeses poseen grandes mercados extranjeros y lideran las ventas de las cervezas de importación en casi todos los países del mundo.
En Holanda se consumen per cápita unos 85 litros de cerveza al año, aproximadamente el mismo nivel que en Estados Unidos, aunque el consumo holandés queda por detrás del alemán y el polaco, con unos niveles tope de 125 litros al año. Para incrementar sus ventas de exportación, los cerveceros holandeses dirigen ahora sus miradas a los crecientes mercados del sur de Europa, Asia, África y Latinoamérica. Las mayores cervecerías producen cerveza en todo el mundo bajo su propia supervisión. La calidad de la cerveza holandesa de exportación permite promover las ventas en el extranjero.

Las artes

Los Países Bajos son sinónimo de arte. Los cielos de los paisajistas holandeses son como los del país mismo.

La tradición artística data del siglo XVII, el Siglo de Oro de Amsterdam, período de florecimiento de pintores tales como Rembrandt, Vermeer y Hals. A veces, estos artistas creaban escuelas para ayudar a finalizar sus propias obras y enseñar a los artistas jóvenes. Sus obras pueden contemplarse en los grandes museos del país entre los que se cuenta el Rijksmuseum de Amsterdam. Existen museos dedicados a un arte más contemporáneo, como el Boymans Van Beuningen de Rotterdam y el Stedelijk de Amsterdam. El museo Kröller-Müller, cerca de Arnhem, posee una amplia y rica colección así como un importante jardín de esculturas. El museo Van Gogh de Amsterdam es uno de los pocos del mundo que están dedicados por entero a un solo artista importante.
Muchos edificios del país figuran en las listas de monumentos, de ellos 7.000 se encuentran en Amsterdam, lo cual ha permitido conservar el centro histórico de la ciudad, en su mayor parte del siglo XVII, que constituye una especie de museo viviente. En cualquier rincón de cualquier ciudad e incluso en los más estrechos caminos vecinales pueden admirarse obras escultóricas. En Holanda son también muy populares la danza, la ópera y los conciertos musicales. El Nederlands Dans Theatre es una famosa compañía de ballet que realiza con regularidad giras por todo el mundo. La Concertgebouworkest de Amsterdam está considerada internacionalmente como una de las mejores, así como su sede, el acústicamente casi perfecto Concertgebouw. La Netherlands Opera, con sede asimismo en Amsterdam, es conocida por sus producciones vanguardistas. En todas partes se fomenta el arte y la cultura. Rotterdam celebra un festival anual de cine y Maastricht un salón de bellas artes. Gran número de objetos artísticos holandeses se sacan a subasta pública en las casas de subastas de Amsterdam y La Haya, dirigidas tanto por las grandes casas de subastas internacionales como por especialistas holandeses. En las casas principales se venden regularmente pinturas, dibujos, objetos de plata, muebles y otros objetos de arte.
Las clases de arte y música son muy populares entre jóvenes y mayores. Existen varias instituciones acreditadas como la Rietveld Academie, que está especializada en pintura, arquitectura y escultura.

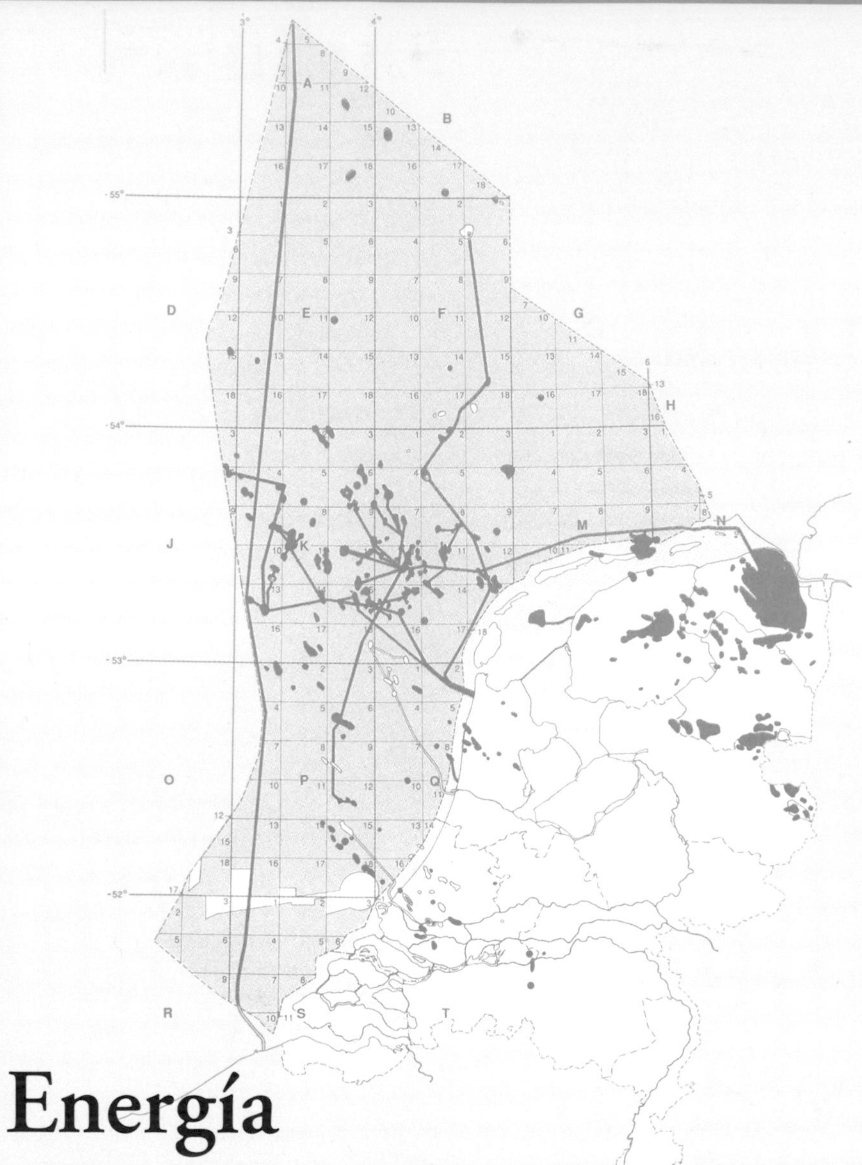

Energía

Los Países Bajos cuentan con las reservas de gas natural mayores de Europa Occidental. El país era un gran productor de carbón hasta los años sesenta en que el descenso de las existencias y los grandes suministros de carbón extranjero barato incitaron al gobierno a tomar la decisión de cerrar las minas de carbón de la provincia de Limburgo.

Aproximadamente en la misma época se descubrió el yacimiento de Groninga en la provincia septentrional del mismo nombre.
Otros descubrimientos subsiguientes de yacimientos de gas natural y petróleo tanto en tierra como en el mar echaron las bases del robusto crecimiento económico del país en las décadas siguientes. Se decidió conservar las reservas de gas adoptando la política de diversificar las fuentes de energía durante los 50 años siguientes. Mientras tanto se fueron desarrollando nuevas técnicas de extracción del gas de yacimientos más pequeños y marginales.
Hoy en día, Holanda exporta al año aproximadamente la misma cantidad de gas natural que consume. Las reservas son suficientes para continuar realizando estos suministros durante décadas. Existen contratos para importar gas natural de Rusia, que posee las reservas más grandes del mundo, y de otros productores, entre ellos, Inglaterra. La exportación futura de gas a otros mercados se regirá por otros contratos.
Se espera que en un futuro próximo Holanda llegará a ser el principal proveedor de gas natural de Europa occidental. Para ello, se han construido redes completas de tuberías que conectan con los mercados importadores y exportadores. El punto de partida es que las reservas de gas de Holanda, conservadas en parte en depósitos subterráneos recientemente construidos, pueden utilizarse para garantizar las exportaciones en el caso de que se interrumpan las importaciones. Esto garantiza un suministro estable de gas a los compradores extranjeros y servirá para evitar problemas económicos tanto a los importadores como a los exportadores.

Centro Financiero

Amsterdam es uno de los centros financieros rectores de Europa y está desempeñando un papel cada vez más importante en la Unión Europea en expansión.

Su fuerte sector de banca y seguros, sus activas bolsas de valores y materias primas, sus innovadores equipos de gestión de activos y su emergente sector de servicios financieros la colocan inmediatamente detrás de Londres, Francfort y París en el liderazgo de centros financieros europeos. Sus raíces son profundas. Las finanzas siempre han sido necesarias para apoyar al comercio, puntal de la economía holandesa durante siglos. En 1602 se creó en Amsterdam la primera sociedad por acciones para reunir fondos para la Compañía Unida de las Indias Orientales, conocida como la VOC, cuyo cometido inicial era transportar especias a Europa desde el archipiélago indonesio, y que más tarde, diversificando sus actividades, se dedicó al comercio de otras mercancías en otras partes del mundo.
A principios del siglo XIX, tras la derrota de Napoleón en Waterloo y la subsiguiente retirada de los franceses de los Países Bajos, el rey Guillermo I favoreció los bancos nacionales.
En 1997, las bolsas de Amsterdam de valores, opciones, materias primas y futuros se fusionaron formando la Amsterdam Exchanges, mejor conocida por AEX, dándose con ello el primer paso para eliminar servicios traslapados y propiciar un perfil fortalecido de estas actividades bursátiles.
La AEX maneja un número significativo de acciones americanas y de otros países extranjeros, constituyendo un eslabón importante en el comercio de valores que se desarrolla ininterrumpidamente durante las 24 horas del día. La bolsa de opciones fue la primera de Europa en manejar acciones internacionales. La AEX está abierta a los bancos y corredores extranjeros y frecuentemente es testigo de nuevas ofertas públicas de valores, siendo ampliamente considerada como un entorno excelente para las pequeñas empresas principiantes.
Los bancos y compañías de seguros holandeses se encuentran entre los mayores del mundo y realizan actividades en todos los lugares del planeta. Muchos de ellos llevan más de 100 años presentes en las Américas y Asia. Expansiones posteriores han sido propiciadas por la entrada en nuevos mercados de las compañías industriales holandesas. Los bancos y las compañías aseguradoras desempeñan un papel primordial en el desarrollo de nuevos productos financieros a escala mundial.

Infraestructura

La infraestructura holandesa de transporte es eficiente y moderna, comunicando con el resto de Europa por carretera y ferrocarril, mientras que, a través de los ríos y las aguas interiores, se desarrolla un amplio tráfico de mercancías nacionales e internacionales.

En la actualidad se están ampliando las redes de carreteras y vías férreas para proporcionar un mejor acceso a las ciudades y a las rutas internacionales.
El aeropuerto de Schiphol, cerca de Amsterdam, es el aeropuerto de más rápido crecimiento de Europa; en su sofisticada terminal única la eficiencia está asegurada. Schiphol es el cuarto aeropuerto de Europa en cuanto a número de pasajeros y el tercero en cuanto a carga. Más de 80 aerolíneas hacen cada día el servicio a 200 destinos. El aeropuerto y sus industrias de apoyo son los empleadores mayores del sector.
Rotterdam es el puerto marítimo mayor del mundo. Todos los puertos marinos holandeses despachan en conjunto alrededor del 50% de las mercancías internacionales que despachan todos los puertos marítimos comprendidos entre Hamburgo y Le Havre. El puerto de Rotterdam goza de una situación inmejorable en la desembocadura de los ríos Rin y Mosa que conducen respectivamente a Alemania, Suiza y Europa Central y a Bélgica y el norte de Francia.
Existen planes para ampliar la infraestructura de forma importante, entre ellos, un plan de ferrocarril de alta velocidad para unir Amsterdam y Rotterdam con Bruselas y París hacia el sur y con Colonia y otros puntos de Alemania hacia el este. Los trenes de pasajeros se cree que constituyen una alternativa viable y eficiente a los viajes por vía aérea, esperándose que puedan reducir la presión sobre los aeropuertos europeos así como proporcionar una forma agradable de transporte entre los centros de las ciudades.
Los Países Bajos siguen con el plan de construir una línea de ferrocarril de mercancías entre el Puerto de Rotterdam y la industrial cuenca del Ruhr en Alemania. Gran parte de las exportaciones alemanas y su abastecimiento de materias primas se realizan ya a través de Rotterdam y esta conexión por vía férrea ofrecerá una alternativa para el transporte de estas mercancías por carretera o vía fluvial.
El aeropuerto de Amsterdam está todavía lejos de saturar su capacidad, pero ya existen propuestas para ampliarlo construyendo un aeropuerto satélite en una isla artificial en el mar del Norte. De la construcción de tal aeropuerto podrían encargarse empresas holandesas de dragado y construcción que han acumulado experiencia en proyectos similares desarrollados en otras partes del mundo.

Distribución

Conocida como la puerta de Europa, Holanda es el centro primario de distribución del continente.

Su emplazamiento en el delta de los ríos Rin y Mosa a orillas del mar del Norte, la región de mayor tránsito marítimo del mundo, ha hecho del país el punto natural de entrada de mercancías procedentes de América del Norte y del Sur, África y Oriente Medio, dando simultáneamente salida a las mercancías que parten de Europa rumbo a destinos extranjeros.
Los transportistas holandeses son expertos en todos los tipos de distribución y numerosas empresas del sector actúan, en calidad de socios, en nombre de firmas extranjeras que intentan acceder al mercado europeo. Europa puede parecer un mercado único, pero entre los europeos existen grandes diferencias de idioma, necesidades y gustos, para superar las cuales se requiere la asistencia de expertos, que Holanda es capaz de proporcionar sin problema alguno.
En un radio de 500 kilómetros de distancia de Rotterdam y Amsterdam viven cerca de 300 millones de personas que constituyen un lucrativo mercado de consumidores de gran poder adquisitivo. Existen excelentes comunicaciones con el resto de Europa por carretera, vía férrea, aire, mar y vía fluvial.
El último instrumento de distribución desarrollado por los holandeses es la Value Added Logistics o VAL (logística de valor añadido), a través del cual se expiden mercancías a granel con destino a unos almacenes donde se revalorizan (por ejemplo, se añaden teclas de lenguas extranjeras a los ordenadores), se embalan, se etiquetan y, en ciertas circunstancias, se montan. Mediante un sistema único de depósitos francos repartidos por el país se logra que no haya que pagar derechos de aduana, ya que las mercancías se hallan aún en tránsito. De las autoridades aduaneras se recibe una excelente cooperación.
Los centros europeos de distribución están ganando cada vez más popularidad. Dentro de este sistema, los productores extranjeros pueden centralizar en un solo lugar sus actividades europeas de distribución. Las ventajas son obvias, ya que las expediciones de exportación pueden adaptarse a las necesidades de cada cliente. Además, para ayudar en los servicios administrativos de respaldo, hay disponible un equipo de personas multilingües instruidas para discutir problemas con clientes de toda Europa en su propia lengua.

Agricultura

El holandés sigue contándose entre los más eficientes agricultores del mundo. En el siglo XVI, la zona producía ya magníficos cultivos de avena para el ganado y proporcionaba alimentos para el invierno y buenos pastos mediante la siembra de trébol y nabos.

Holanda no es una región agrícola natural, pues su suelo es árido y arenoso, pero el holandés le ha sacado provecho alternando los cultivos para subvenir a su alimentación.
El moderno granero holandés de acero y hierro galvanizado puede contemplarse en todo el mundo ya que los granjeros holandeses se mudaron a menudo en busca de pastos más verdes.
En 1890 la agricultura y la ganadería empleaba a un tercio de la población trabajadora. Hoy en día esta cifra es inferior al 10% pero los resultados son impresionantes. Holanda es, después de Estados Unidos, el país exportador de productos agrícolas mayor del mundo.
La cría de ganado vacuno y porcino está muy extendida en Holanda, donde las granjas a gran escala no son una excepción. Las vacas holandesas producen los mayores índices de leche del mundo. La exportación de vacuno y porcino en carne y en vivo es también muy alta. Otro producto importante de exportación son las patatas de siembra.
Los holandeses han sido siempre líderes en la elaboración de alimentos. A un tal Willem Breukels de la provincia de Zelanda le cabe el honor de haber sido el primero en salar arenques para conservarlos en el siglo XIV.
La margarina se produjo por primera vez extensamente en Holanda hace 100 años.
Gran parte de la producción de leche se transforma en mantequilla, queso y leche condensada y en polvo, a menudo en cooperativas propiedad de los mismos granjeros.
El queso es un producto importante de exportación, los quesos de Gouda y Edam se venden en todo el mundo.
Otro producto de exportación son las frutas y verduras. En tiendas de todo el mundo se venden tomates, coles, zanahorias y pimientos holandeses frescos y a menudo más baratos que los producidos localmente. Transportistas especializados se encargan de que la fruta y la verdura madure y se transporte en magníficas condiciones.

Laboratorio de la Universidad de Twente

Investigación y desarrollo

En Holanda existe una larga tradición científica. Nacido en Rotterdam, el humanista holandés Desiderio Erasmo a principios del siglo XVI se esforzó más que nadie por fomentar el conocimiento.

Los primeros descubrimientos científicos holandeses están relacionados principalmente con la navegación, ya que los comerciantes trataban a toda costa de fortalecer su posición en las rutas mercantiles. De ahí el elevado nivel que alcanzó el arte de la cartografía.
También a los holandeses se les debe el descubrimiento de diversos métodos quirúrgicos totalmente innovadores.
Hoy en día, Holanda es el centro de un vasto complejo de investigación y desarrollo. El gobierno financia diversos institutos de I+D que a su vez funcionan en estrecha cooperación con el sector privado. Las universidades holandesas más importantes gestionan sus propios centros de I+D adaptados a sus especialidades: agricultura en Wageningen, medicina en Utrecht, biotecnología en Amsterdam, etc. En diversas instituciones universitarias y financiadas por el gobierno se realizan investigaciones en el campo de las humanidades.

La subasta de Poeldijk se alberga en este reciente edificio

También el sector privado posee numerosos centros de I+D repartidos por todo el país. Holanda es a menudo seleccionada para tales actividades por el gran número de graduados multilingües que salen cada año de sus universidades, existiendo un amplio intercambio de conocimientos entre los distintos centros de I+D.
En cualquier lugar se encuentran parques científicos, que el gobierno estimula a fin de fomentar el surgimiento de nuevos avances en la industria y los servicios. Los llamados parques de cerebros han atraído la atención internacional, ya que permiten a las industrias particulares cooperar y hacer uso de productos e ideas desarrolladas in situ. El concepto incluye parques de investigación establecidos en universidades para promover los lazos entre la universidad y los negocios y parques tecnológicos diseñados para la explotación comercial de la alta tecnología.
El gobierno ha reconocido como tales varios 'centros de excelencia' en campos tales como la agricultura y la química. La idea en la que se fundan estos centros es fomentar la investigación y propiciar el desarrollo de nuevos productos.

A indústria química

A indústria química com mais de 80.000 operários é uma das maiores indústrias da Holanda. Três grandes multinacionais têm aí a sua sede principal. Além disto, um grande número de industrias químicas estrangeiras desenvolvem grandes actividades na Holanda.

E, finalmente, há um certo número de pequenas empresas holandesas especializadas que também desenvolvem actividades neste sector.
Na Holanda, o preço da energia para grandes indústrias é dos mais baixos na Europa. Tal preço forma globalmente 60% do preço de custo da maioria dos produtos químicos. Além disto, a Holanda tem grandes estoques de gás natural e sal, elementos chaves de muito produtos químicos.
O vasto complexo de refinarias em Roterdão providencia um grande número de matérias-primas para o fabrico de produtos químicos. Muitas empresas químicas são estabelecidas no porto por onde não apenas as matérias-primas chegam à Holanda mas também os produtos acabados são despachados sem qualquer problema. Os produtos químicos são transportados não apenas por vias marítimas e através do Reno, mas também por meio duma vasta rede europeia de tubos canalizados, ligados às redes nacionais em outros sítios na Europa. Uma canalização especial para produtos químicos liga Roterdão à zona do Ruhr na Alemanha. Em breve, vai haver uma nova canalização de tubos entre Roterdão e Antuérpia, o maior centro de indústria química na Bélgica. Em Roterdão encontra-se também o maior complexo de tanques de armazenagem onde empresas especializadas armazenam temporariamente tipos de especiais produtos químicos.
Após a segunda guerra mundial Roterdão ressurgiu da catástrofe causada pelos bombardeamentos e ficou o maior centro petroquímico da Europa.
O sector químico holandês produz a escala integral de produtos químicos, destinados a mercados do mundo inteiro. Fundaram centros de formação específica para a indústria química. Além disto, há centros de Investigação e Desenvolvimento estabelecidos pelo Governo. Muitas empresas dispõem, na Holanda, de facilidades próprias para a Investigação e o Desenvolvimento.
Para os próximos decénios prevêem-se investimentos consideráveis em novas fábricas e facilidades de armazenagem e transporte actualizadas.
O Governo Holandês promove activamente os investimentos neste sector. As prescrições dadas com o intuito de fazer com que a indústria química não seja causa de grande poluição do ambiente, são muito rigorosas.

A parte pré-fabricada do casco é levada para fora da oficina

Os estaleiros holandeses

A construção naval é uma das mais antigas indústrias da Holanda. Visto a relação de ódio/amor dos holandeses para com as águas assim como a situação geográfica da Holanda com os grandes rios europeus que desaguam no Mar do Norte e a tradição comercial, os navios eram e são essenciais para a economia.

Já na Idade Média havia estaleiros por toda a parte: mesmo nas mais pequenas povoações havia pessoas que sabiam construir barcos. Quando o comércio com os Países Bálticos começou a ter certa importância, pequenas embarcações de madeira à vela percorriam a distância que separava os grandes estabelecimentos da Holanda dos da Europa do Norte. Começaram a construir navios maiores quando as rotas comerciais foram estendidas para a Europa do Sul e mais tarde para as Índias Orientais e Ocidentais.
Durante séculos a Holanda foi uma nação marítima muito importante: os navios de guerra holandeses protegiam as mais vitais rotas comerciais e costas marítimas, principalmente contra os Ingleses. A frota comercial holandesa continua a ser respeitada, embora a frota ficasse consideravelmente menor devido à maior tonelagem dos navios. A construção naval holandesa foi modernizada recentemente e classificada agora como uma das mais eficientes e competidoras do mundo. Nos anos sessenta os estaleiros navais holandeses construíam qualquer tipo de navio, variando dos mais sofisticados navios tanque até submarinos. Neste momento a reduzida indústria naval orienta-se para o que se sabe mais equipada: navios mercantis de tamanho médio como navios contentores, navios frigoríficos, barcos de passagem, rebocadores e navios de abastecimento. O maior grupo de construção naval constrói mesmo barcos para serem montados em outro sítio. Nas grandes e modernas oficinas industriais os módulos são fabricados exactamente de acordo com as medidas indicadas pelo cliente. Os estaleiros holandeses têm a produção mais alta por operário do mundo inteiro.
Também a construção de iates constitui uma especialidade holandesa. Os iates holandeses são conhecidos devido à sua qualidade, luxo e navegabilidade no mar. A alta sociedade internacional encomenda na Holanda os seus grandes iates a motor. Iates a vela são frequentemente encomendados por iatistas que participam em corridas transatlânticos assim como pelos amantes da vida boa que gostam de atravessar os mares num estilo confortável. Tal como os navios mercantis os iates são considerados os melhores do mundo.

A exportação de cerveja

As águas salobras da Holanda eram consideradas na Idade Média inadequadas para o consumo humano. Por conseguinte, todos, homens, mulheres e crianças tomavam uma fraca espécie de cerveja.

A técnica de fazer cerveja era oriunda da Alemanha, mas os Holandeses começaram bem rapidamente a produzir as suas próprias cervejas e melhoraram o processo de fabrico. No século 16 havia cervejarias em todas as cidades. A maioria dos bairros das cidades tinha as suas próprias cervejarias pois a cerveja era fabricada todos os dias e não podia ser conservada.
No fim do século 18 havia só na província de Limburgo 512 cervejarias, uma por cada 290 habitantes. Em 1900 restavam apenas 132, um número não pequeno se se toma em consideração o total de 500 cervejarias no país inteiro.
Com a vinda da refrigeração as cervejarias começaram a concentrar a produção. Já não era preciso restringir a venda dos produtos à vizinhança imediata da fábrica. Quando os mercados começaram a crescer, a produção ficou limitada a um número cada vez menor de fabricantes. O total de fábricas de cerveja decresceu drasticamente. Neste momento 95 % da cerveja nacional é produzido por algumas grandes fábricas de cerveja.
As pequenas cervejarias conseguiram um lugar nos mercados exclusivos, em geral com bons resultados.
Tal como acontece com muitos outros produtos o mercado holandês é considerado demasiadamente pequeno para produções de grande escala. As fabricas holandesas de cerveja orientam-se para grandes mercados ultramarinos e ocupam em quase todos os países o primeiro lugar na venda de cerveja importada.
Na Holanda, o consumo anual de cerveja é mais ou menos 85 litros por pessoa, quase o mesmo que nos Estados Unidos. No entanto, o consumo holandês é inferior ao da Alemanha e da Polónia onde os habitantes consomem 125 litros por ano. Neste momento os fabricantes de cerveja holandeses estão extremamente interessados nos mercados de crescimento na Europa do Sul, na Ásia, África e América Latina. As grandes cervejarias fabricam cerveja no mundo inteiro, mas sempre sob a sua própria supervisão. A qualidade da cerveja holandesa constitui um elemento muito importante na venda no estrangeiro.

Artes

Quem fala da Holanda, fala das belas artes. Nos quadros dos pintores holandeses há muito céu a admirar como aliás também nas paisagens da própria Holanda.

A tradição artística remonta ao século 17, o Século de Ouro de Amsterdão, o período áureo dos pintores como Rembrandt, Vermeer e Hals. Às vezes os pintores fundaram escolas a fim de, juntamente com os seus discípulos, poderem acabar as suas próprias obras mas também para instruir jovens artistas.
As suas obras podem ser vistas nos muitos museus que a Holanda possui, um dos quais é o Museu Nacional (Rijksmuseum) em Amsterdão. Alguns museus são dedicados à arte contemporânea como o museu Boymans-Van Beuningen em Roterdão e o museu 'Stedelijk' em Amsterdão. O museu Kröller-Müller na vizinhança da cidade de Arnhem tem uma vasta e variada colecção de obras assim como um jardim importante com esculturas. O Museu Van Gogh é um dos poucos museus, dedicados a um único artista. Por toda a parte no país existem edifícios que fazem parte do património artístico. Desta forma os centros históricas das cidades que em geral remontam ao século 17, são conservados como uma espécie de museu ao ar livre.
Também o bailado, os concertos e óperas são muito populares na Holanda. O 'Nederlands Dans Theater' (Teatro de Bailado Neerlandês) é um conjunto de bailarinas e bailarinos muito famosos que frequentemente faz digressões artísticas no mundo inteiro. A 'Concertgebouworkest' (Filarmónica) de Amsterdão é internacionalmente considerada uma das melhores orquestras do mundo e a Sala dos Concertos de Amsterdão com a sua perfeita acústica causa internacionalmente sensação Em Amsterdão encontra-se também a Opera Neerlandesa que é muito conhecida graças às suas produções avançadas. Por toda a parte a vida cultural é estimulada. Anualmente tem lugar em Roterdão o Festival do Cinema e na cidade de Maastricht há todos os anos uma feira de antiguidades.
Frequentemente os objectos de arte holandesa são leiloados nas agências de leilão em Amsterdão e Haia sob a orientação de agências internacionais, especializadas em leilões de obras artísticas mas também com a ajuda de peritos holandeses.
Os cursos de arte e música são muito apreciados tanto por jovens como por idosos, Há uma série de instituições oficialmente reconhecidas como a Academia Rietveld que se dedicam à pintura, escultura e arquitectura.

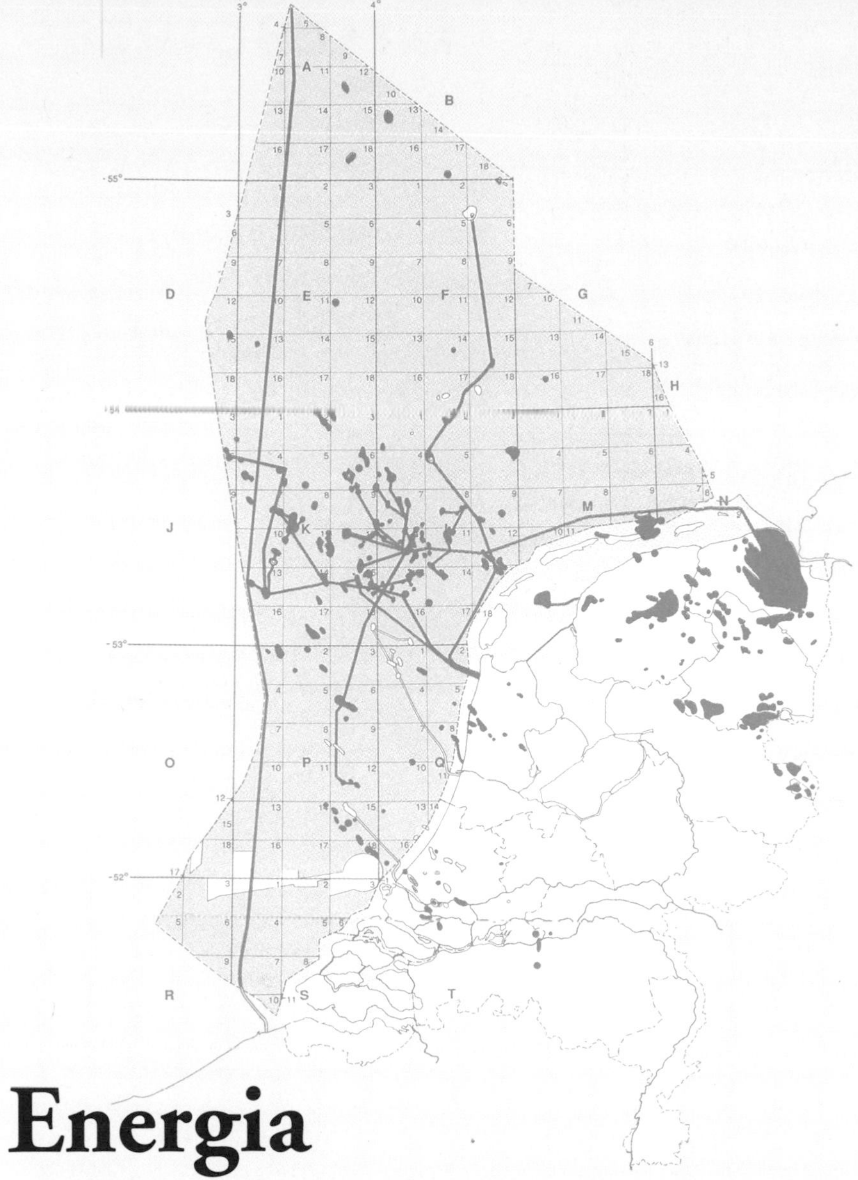

Energia

A Holanda tem as maiores reservas de gás-natural na Europa. Até aos anos de sessenta a Holanda era um grande produtor de carvão. Mas devido ao facto de as reservas decrescerem e as ofertas de carvão proveniente do estrangeiro serem cada vez mais baratas, o Governo decidiu encerrar as minas de carvão na Província de Limburgo.

Mais ou menos ao mesmo tempo foi descoberto um grande depósito subterrâneo de gás natural na Província de Groningen. Descobertos posteriores de mais depósitos de gás natural e óleo tanto na terra como no mar foram a causa de um crescimento económico muito forte nos subsequentes decénios. Resolverem poupar as reservas de gás natural adotando ao mesmo tempo uma política que visava empregar, nos próximos 50 anos, as outras fontes de energia. Entretanto, foram desenvolvidas novas técnicas para tirar gás de depósitos de menor volume. Neste momento, o volume de gás exportado é o mesmo que se gasta no próprio país. As reservas são suficientes para poder continuar a mesma política nos próximos decénios. Celebraram contratos para importar gás de outros países, por exemplo da Rússia que tem as maiores reservas de gás do mundo, e também da Inglaterra. Ainda outros contratos regulam a exportação do gás natural. Espera-se que a Holanda se torne no próximo futuro o mais importante fornecedor de gás natural na Europa. Para tal fim foi elaborada uma rede completa de canalizações. A ideia atrás disto é que as próprias reservas de gás da Holanda que se encontram parcialmente armazenadas em depósitos subterrâneos recentemente construídos, poderão ser empregadas para fins de garantia se, inesperadamente, a importação de gás venha a ser anulada. Com isto, a continuidade fica garantida. Tanto os importadores como os exportadores tiram proveito desta política.

Centro Financeiro

Amsterdão, um dos principais centros financeiros da Europa, está a desempenhar um papel cada vez mais importante na União Europeia.

Tradicionalmente, Amsterdão possui fortes sectores bancários, companhias de seguros, bolsas de acções e mercadorias, companhias inovadoras no campo de investimentos e serviços financeiros que crescem cada vez mais. Desta forma, Amsterdão é classificado imediatamente atrás de Londres, Francoforte e Paris como centro financeiro dirigente da Europa. As razões vêm de longe: os financiamentos sempre têm sido necessários para assegurar o comércio, ponto de apoio da economia holandesa durante séculos. Em 1602 a primeira sociedade por acções foi fundada em Amsterdão a fim de arranjar fundos para a Companhia das Índias Orientais Unidas, conhecida como a VOC. A VOC foi erigida com o fim de levar para a Europa especiarias do Arquipélago Indonésio. Mais tarde, estendeu-se e dedicou-se também ao comércio de outras mercadorias em outras partes do mundo. Os bancos do país receberam um impulso do Rei Guilherme I no princípio do século 19 após a derrota de Napoleão em Waterloo e a conseguinte retirada dos Franceses da Holanda.

Em 1997 as bolsas de acções, opções e mercadorias assim como os mercados a termo foram unidos para formar os 'Amsterdam Exchanges', melhor conhecidos como os AEX. A mudança foi feita com o intuito de eliminar serviços dobrados e de realizar uma presença mais forte das actividades de bolsa. Os AEX negociam uma quantidade considerável de títulos Americanos e títulos de outros países e formam uma importante elo no comércio de 24 horas de muitas emissões. O comércio de opções foi o primeiro na Europa que começou a negociar emissões internacionais. Os AEX estão abertos para bancos e corretores estrangeiros. Ofertas públicas iniciais são bastante frequentes nos AEX que, em grande escala, são conhecidos como excelente oportunidade para pequenas empresas que começam com as suas actividades.

Os bancos e companhias de seguro holandeses encontram-se entre os maiores do mundo e são activos em todos os continentes. Vários destes bancos têm desenvolvido as suas actividades durante mais de 100 anos nas Américas e na Ásia. As expansões posteriores foram possíveis graças à presença das companhias industrias holandesas em novos mercados. Os bancos e as companhias de seguro constituem um elemento chave na inovação de novos produtos financeiros no mundo inteiro.

PORTUGESE

Infra-estrutura

A infra-estrutura do transporte na Holanda é moderno e eficiente. As auto-estradas e caminhos de ferro estão em comunicação com o resto da Europa. Uma grande parte dos transportes de mercadorias nacionais e internacionais é realizada através de rios e vias fluviais.

A rede de auto-estradas e caminhos de ferro está sendo, neste momento, aumentada com vista a um melhor acesso ainda das cidades e rotas internacionais.
Schiphol Airport, perto de Amsterdão, é o aeroporto que mais cresce na Europa; e o sistema 'single terminal' garante uma alto grau de eficácia. Schiphol é o quarto aeroporto da Europa quando se trata do número de passageiros e o segundo, tratando-se do transporte aéreo de mercadorias. Mais de 80 companhias realizam diariamente voos para 200 destinos. O aeroporto e os ramos industriais de apóio constituem uma das maiores entidades patronais na região.
Roterdão é o maior porto marítimo do mundo. Juntos, os portos marítimos holandeses despacham por volta de 50% de todos os transportes de mercadorias realizados em todos os portos do Mar do Norte, situados entre Hamburgo e le Havre. O porto de Roterdão encontra-se situado num lugar excelente junto da embocadura do Reno e da Mosa que conduzem para a Alemanha, Suíça e Europa Central, Bélgica e o Norte da França respectivamente.
Existem planos para aumentos consideráveis da infra-estrutura. Desta forma, pretende-se ligar Amsterdão/Roterdão a Bruxelas e Paris no sul e a Colónia e a outras cidades da Alemanha no Leste mediante comboios de alta velocidade.
O transporte por caminho de ferro é visto como uma alternativa realística e eficiente, adequada para substituir transportes aéreos. Desta forma, a pressão nos aeroportos europeus pode ser diminuída consideravelmente e inspirar, ao mesmo tempo, os passageiros a empreenderem as suas viagens entre os centros citadinos da Europa de maneira mais agradável.
Neste momento está-se a construir na Holanda uma linha de comboio, destinada exclusivamente ao transporte de mercadorias entre o porto de Roterdão e a zona industrial do Ruhr na Alemanha. Uma grande parte da exportação e da importação alemãs das matérias primas já vai pelo porto de Roterdão. A nova ligação por comboio vai constituir uma alternativa para o transporte existente por auto-estradas e vias fluviais.
O aeroporto de Schiphol ainda não atingiu a sua máxima capacidade. Existem planos para aumentar a capacidade do aeroporto mediante um aeroporto-satélite numa ilha artificial no Mar do Norte. A construção dum tal aeroporto podia ser realizada por empresas holandesas de dragagem e construção que desenvolveram técnicas específicas em projectos semelhantes no estrangeiro.

Distribuição

Conhecida com a porta da Europa, a Holanda é o centro de distribuição mais importante do continente.

A sua locação na delta do Reno e da Mosa, a região de navegação mais intensa do mundo, fez com que o país se tornasse o ponto natural da entrada de mercadorias provenientes da América do Norte e do Sul, da Ásia, África e Médio Oriente. Ao mesmo tempo as mercadorias europeias são levadas para fora através dos portos holandeses.
Os transportadores holandeses encontram-se equipados para qualquer forma de transporte e muitas companhias estão habilitadas para servirem de sócios para firmas estrangeiras desejosas de terem acesso ao mercado europeu. À primeira vista a Europa pode apresentar-se como mercado único, mas existe uma variedade de línguas, necessidades e preferências diferentes entre os Europeus. Ajuda especializada é frequentemente necessária e está prontamente à disposição na Holanda. Dentro dum raio de 500 quilómetros de Roterdão e Amsterdão vive uma população de cerca de 300 milhões de pessoas. Trata-se dum mercado lucrativo onde os consumidores dispõem dum alto poder de compra. As ligações para o resto da Europa através de auto-estradas, caminhos de ferro e vias aéreas, marítimas e fluviais são excelentes.
A Logística de Valor Acrescentado ou seja o LVA, é um instrumento de transporte que recentemente está a ser desenvolvido pelos holandeses. No âmbito do LVA, as mercadorias são carregadas em massa para um armazém onde são adaptadas às circunstâncias locais (por exemplo, os computadores são munidos de teclados apropriados para línguas estrangeiras), empacotadas, previstas de rótulos e, em certas circunstâncias, montadas. Este sistema único de armazéns de depósito, existentes através do país, faz com que a taxa de importação não precise ser paga porque as mercadorias continuam a encontrar-se em trânsito. As autoridades alfandegárias cooperam de forma excelente.
Os Centros Europeus de Distribuição estão a ficar cada vez mais populares. Com ajuda deste sistema os produtores estrangeiros de mercadorias centralizam as suas actividades de distribuição europeia num só lugar. As vantagens são óbvias visto que os despachos de exportação podem ser adequados às necessidades de cada cliente. Além disto, um quadro de pessoal multilingue está à disposição para ajudar nas operações de ordem administrativa daí decorrentes. O pessoal está treinado para discutir problemas com os utentes em toda a Europa na sua própria língua.

Agricultura

Os holandeses são contados entre os mais eficientes agricultores do mundo. No século 16 a região já produzia magníficas colheitas de aveia para o gado, boa alimentação para o inverno e bons pastos devido a facto de o trevo e o nabo serem semeados em solos rasos.

A Holanda com o seu solo de areia estéril não é por natureza uma área de agricultura. Mas os holandeses conseguiram melhorar a sua terra alternando as colheitas com o intuito de produzir substâncias nutritivas. Os modernos celeiros holandeses de aço e ferro galvanizado tornaram-se conhecidos no mundo inteiro quando os agricultores holandeses mudaram para pastos mais verdes. Em 1890 a agricultura e lavoura ofereciam trabalho a um terço da população activa. Hoje, o total é menos de 10% da população activa, mas o resultado é impressionante. A Holanda é o segundo exportador de produtos agrícolas do mundo depois dos Estados Unidos.

A criação de gado e porcos está muito espalhada na Holanda; criações em grande escala são muito comuns. As vacas holandesas produzem o rendimento mais alto de leite do mundo. A exportação de gado e porcos vivos assim como a de carne é muito elevada. Batatas de semente constituem também um dos maiores elementos da exportação.

A Holanda sempre tem desempenhado um papel importante no processamento de alimentos. Um certo Willem Breukels que vivia no século 14 na Província de Zelândia é considerado ter sido o primeiro a salgar arenques para os conservar. Foi na Holanda que, cem anos atrás, a margarina foi pela primeira vez largamente produzida.

Uma grande parte do leite é transformada em manteiga, queijo e em leite condensado e em pó, frequentemente por cooperativas que são propriedade dos agricultores. O queijo é um dos mais importantes produtos de exportação. Os queijos do tipo Gouda e Edam podem ser comprados no mundo inteiro.

Fruta e verdura constituem um outro produto de exportação. Os tomates da Holanda, as cenouras, couves e pimentões estão à venda no mundo inteiro, frescos e frequentemente mais baratos que os produtos locais. Os especialistas de transporte fazem com que a fruta e as verduras sejam despachadas em óptimas circunstâncias de forma que possam amadurecer adequadamente.

Um dos laboratórios da Universidade de Twente

Investigação e Desenvolvimento

A Holanda tem uma longa tradição nos campo das ciências. O humanista Desidério Erasmo, nascido em Roterdão, fez mais que qualquer outro cientista no princípio do século 16 para promover o ensino.

Uma grande parte da antigas descobertas científicas holandesas dizia respeito à navegação. O motivo é que os mercadores holandesas tentavam fortalecer a sua influência nas rotas comerciais. Não é de admirar que a cartografia holandesa tinha um alto nível. Também no campo da cirurgia os holandeses desenvolveram métodos pioneiros.

Hoje em dia a Holanda é um importante centro de investigação e desenvolvimento. O Governo fundou vários institutos de investigação e desenvolvimento que, por sua vez, trabalham em estreita colaboração com o sector privado. As mais importantes universidades holandesas têm centros de investigação e desenvolvimento focalizados nas suas próprias especialidades: agricultura em Wageningen, medicinas em Utreque, biotecnologia em Amsterdão etc. As pesquisas no campo das letras são empreendidas por diversas instituições académicas, subsidiadas pelo Governo.

O novo edifício da arrematação em Poeldijk

O sector privado tem muitos Centros de Investigação e Desenvolvimento em todo o país. Frequentemente opta-se pela Holanda para tais actividades devido ao grande número de académicos multilingues que todos os anos são formados pelas universidades. O intercâmbio de conhecimentos entre os diversos Centros de Investigação e Desenvolvimento é muito frequente.

Centros científicos encontram-se por toda a parte. O Governo holandês está a desenvolver uma política de encorajamento de expansão dos mesmos a fim de promover novas evoluções na indústria e nos serviços. Os assim chamados centros de conhecimentos têm atraído um grande número de interessados estrangeiros. Estes centros permitem que serviços individuais colaborarem e façam uso de produtos e ideias desenvolvidos nesses lugares. No conceito estão incluídos não apenas os centros de investigação estabelecidos nas universidades que procuram pôr em contacto o comércio e a ciência mas também os centros técnicos fundados para a exploração comercial da alta tecnologia.

O Governo tem reconhecido vários 'centros de excelência' em diversos sectores, inclusive no campo da agricultura e da química. A ideia atrás destes centros visa encorajar pesquisas ulteriores nessas áreas e estimular a evolução de novos produtos.

Illustratieverantwoording:

Amsterdam Airport Schiphol 116,117
Bloemenveiling Aalsmeer 118,119
Nationaal Visbureau 122,123, 124, 125
Jan Vermeer 129, 149
N.V. Nederlandse Gasunie 132, 133
KPN Telecom 135
The Greenery 140, 141
Nederlands Zuivelbureau 143, 144
Projectorganisatie HSL-Zuid 144, 145
NS Railinfrabeheer 144, 145
Kon. Schelde Groep (Lex de Meester) 150, 151, 162, e.v.
Sectie Foto AVD-Koninklijke Marine 150,151
ECT Corporate Communications 154, 155
Heineken Nederland B.V.163, e.v.